Reforming Infrastructure

Privatization, Regulation, and Competition

A World Bank
Policy Research Report

Reforming Infrastructure

Privatization, Regulation, and Competition

Ioannis N. Kessides

A copublication of the World Bank
and Oxford University Press

9316807

© 2004 The International Bank for Reconstruction and Development / The World Bank
1818 H Street, NW
Washington, DC 20433
Telephone 202-473-1000
Internet www.worldbank.org
E-mail feedback@worldbank.org

1 2 3 4 07 06 05 04

A copublication of the World Bank and Oxford University Press.

This volume is a product of the staff of the World Bank. The findings, interpretations, and conclusions expressed herein do not necessarily reflect the views of the Board of Executive Directors of the World Bank or the governments they represent.

The World Bank does not guarantee the accuracy of the data included in this work. The boundaries, colors, denominations, and other information shown on any map in this work do not imply any judgment on the part of the World Bank concerning the legal status of any territory or the endorsement or acceptance of such boundaries.

Rights and Permissions

Library of Congress Cataloging-in-Publication Data

Reforming infrastructure : privatization, regulation, and competition.
    p. cm. — (A World Bank policy research report)
  Includes bibliographical references.
  ISBN 0-8213-5070-6
  1. Public utilities.   2. Privatization.   3. Public utilities—Government policy.
4. Infrastructure (Economics) I. World Bank. II. Series.

HD2763.R427 2004
363.6—dc 22

2004043841

Cover photos (clockwise from top left): © Adrian Lyon/Getty; World Bank Photo Library; © Corbis; World Bank Photo Library
Cover designed by Richard Fletcher of Fletcher Design

Contents

Figures

Tables

Foreword

INFRASTRUCTURE INDUSTRIES AND SERVICES ARE CRUCIAL FOR generating economic growth, alleviating poverty, and increasing international competitiveness. Safe water is essential for life and health. Reliable electricity saves businesses and consumers from having to invest in expensive backup systems or more costly alternatives, and keeps rural women and children from having to spend long hours fetching firewood. Widely available and affordable telecommunications and transportation services can foster grassroots entrepreneurship and so are critical to generating employment and advancing economic development.

Recognizing infrastructure's importance, many countries have implemented far-reaching reforms over the past two decades—restructuring, encouraging private participation, and establishing new approaches to regulation. This report identifies the challenges involved in this massive policy redirection within the historical, economic, and institutional context of developing and transition economies. It also assesses the outcomes of policy changes and suggests directions for policy reform and research to improve infrastructure performance.

In most developing and transition economies, private participation in infrastructure and restructuring have been driven by the high costs and poor performance of state-owned network utilities. Under state ownership, services were usually underpriced, and countries often could not afford the substantial investments required to expand services to large parts of their populations. Deficiencies in infrastructure quantity and quality imposed a heavy penalty in terms of growth and welfare.

Although privatization, competitive restructuring, and regulatory reforms improve infrastructure performance, several issues must be considered and conditions met for these measures to achieve their public interest goals. There is no universal reform model; every restructuring and private participation program must take into account the sector's features and the country's economic, institutional, social, and political characteristics. Telecommunications offers perhaps the most compelling case for privatization, and in many transportation segments—railways, ports, trucking, airlines, interurban busing—competition within and between modes is often sufficient to justify aggressive liberalization. However, the case for privatizing transport network facilities is much less compelling. Electricity is more dependent on administrative ability and therefore quite challenging, but not more so than telecommunications. And the scope for introducing competition in water supply is more limited than in other network utilities (although there are opportunities to introduce competition in sewage treatment).

While the links between infrastructure reforms and subsequent performance are complex, several conclusions can be drawn. First, reforms have significantly improved performance, leading to higher investment, productivity, and service coverage and quality. Prices have become better aligned with underlying costs. And services have become more responsive to consumer and business needs and to opportunities for innovation.

Second, effective regulation—including the setting of adequate tariff levels—is the most critical enabling condition for infrastructure reform. Protecting the interests of both investors and consumers is crucial to attracting the long-term private capital needed to secure adequate, reliable infrastructure services and to getting social support for reforms. Regulation should clarify property rights, allocate them sensibly, and assure private investors that their investments will not be subject to regulatory opportunism. Crafting proper regulation is the greatest challenge facing policymakers in developing and transition economies.

Third, for privatization to generate widely shared social benefits, infrastructure industries must be thoroughly restructured and able to sustain competition. The benefits from privatizing infrastructure monopolies are much smaller than those from introducing competition. It is often hard or costly to change structural choices—such as the degree of vertical and horizontal integration—after privatization. Thus restructuring to introduce competition should be done before privatization, and regulation should be in place to assure potential buyers of both competitive and monopoly elements.

There is a clear discrepancy between scholarly assessments and public perceptions of privatization. In recent years the alleged failures of privatization have led to street riots, skeptical press coverage, and mounting criticism of international financial institutions. Concerns are increasingly being expressed about the distributional consequences of privatization and market liberalization—especially their effects on basic services for poor households and other disadvantaged groups.

The critics are right in pointing out the cases where privatization was undertaken without institutional safeguards and conducted in ways widely considered illegitimate. Thus there is an urgent need for more comprehensive welfare assessments of infrastructure reforms and for both retrospective and forward-looking analyses to clarify the successes and failures associated with reforms and to identify better instruments and policies to guide ongoing and future efforts. In addition, extensive information is required to analyze the links between specific policy reforms and infrastructure outcomes, including their distributional dimensions. Because comprehensive data on distributional dimensions of costs and benefits are currently unavailable, it is imperative that a systematic cross-country data collection effort be undertaken.

In sum, infrastructure restructuring, privatization, and regulatory reform offer substantial potential benefits for governments, operators, and consumers. And there is sufficient experience to guide these institutional reforms. Still, they should not be pursued blindly in a specific country or industry without carefully assessing the institutional and structural prerequisites and without explicit attention to the concerns they raise.

François J. Bourguignon
Senior Vice President and Chief Economist
The World Bank

Michael U. Klein
World Bank–IFC Vice President,
Private Sector Development
and Chief Economist,
International Finance Corporation

Nemat Talaat Shafik
Vice President and Head of Infrastructure Network
The World Bank

March 2004

The Report Team

THIS POLICY RESEARCH REPORT WAS WRITTEN BY IOANNIS Kessides (Lead Economist, Development Research Group) under the supervision of François Bourguignon (Senior Vice President and Chief Economist) and David Dollar (Senior Adviser), with guidance from an advisory board comprising Paul Joskow (Massachusetts Institute of Technology), Michael Klein (World Bank–IFC Vice President and Chief Economist, IFC), David Newbery (University of Cambridge), and Roger Noll (Stanford University).

Extremely helpful comments on earlier drafts were provided by peer reviewers Antonio Estache, Luis Guasch, and Bernard Tenenbaum, as well as by many others including Ian Alexander, Mark Armstrong, Varadarajan Atur, Nancy Benjamin, John Besant-Jones, Harry Broadman, George Clarke, Shantayanan Devarajan, Janet Entwistle, Indermit Gill, Philip Gray, Kenneth Gwilliam, Luke Haggarty, Jonathan Halpern, Aira Htenas, Gregory Ingram, Philip Keefer, Christine Kessides, Frannie Leautier, Ira Lieberman, Laszlo Lovei, Abel Mejia, Richard Messick, Pradeep Mitra, Gobind Nankani, Paul Noumba Um, Takis Papapanagiotou, Luiz Pereira Da Silva, S. Ramachandran, Hossein Razavi, Jamal Saghir, Luis Serven, Zmarak Shalizi, Mary Shirley, Peter Smith, Warrick Smith, Jon Stern, Helen Sutch, Louis Thompson, Lee Travers, Cecilia Valdivieso, Jos Verbeek, Scott Wallsten, Bjorn Wellenius, and Colin Xu. The author is also grateful for the excellent work of Paul Holtz, who edited the report; Polly Means, who managed the art files; Dimitrios Mantoulidis and Periklis Saragiotis, who provided research assistance; Paulina Sintim-Aboagye, who processed the report; and those involved from the Office of the Publisher of the World Bank—Susan Graham, Stuart Tucker, and Monika Lynde—for their management of the book production process.

Executive Summary

OR MUCH OF THE 20TH CENTURY AND IN MOST COUN-
tries, network utilities—electricity, telecommunications,
railroads, water supply, natural gas—were vertically and
horizontally integrated state monopolies under ministerial control.[1] Infrastructure's enormous economic importance, a desire to protect the public interest in industries supplying essential services, and concerns about private monopoly
power led governments to conclude that control over these services
could not be entrusted to the motivations and penalties of free markets. Governments also believed that, given the large investments involved, public resources were required to increase infrastructure coverage. Accordingly, a single public entity usually controlled every aspect
of a utility—facilities, operations, and administration—and determined
which services to provide to essentially captive customers.

The past decade has seen dramatic change in views about how network utilities should be owned, organized, and regulated. The new
model calls for increased reliance on private infrastructure to improve
efficiency, promote innovation, and enhance services. But after a series
of financial crises, corporate scandals, and stock market collapses, the
California electricity crisis, and blackouts around the world, clear guidance is needed on what should be done for infrastructure—as well as
reassurance about (or qualifications of) earlier, more confident messages. What are the promises and perils of the new model? And what
principles should guide future efforts to restructure, regulate, and expand infrastructure?

State-owned Monopolies Often Exhibited Poor Performance...

THE PERFORMANCE OF STATE-OWNED INFRASTRUCTURE monopolies varied considerably across countries. In many developing and transition economies these entities suffered from low labor productivity, deteriorating fixed facilities and equipment, poor service quality, chronic revenue shortages and inadequate investment, and serious problems of theft and nonpayment. In addition, large portions of the population lacked services in developing countries—though not in transition economies, many of which achieved fairly high service coverage. Moreover, prices varied considerably across sectors. In telecommunications they were typically high, while underpricing was common in electricity and certain segments of transportation, and especially serious in water.

Infrastructure performance was generally much better in advanced industrial countries. Still, high construction costs (caused by delays and changing environmental and safety requirements) and expensive, politically driven programs led to problems in the electricity sector. State-owned telecommunications entities were forced to adopt inefficient pricing structures and were used to generate revenue for governments and support excessive employment—delaying investment and modernization and undermining efficient operations and universal service. In almost all countries railroads failed to earn adequate revenue, had difficulties adjusting to changes in markets, experienced declining market shares for passenger and freight traffic, and exhibited poor productivity relative to technological opportunities.

Underinvestment—largely caused by underpricing—was the key problem of the state-owned utility model

In developing and transition economies a main cause of deteriorating infrastructure performance was underinvestment, which was largely due to the failure of governments to prescribe cost-reflective tariffs, especially during periods of high inflation. Under state ownership, prices fell to levels that could not cover the investment needed to meet growing demand. This problem was deferred as long as governments were able to provide subsidies and international financial institutions were willing to bail them out. But years of underfunding and failure to address systemic problems led to a significant infrastructure deficit in the developing world, generating substantial welfare losses. Infrastructure inefficiencies constrained domestic economic growth, impaired international competitiveness, and discouraged foreign investment.

In the early 1990s, for example, developing countries incurred annual losses of about $180 billion due to mispricing and technical inefficiency in water, railroads, roads, and electricity—nearly as much as annual investments in these sectors (World Bank 1994b). With growing budget deficits and the resulting inability of governments to maintain and expand infrastructure services, most developing and transition economies simply could not sustain state-owned utilities. Debt and fiscal crises, combined with extraordinarily weak performance, stimulated strong pressures for infrastructure reform.

...Leading to a New Model for Financing and Providing Infrastructure

RECOGNIZING THE PERFORMANCE PROBLEMS OF STATE-owned, monolithic network utilities—and driven by technological progress, advances in economic thinking, and mounting evidence on the high costs of government intervention—nearly all industrial and many developing and transition economies have implemented far-reaching infrastructure reforms. These institutional reforms have entailed a combination of competitive restructuring, privatization, and establishment of regulatory mechanisms.

Because of their financial, technical, and managerial resources, private entities are seen as having a comparative advantage in the rapidly changing markets and technologies of network utilities. Thus rebalancing of the roles of the private and public sectors has been an integral part of every infrastructure reform program. A key attraction of privatization is that it places the realignment of prices with underlying costs at the center of the reform agenda. Investors demand cost-reflective tariffs before they will commit their capital and expand networks.

Moreover, network utilities are no longer seen as monolithic natural monopolies, but rather as encompassing distinct activities with entirely different economic characteristics. Thus most analysts now believe that network utilities should be unbundled, horizontally and vertically, with potentially competitive segments under separate ownership from natural monopoly components:

- In electricity, transmission and distribution should be unbundled from generation.

The monolithic, state-owned utility option is largely a strawman from today's perspective—no one would choose it for the public interest

3

- In telecommunications, the local loop should be split from long-distance, mobile, and value added services.
- In natural gas, high-pressure transmission and local distribution should be separated from production, supply, and storage.
- In railroads, tracks, signals, and other fixed facilities should be separated from train operations and maintenance.

Competition should be pursued where feasible, and regulation confined to core natural monopoly activities

Under this view, in competitive or contestable segments any interference with market mechanisms should be minimized and privatization and competitive entry should be fully exploited. Only segments where natural monopoly conditions persist and are unavoidable (generally because they involve substantial sunk capital) should be regulated and perhaps operated by the public sector.

The New Model Poses Risks—But Also Holds Considerable Promise

THE GLOBAL WAVE OF INFRASTRUCTURE PRIVATIZATION AND liberalization in the 1990s was a significant departure from previous economic consensus. This departure did more than just question the need for state ownership of network utilities. It also reconsidered—and often replaced—long-standing notions about natural monopolies and related regulatory interventions. As a result it has become widely accepted that the monopoly utility model no longer applies—and perhaps never should have been applied—to all network industries. Moreover, if these industries are properly restructured, substantial competition can emerge in many activities.

Yet today's industrial countries relied on the old, vertically integrated model to develop good infrastructure and have only recently pursued unbundling. So why should developing and transition economies take this new approach? This question is especially relevant given that the new model poses significant risks if not accompanied by appropriate structural and regulatory safeguards.

Institutional reforms—restructuring, privatization, establishment of effective regulation—can significantly improve performance

The simple answer is that the new model, implemented correctly, offers benefits too big to ignore—for governments, operators, and consumers. And there is enough experience to guide its implementation. Still, it should not be pursued in a specific country or industry without carefully assessing its institutional and structural prerequisites and without explicit attention to the concerns it raises.

Unbundling Is No Panacea...

The primary virtue of unbundling is that it promotes competition, ensuring that firms provide their services at efficient prices. Unbundling is likely to be particularly attractive when market size and density permit many operators to function, providing both active and potential competition.

But in many developing countries markets are too small for substantial competition to emerge. In electricity, for example, 60 developing countries have peak system loads below 150 megawatts, another 30 between 150 and 500 megawatts, and possibly another 20 between 501 and 1,000 megawatts. Even a 1,000-megawatt system is small for introducing competition. Thus the benefits of competition that come from unbundling will be limited in many developing and transition economies.

Moreover, provision of many innovative, market-responsive utility services requires investments in physical infrastructure. In unbundled systems it may be difficult for providers of competitive final services to coordinate with monopoly owners of infrastructure networks—especially if their incentives for investments are not in harmony. Thus another factor required for unbundling is a mature, well-developed set of network facilities, so that there is little need for new investments where incentive problems are more likely. Yet circumstances in most developing and transition economies are exactly the opposite. These countries require substantial new infrastructure investments, either because their networks are underdeveloped or because they have not been adequately maintained or modernized (or both).

The competitive advantages of unbundling and the potential economies of vertical integration must be carefully balanced

... And Requires Careful Regulation

Unbundling can reduce the need for regulation by isolating monopoly segments, containing their damaging consequences, and replacing regulation with competition. But even though fewer activities require regulatory oversight in unbundled systems, performance becomes much more sensitive to regulatory efficacy. In fact, some inefficient practices (such as internal cross-subsidies) that were tolerable in a monopoly environment can cause much more damage in the new setting.

To obtain the benefits of unbundling, policies need to harmonize regulatory oversight of monopoly activities with increasing competi-

Regulating unbundled utilities is harder than regulating vertically integrated utilities, and may require aggressive pro-competitive policies

Infrastructure networks offer more opportunities for market manipulation than do ordinary markets. Ensuring efficient entry conditions is challenging

tion. Otherwise, the interface between bottleneck components (those essential to the provision of final services and too costly to duplicate) and competitive segments can create such severe distortions that the mixed system is the worst of both worlds. Thus unbundling makes the regulatory task more complex, which is likely to be a problem in environments with weak institutional capacity—as in most developing and transition economies.

Privatization Has Been Oversold and Misunderstood

As with all economic elixirs, privatization has been oversimplified, oversold, and ultimately disappointing—delivering less than promised

Just a few years ago, privatization was heralded as an elixir that would rejuvenate lethargic, wasteful infrastructure industries and revitalize stagnating economies. But today, privatization is viewed differently—and often critically. Skepticism and outright hostility toward privatization are not limited to a few radical protesters. Opinion polls in several developing and transition economies, especially in Latin America, reveal growing public dissatisfaction with privatization. Disapproval ratings were higher in 2002 than in 2000, and higher in 2000 than in 1998. In 2002 almost 90 percent of Argentines and 80 percent of Chileans surveyed disapproved of privatization.[2]

Public discontent with privatization has been fueled by price increases, job reductions, and the high profits of firms that have improved operating performance—as well as by economic and political crises that had little to do with government policy toward infrastructure. But these adjustments have been necessary for privatization to achieve its public interest objectives. As noted, inadequate revenue was a key problem of the old model. The choice was either higher prices or more taxation. Higher prices generally fall on those benefiting from services—in many developing countries, the middle and upper classes—while higher taxes are likely to occur partly through inflation taxes that hurt poor people and other vulnerable groups. Thus a sensible, and arguably less regressive, response is to realign prices with costs. That privatization makes such adjustments mandatory—to attract investors—is one of its main appeals.

As for layoffs, state utilities in most developing and transition economies had high excess employment before reforms. Efficiency and competitiveness require eliminating redundant jobs. Efficiency is especially important in infrastructure because such services are critical for manufacturing, transportation, and commerce—and so essential to boosting economic activity.

Moreover, the market's primary incentive is the prospect of profits for firms that succeed. So, while preventing monopoly profits is a legitimate goal for public policy, it should not lead to artificial limits on post-privatization profits or restrict such returns based on mechanistic formulas or populist demands. Otherwise, incentives for investment, innovation, efficiency, and productive growth—badly needed in the network utilities of most developing and transition economies—would be undermined or eliminated.

Finally, the role of institutions cannot be overlooked. Most developing and transition economies have suffered from much worse infrastructure performance than have advanced industrial economies. But the structure of ownership has not been the key explanatory variable for the differences in performance. After all, for many years state ownership prevailed in most advanced economies. The true explanation lies in the broader institutional context.

It can be argued that the performance of state-owned network industries reflects a variety of country characteristics both observable and unobservable, including institutional capacity, business culture, nature of organized interest groups, patterns of social conflict, and codes of conduct. It would be unrealistic to expect such features to change on a timescale comparable to that of privatization transactions—or to think that less attractive attributes would disappear overnight.

Strong institutions took a long time to develop even in advanced industrial economies. It is difficult to create such institutions overnight in societies that do not have the constitutional, political, and legal traditions required to support them. Thus achieving the public interest objectives of privatization will take longer than has elapsed since such reforms were introduced in most developing and transition economies. Even in East Asia's "miracle" economies it took several decades of concerted efforts to produce notable results.

Reforms Require Proper Sequencing . . .

It is often hard or costly to change structural choices—such as the degree of vertical and horizontal integration—after privatization. Moreover, the absence of regulation that clarifies the rules of the game for

Restructure and regulate— and only then privatize

potential investors may cause them to demand risk premiums that could later appear unreasonably high and generate public backlash against privatization, possibly leading to policy reversals. So, restructuring to introduce competition should occur before privatization, and regulation should be in place to assure potential buyers of both competitive and monopoly elements. But it is also important to keep options open—and to delay irreversible changes until their benefits outweigh their potential costs. State ownership may be undesirable, but at least it retains the option of well-designed future privatization.

. . . And Each Sector Must Choose Among Imperfect Options

There is no universally appropriate model for restructuring network utilities. And the fact that state ownership is flawed does not mean that privatization is appropriate for all infrastructure activities and all countries. Before state ownership is supplanted by another institutional setup, it is essential to assess the properties and requirements of the proposed alternative—taking into account the sector's features (its underlying economic attributes and the technological conditions of its production) and the country's economic, institutional, social, and political characteristics.

The telecommunications sector offers perhaps the most compelling case for privatization and liberalization in developing and transition economies. Prices are typically too high and investment and penetration too low. In many countries the economic implications of efficient telecommunications are extensive but underappreciated. Thus the benefits from relaxing restrictions on entry are potentially substantial. Issues of regulatory commitment to safeguard private investors are probably less important than issues of regulatory design to facilitate competitive entry and price reductions.

In many segments of the transportation sector—railways, ports, trucking, airlines, interurban busing—competition within and between modes is sufficient in most countries to justify substantial liberalization and privatization. But the case for privatizing transport network infrastructure is much less compelling than that for privatizing services operating on the network. Rail track, basic and access port infrastructure, and certain portions of airport facilities, where monopolies are unavoidable and substantial amounts of sunk capital are involved, must be regulated or even operated by the public sector.

In the United States railroad liberalization worked splendidly because rail is competitive with roads for freight carried over long distances. In most other countries (except perhaps Argentina, Brazil, China, India, the Russian Federation, and parts of Africa) rail is uncompetitive for freight except for bulk items, many of which are in decline. In these countries "liberalization" is often code for restructuring, downsizing, and reorienting transportation toward roads.

In electricity, wholesale competition has worked well in industrial countries because of excess capacity, moderate demand growth, and the availability of natural gas (which enabled the entry of gas-fired plants at modest scale and relatively low cost). In contrast, electricity markets in many developing countries face capacity shortages, enormous excess demand, and periodic blackouts. Thus electricity restructuring and privatization are more problematic and dependent on administrative ability. California's experience has shown that market liberalization under conditions of tight demand can lead to serious problems: market-clearing prices would be politically unacceptable and would likely derail attempts at radical liberalization.

The scope for introducing competition in the supply of water is far more limited than in other network utilities. Local networks of pipes and sewers remain quintessential natural monopolies. Moreover, unbundling is not as attractive because increased competition in supply will likely provide far fewer benefits than in other network utilities—the costs of producing water (a potentially competitive activity) are low relative to the value added at the transportation stage (where natural monopoly prevails), though this may vary across countries. Greater opportunities exist to introduce competition in sewage treatment. Overall, concessions and leases will likely be the most effective way of increasing competition in this sector.

What Effects Have Reforms Had?

THIS REPORT EVALUATES THE EFFECTS OF INSTITUTIONAL REforms—vertical and horizontal restructuring, privatization, establishment of effective regulation—in the network utilities of developing and transition economies using three criteria: the resulting levels of investment (and thus service expansion), operating efficiency, and allocative efficiency (as indicated by the rebalancing of tariffs). But no public policy can be justified on purely economic grounds if a country's population considers its results unjust. Thus the report also assesses the distributional consequences of reforms—especially their impacts on basic services for poor households and other disadvantaged groups.

Although experiences have varied considerably across countries and sectors, for the most part these reforms have significantly improved infrastructure performance. Investment and service coverage have increased. Productivity and cost-effectiveness have risen. Service quality has improved. Prices have become more closely aligned with underlying costs. And services have become more responsive to consumer and business needs and to opportunities for innovation.

Effects on Investment and Service Expansion

Between 1990 and 2001 more than $750 billion was invested in 2,500 private infrastructure projects in developing and transition economies. This investment varied enormously across regions, with nearly half going to Latin America and the Caribbean (mainly through divestitures) and more than a quarter going to East Asia and the Pacific (mainly in greenfield projects; figure 1). Meanwhile, Sub-Saharan Africa and the Middle

Figure 1   In 1990–2001, Latin America and East Asia Received the Most Private Investment in Infrastructure

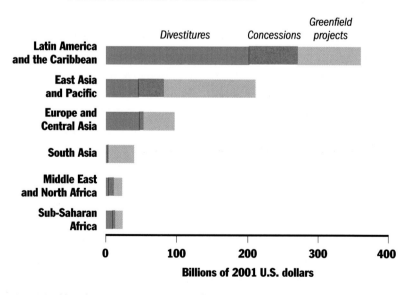

Source: World Bank, Private Participation in Infrastructure Project database.

Figure 2   Private Investment in Infrastructure in Developing and Transition Countries Peaked in 1997

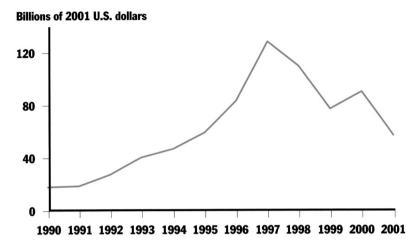

Billions of 2001 U.S. dollars

Source: World Bank, Private Participation in Infrastructure Project database.

East and North Africa each received just 3 percent of private investment—reflecting much weaker reforms. Investment also varied considerably by sector, with most going to telecommunications and power.

Investment peaked at around $130 billion in 1997, but by 2001 had fallen to about $60 billion (figure 2). This sharp drop was mainly due to the deteriorating global market for private financing of infrastructure assets—reflecting financial crises, stock market collapses, and corporate scandals—though lack of economic reforms might also have played a role. Whatever the cause, utility operators around the world are having an extraordinarily hard time securing the financing needed to maintain and expand services. Even with effective regulation and attractive domestic conditions, foreign direct investment in the infrastructure sectors in these countries would be at risk. Thus there is a legitimate question of whether there is a new role for international financial institutions in finding ways to support investment in these sectors.

Reforms have expedited service expansion in a variety of sectors and countries. Telecommunications coverage has seen the largest jump, but significant increases have also occurred in electricity, transportation, and access to safe water (figure 3). The size of such changes depends enormously on the extent to which the market is liberalized and the effectiveness of regulation. For example, increased competition has been particularly powerful in boosting telecommunications coverage. In Latin

Reforms have significantly increased private investment in infrastructure—one of the key goals of restructuring

11

Figure 3   Privatized Services Have Increased Access to Safe Water in a Variety of Cities and Countries

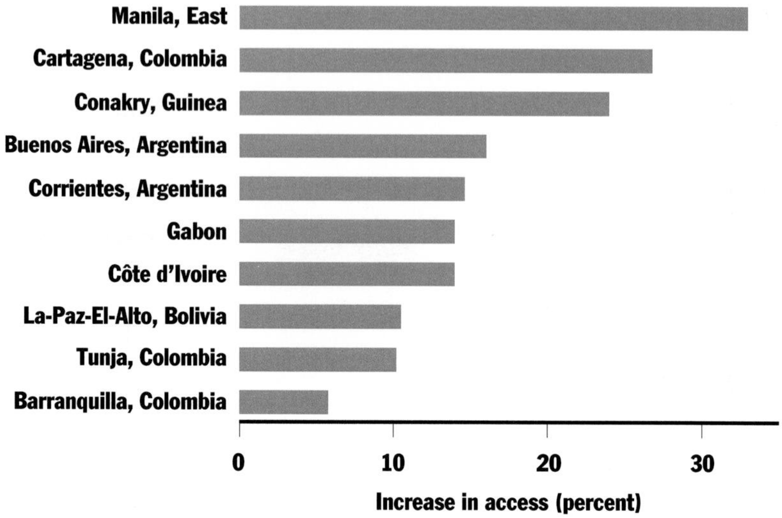

Source: Harris (2003).

American countries that have allowed competition in telecommunications after privatization, networks have expanded almost twice as quickly as in countries that simply converted to private monopolies. But even private monopolies have expanded faster than public ones (figure 4).

Effects on Operating Efficiency

Restructuring, privatization, and deregulation have made network utilities much more efficient in developing and transition economies. Many of these gains have resulted from policy options previously denied to state enterprises. As part of their privatization contracts, new operators could generally start shedding excess employees—one of the most vexing problems facing state-owned utilities in nearly every developing and transition economy. As a result reforming countries have often seen dramatic improvements in labor productivity (figure 5).

A key argument for privatization is that, relative to state-owned utilities, private owners and operators who face competition have stronger incentives and are better able to control costs, respond to consumer

Figure 4   In 1989–94, Privatization Contributed to Faster Growth in Phone Lines in Latin America

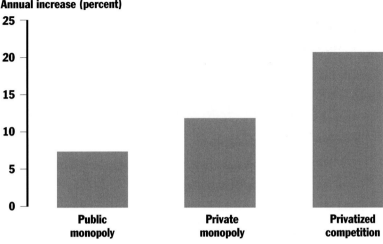

Source: Wellenius (1997b).

needs, and adopt new technologies and management practices. Privatization and deregulation have significantly improved physical performance, service quality, and other aspects of efficiency in many developing and transition economies. Although the most dramatic gains have been in telecommunications (due to revolutionary technological changes and the sector's substantial scope for competitive entry), other infrastructure sectors have also made swift advances.

In telecommunications privatization and related reforms have lowered repair requests and raised call completion rates and the probability of receiving a dial tone. In railroads they have increased locomotive availability. In ports they have shortened waiting times for vessels and increased crane handling rates. And in electricity they have lowered energy losses, outages per customer, and rates of plant unavailability.

Effects on Allocative Efficiency

Before reforms, the failure of many governments to adequately increase service rates, especially during periods of high inflation, effectively de-

Figure 5   Railway Concessions Sharply Increased Labor Productivity in the 1990s

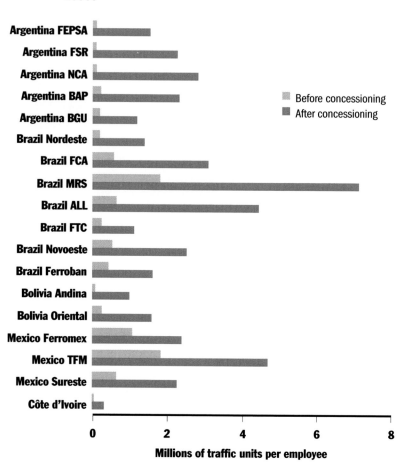

Source: Thompson and Budin (2001).

capitalized their infrastructure systems. Thus one of the main attractions of infrastructure privatization is the expectation that it will make price reform a policy priority. The assumption is that private investors will be unwilling to invest in infrastructure unless governments agree to implement prices that reflect costs. And indeed, many countries are dismantling long-standing policies of underpricing and cross-subsidies. But in some countries price reform has been slow, with infrastructure prices still far removed from their underlying costs. For example, in 2000 household electricity prices still covered less than 50 percent, and

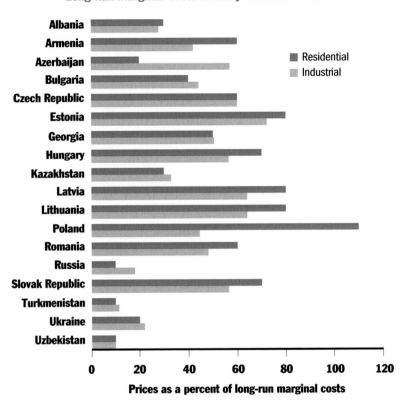

Figure 6 In 2000, Electricity Prices Covered a Small Fraction of Long-Run Marginal Costs in Many Transition Economies

Prices as a percent of long-run marginal costs

Source: Stern (2002).

industrial prices less than 70 percent, of long-run marginal costs in most transition economies (figure 6).

Effects on Distributional Equity

To mitigate the public discontent associated with restructuring and privatization, more comprehensive assessments are needed of their welfare effects—moving beyond standard analyses of their impacts on firm profitability and industry performance to include their effects on workers and households at different income levels. Moreover, distinctions between low- and middle-income countries need to be made more carefully. In low-income countries nearly all rural and many poor urban residents lack access to basic infrastructure services. Thus the policy reforms that normally accompany restructuring and privatization—such as eliminating cross-subsidies and moving toward cost-reflective prices—mainly affect higher-income groups. But in middle-income countries—such as those in Latin America and especially transition economies—such reforms can hurt poor people because many of them (mainly in urban areas) have access to basic services. The solution is not to halt the needed reforms but to put in place safety nets and tariff rebalancing schemes that do not involve radical, across-the-board price increases.

Recent empirical work offers insights on the distributional effects of infrastructure reforms. Studies in Argentina, for example, have found that all income classes benefited from the efficiency, quality, and access improvements resulting from the utility privatizations that began in 1990. More efficient infrastructure services also affect most other economic activities and promote general economic growth—enhancing economic opportunities for poor people. When these general effects are taken into account, the poorest groups seem to benefit the most from the increased productivity and access brought about by privatization and related reforms (Benitez, Chisari, and Estache 2003).

Recent research analyzing the welfare effects of utility privatizations in four Latin American countries (Argentina, Bolivia, Mexico, Nicaragua) found no clear pattern in price changes—in about half the cases, prices fell (McKenzie and Mookherjee 2003). But there were adverse distributional effects on the bottom half of the income distribution due to job cuts in the privatized utilities. (Though the utilities accounted for only a small share of employment in these countries, so privatization cannot be blamed for any significant increases in national unemployment.) Still, the negative distributional effects of layoffs and price adjustments were more than offset by improvements in service quality, increased access for poor people, and the changed structure of public finances, which benefited poor people more.

Negative popular perceptions of privatization might also reflect a process that has at times been deeply flawed. For privatization to achieve its public interest objectives, significant institutional preconditions must be met. For example, effective regulation is needed to balance the interests of consumers and operators—to protect consumers lacking competitive alternatives while allowing operators to earn a fair return on prudent investments. But creating regulatory institutions that render

Fears that restructuring and privatization would hurt poor people have proven largely unfounded . . .

. . . In fact, these reforms have increased coverage, often delivering the biggest benefits to poor households

decisions legitimate to citizens and credible to investors has proven to be the most vexing problem of every infrastructure reform program.

Given the importance of network utilities, removing pricing distortions is crucial to economic reform in developing and transition economies. Still, there are good reasons to avoid overly abrupt, across-the-board price changes, which can cause large, unnecessary adjustment costs for consumers and firms alike. Even optimal prices, if instituted extremely quickly and without sufficient notice, can lead to a difficult transition process that is far from optimal. Thus policymakers should plan from the outset for a smooth, well-planned transition to efficient pricing levels and structures.

Developing Good Regulation Remains a Major Challenge

AMONG THE MOST CRITICAL TASKS FOR POLICYMAKERS IN developing and transition economies is designing and implementing stable, effective regulation for network utilities. In many advanced industrial economies the challenge has been reforming existing regulations and reducing unwarranted governmental intrusion. By contrast, in nearly every developing and transition economy the most pressing issue is designing—from scratch—regulatory mechanisms for privatized utilities.[3]

Regulation that provides a credible commitment to safeguarding the interests of both investors and customers—particularly when economic shocks create political pressure to shift the balance of power among competing interest groups—is crucial to attracting the long-term private capital needed to secure an adequate, reliable supply of infrastructure services. Successful reform requires regulation that clarifies property rights, allocates them sensibly, and assures private investors that their sunk investments will not be subject to regulatory opportunism.

For regulation to promote welfare by facilitating investment, innovation, and allocatively efficient pricing, its institutional design and substantive content must be consistent with country circumstances—particularly the country's size, institutional endowments (including checks and balances), technical expertise, auditing technologies, fiscal condition and tax system efficacy, and the economic characteristics of its industries. Thus it is inappropriate and often costly for developing

Credible regulation is essential

17

and transition economies to try to uncritically replicate the regulatory frameworks of advanced industrial countries.

What Makes for Effective Regulation?

Regulatory procedures must be predictable, accountable, and transparent. Regulatory bodies should:

Competent regulatory institutions are the linchpins of successful reform . . .

- Have competent, nonpolitical, professional staff—expert in relevant economic, accounting, engineering, and legal principles and familiar with good regulatory practices.
- Operate in a statutory framework that fosters competition and market-like regulatory policies and practices.
- Be subject to substantive and procedural requirements that ensure integrity, independence, transparency, and accountability.

. . . Yet many developing and transition countries have paid inadequate attention to creating such institutions

Where Do Things Stand?

Political interference has undermined regulatory independence in many developing and transition economies. Governments, especially line ministries, have been reluctant to consign important regulatory functions to independent agencies. Instead, many regulatory agencies report to sector ministries and are filled with government representatives.

Recent surveys indicate that most regulatory agencies in developing and transition economies are not legally required to hold open meetings. Nor are they obligated to provide written justifications for their decisions. And in many countries the regulatory framework lacks coherence, with responsibilities splintered among regulatory agencies and line ministries.

The label "independent" is often applied too quickly to regulators in developing and transition economies

One emerging lesson is that although formal requirements for integrity, independence, transparency, and accountability are essential for effective regulation, they are far from sufficient. The experience so far raises doubts that governments will observe the spirit of the law and implement proper, consistent regulatory procedures—especially when their choices are influenced (and constrained) by external pressures and loan conditions.

Still, it is important to remember that it took many years for advanced economies to achieve regulatory effectiveness. For example, it took decades for the United States to reach an equilibrium in which the independence of regulatory agencies was recognized and supported by administrative procedures, ex parte rules, and judicial review. In developing countries regulatory structures have been created from scratch and are still in early stages of development. And although progress towards regulatory effectiveness has been slow, at least the trend is in the right direction—greater independence, accountability, and transparency than under state ownership.

Many Prices and Subsidies Still Require Reform

S TATE-OWNED INFRASTRUCTURE MONOPOLIES IN DEVELOPING countries often failed to achieve widespread service coverage. Thus infrastructure reform must be designed to increase access to affordable services for previously unserved customers—mainly poor and rural groups. Pricing policies and subsidy mechanisms play a crucial role in achieving this goal.

Past pricing policies and subsidy mechanisms were seriously flawed and usually failed to achieve their stated objectives. Rather than providing affordable infrastructure services to poor people, they undermined the financial viability of utilities, resulted in rationing of services, and actually exacerbated inequality. Thus there is an urgent need for tariff and subsidy mechanisms that do a better job of achieving economic efficiency and social equity.

Moving toward Efficient, Equitable Pricing

Most developing and transition economies have been slow to implement cost-reflective prices for infrastructure services. Moreover, many infrastructure prices contain significant cross-subsidies that cannot be defended on social equity grounds.

Infrastructure services are often considered essential both to the public and to the effective functioning of the economy. Because some of these services are extremely price and income inelastic, their pricing has important distributional implications. Subsidizing basic services such as electricity and water is politically attractive because it can approximate a lump-sum grant based on the number of household members.

Conversely, raising the price of basic services appears like a lump-sum tax bearing heavily on poor and elderly people and large households. Not surprisingly, moves toward cost-reflective tariffs often encounter strong political opposition. As a result most governments that have liberalized infrastructure have not accorded sufficient prominence to adjusting infrastructure prices.

Deviations from optimal pricing also reflect lack of appreciation of how alternative pricing schemes could strike a better balance between economic efficiency and social equity. In particular, price differentiation and competitive pricing flexibility, potentially valuable tools for achieving adequate revenue and expanding service to poor people, have not been sufficiently exploited in developing and transition economies.

Most developing and transition economies have used cross-subsidies ostensibly to promote desirable social goals (such as helping disadvantaged customers) and positive economic externalities (such as those associated with universal service). In telecommunications, rates for access and for local calls have been low, while those for domestic and international long-distance calls have been high (relative to underlying long-term costs). Similarly, residential electricity has often been priced below its incremental cost—while service for industrial users has been priced above its stand-alone cost.[4] But because of poor targeting, a large portion of such subsidies flow to people other than the intended beneficiaries. Furthermore, distorted prices impose significant costs by sending the wrong economic signals to consumers, suppliers, and investors. And economic theory and regulatory experience suggest that cross-subsidies are incompatible with open entry and competition.

Even though cross-subsidies can create significant distortions leading to welfare and financial losses, they should not be eliminated in all circumstances. It is true, for example, that using general tax revenue to support social goals can be less distortive than internal cross-subsidies. But in many developing and transition economies the cost of public funds can be very high because government revenue is raised with distortive taxes. So, in developing countries with especially inefficient tax systems, reliance on cross-subsidies might be preferable. Moreover, alternative subsidy mechanisms could require elaborate administrative systems that are costly or unavailable. In such cases cross-subsidies might have to be tolerated as a second-best solution.

Targeting Subsidies Better

Government subsidies for infrastructure services are common in developing and transition economies. For example, India's federal and state governments spend more than $1 billion a year subsidizing water services. The purported rationale for such support mechanisms is to ensure that essential services remain affordable to poor segments of society. Yet many subsidy programs involve almost no targeting: price structures do not discriminate between rich and poor people, so everyone benefits. In fact, because many poor people do not have access to infrastructure services (such as private water connections), poor households capture only a small fraction of subsidy resources.

As an alternative to traditional subsidies, direct subsidies have been proposed using various targeting mechanisms. These alternative mechanisms have several advantages: they are transparent, explicit, and minimize distortions in the behavior of the utility and its customers. Targeting based on location or housing characteristics can substantially reduce subsidy leakage and so substantially increase the share of subsidy resources captured by poor households. Moreover, targeted connection subsidies appear to perform better than targeted consumption subsidies.

An Agenda for Action—From Institution Building to Policymaking

THERE IS MUCH TO APPLAUD IN THE RESTRUCTURED AND privatized network utilities of developing and transition economies—from their new architectures to the commitment of those who crafted them, who operate in them, and who regulate them. But even in countries where restructuring has been carried out in a way that promotes the public interest, a host of significant problems have emerged.

Many of these second generation problems are endemic to infrastructure everywhere and largely reflect issues that arise after privatization, especially when combined with unbundling. Yet lack of resources (especially economic, accounting, and other technical expertise), inexperience with regulating private utilities, and preoccupation with institution building during the first stage of reform have created some unique challenges in these countries.

Designing Retrospective Analysis and Data Collection

Infrastructure restructuring and privatization are undergoing a multifaceted revisionism. Choosing the right restructuring strategy is harder than early optimists claimed, and privatization and related institutional reforms are less impressive in practice than earlier believed. Growing public discontent with these reforms may partly be the result of the failure of some governments to publicly articulate the economic and social rationales, prerequisites, and expected outcomes. Thus it may simply reflect public misunderstanding. Still this discontent points to the importance of careful analysis of what works, what can go wrong, and why.

Lack of empirical knowledge is among the main hindrances to infrastructure policy analysis and reform in developing and transition economies. Given that most reforms began in the early 1990s, until recently there were not enough data to evaluate different ownership, structural, and regulatory options and their dependence on country circumstances. But there is now a growing list of experiments in infrastructure reform—putting us in a better position to reflect on lessons and identify the most important issues to address and options to consider.

Empirically untangling the links between distinct policy decisions and ultimate industry performance will require systematic collection of cross-country infrastructure data. International financial institutions—which at times have imposed covenants to address performance in these sectors, and have collected financial and other data to monitor those efforts—are ideally suited to undertaking this effort. However, in many cases the data have not been collected consistently with a view to supporting the needed types of analysis.

Addressing Second Generation Reforms

Experience and economic logic suggest that post-privatization improvements in performance will be limited, and probably unsustainable, unless accompanied by appropriate second generation regulatory reforms. These include:

- Designing pricing policies that strike a balance between economic efficiency and social equity.
- Developing rules governing access to bottleneck infrastructure facilities.
- Adapting regulation to address emerging problems, changing circumstances, and new information in regulated infrastructure sectors.
- Finding new ways to increase poor people's access to services.

Many of the rules and principles for resolving second generation regulatory issues have been developed in the context of advanced industrial economies. To be effective in developing and transition economies, they must be modified.

Price reform.   Price reform is among the most important and challenging tasks facing policymakers in developing and transition economies. In most of these countries price structures continue to conflict with economic efficiency. Ministries still conduct old-style centralized price setting, in part in an effort to control inflation. Some deviations from optimal policy are due to political and social constraints—noneconomic and equity considerations inevitably intrude when economically efficient prices are devised and administered. But other deviations are due to lack of appreciation of the power of alternative pricing schemes, which could strike a better balance between economic efficiency and social equity.

Policy solutions consistent with both economic efficiency and social equity are not always available or politically feasible. Thus policymakers in the transition and developing economies face no greater challenge than to design and implement price reforms that better manage the tradeoffs between these two goals. The literature provides little guidance for managing the move to cost-reflective prices. Specific challenges include what standards to apply, how fast to proceed, and how to promote universal service in a competitive environment. In particular, there is need for further applied policy research to evaluate the potential use of price differentiation and price flexibility for achieving revenue adequacy and expanding services to poor people.

Access to bottleneck infrastructure facilities.   A vexing task for regulators is designing terms and conditions of access to bottleneck infrastructure facilities by competing service providers. These facilities are essential inputs in the production or delivery of final products, and cannot be economically duplicated. Examples include the local loop ("final mile") in telecommunications, the transmission grid in electricity, the network of pipelines in natural gas, and the track in railroads. Access policy is the keystone of the contemporary response to the problem of residual monopoly in infrastructure. Indeed, it is at the fore of discussions of ways to facilitate competitive entry into activities that have traditionally been run by franchised monopolies. The access issue is especially difficult in situations where several firms compete in the sale of a final product, but one is the monopoly owner of an input that is indispensable in the supply of that product. The problem is how competition in the final product market can be preserved and not tilted to favor either the owner of the bottleneck input or its rivals.

The economic literature offers two main approaches to efficient pricing of essential input facilities: the efficient component pricing rule (also known as parity pricing) and the Ramsey pricing rule. But despite their internal consistency and powerful theoretical results, it is difficult to translate either approach (especially the Ramsey pricing rule) into workable rules and access pricing schedules. Given circumstances in developing and transition economies, there is a need for further research to identify variants of these rules that are less complex technically and less demanding informationally.

Regulatory adaptation and contract renegotiation.   Regulation needs to adapt to emerging problems, changing circumstances, and new information and experiences in regulated sectors. Regulatory flexibility is especially imperative in sectors experiencing rapid technological and market changes.

Inflexibilities built into privatization agreements are often a severe impediment to solving post-privatization regulatory problems. Such inflexibilities were probably needed to create commitments to reform, protect consumers, and attract the private capital required for privatization. But they also make it difficult to solve emerging problems, because many parties find adaptations threatening to the privatization commitments that protect their interests and the entire fabric of reform.

To solve this problem, the regulator should articulate a set of fundamental principles that serve as a transparent basis for policy analysis and decisions. These principles should protect the interests of investors at the levels established by privatization agreements, protect consumer interests, ensure economically efficient competition, and so on. International financial institutions could make an important contribution in this area by helping to develop guidelines for revising regulatory mandates and rules, and for renegotiating privatization contracts—guidelines that adhere to accepted principles of the economic public interest and embody much of the best available economic learning.

Increasing poor people's access.   In addition to reducing distortions and adjustment costs, pricing policies must be designed to maximize efficiency—subject to meeting certain social policy goals, such as universal access for rural and poor urban consumers. When considering and undertaking reforms, policymakers need to know existing service levels for these groups, how policy proposals will affect them, and how to enhance their access. Although low coverage among low-income and rural households suggests that public monopolies have not successfully provided these households with access to infrastructure services in most developing countries, it is not clear that privatization and liberalization will automatically benefit them either.

In the pre-reform era, universal service obligations were funded, at least in theory, by subsidies and, more commonly, cross-subsidies. But with privatization and market liberalization it is impossible to maintain significant cross-subsidies in the structure of prices. So, either new sources of subsidy must be found or rates below incremental costs must be raised to compensatory levels.

In the United States, after the deregulation of key sectors of the economy, substantial effort was put into designing competitively neutral mechanisms to promote universal service. The need to adopt support mechanisms sufficient to advance universal service, and to help consumers who would otherwise be disadvantaged, is even more pronounced in developing and transition countries reforming their infrastructure sectors.

The requisite policy approach for pursuing universal service goals in a specific industry is likely to be sensitive to the country's political and institutional endowment and fiscal condition, consumer incomes and preferences, and the industry's economic characteristics. Additional work is needed to understand how these factors affect the optimal design of support mechanisms: whether support for universal service should be funded out of general tax revenues, or perhaps out of a broadly based tax on revenues from the industry's products and services; the extent and scope of subsidies; and more targeted methods for delivering subsidies without distorting competition.

Designing Effective and Practical Regulatory Regimes

Empirical assessment of economic regulation reveals that in a variety of circumstances its effects deviate substantially from efficiency. Regulatory failure arises from a combination of the information problems facing regulators and the complex agency relationships inherent in the control structure of every regulatory setting. Even in the United States, where regulatory oversight has been supported by expert economic analysis, the disappointing performance that followed the economic regulation of the 1960s and 1970s raised doubts about time-honored regulatory solutions to allocative problems.

In developing and transition economies regulatory failure is exacerbated by lack of technical and economic expertise in critical areas. This may require regulators to avoid sophisticated interventions that impose significant informational and analytical requirements. Indeed, in some circumstances in these countries the costs of regulation may exceed its benefits, and the public could be better off relying on unfettered competitive market forces.

There is an urgent need to:

- Deepen understanding of how to design effective and practical regulatory mechanisms in the face of scarce technical and economic expertise.
- Identify options for the structural reorganization of industries that reduce the need for regulatory oversight.
- Develop more precise criteria distinguishing between cases where regulatory intervention is required and those where it is not.
- Develop models for optimal allocation of scarce regulatory resources among firms and sectors with different sizes, technologies, information asymmetries, and political constraints.

- Identify appropriate, perhaps less sophisticated, tools of intervention better suited to regulators in the developing and transition countries.

Notes

1. This refers mainly to the period after World War II. Private ownership in electricity was initially the norm in many countries in Europe and North and South America. State ownership spread later, especially after World War II, either for ideological reasons (as in England and France) or because political constraints on prices forced private firms into bankruptcy (as in Latin America). Similar situations prevailed for railroads and water in many countries. Telephone services became captive of state-owned post offices in Europe and Japan, but not in Canada, the United States, or, initially, Latin America.

2. The results of such polls can be very sensitive to how the questions are asked. As Klein (2003) notes, according to such polls only 21 percent of Peruvians seemed to generally support electricity privatization. But when asked specifically about privatization implemented transparently and accompanied by increased investments as well as prices set by a regulatory process, more than 60 percent favored it.

3. The regulatory function was not entirely avoided under state ownership. For example, service quality still had to be monitored, and prices for infrastructure services had to be set. The main difference lies in the characteristics of the regulatory process, which was ad hoc and opaque under the old regime—while it is necessary to adhere to certain transparent requirements of due process in the new setting.

4. A service's incremental cost is the addition (per unit of the service's additional output) to a firm's total costs when output of the service expands by some preselected increment. The stand-alone cost of a service (or combination of services) is the cost that would be incurred by an efficient entrant if it were to produce only that service or combination of services—that is, the cost of producing "standing alone" (Baumol and Sidak 1994).

CHAPTER ONE

The New Paradigm for Network Utilities

FOR MUCH OF THE 20TH CENTURY MOST COUNTRIES relied on government ownership and regulation to promote socially equitable access to network infrastructure services—including electricity, telecommunications, water and sewerage, natural gas, and transportation—using mechanisms such as nonexploitive pricing, nondiscriminatory coverage, and universal service.[1] Reflecting infrastructure's strategic importance and concerns about monopoly power, it was widely believed that these sectors could not be entrusted to the signals, motivations, and penalties of free markets. In addition, most governments relied on this public utility paradigm because they were convinced that state resources were required to finance large investments in service coverage.

But in recent decades this consensus has changed, resulting in far-reaching restructuring, privatization, and other reforms of crucial infrastructure sectors and services. This chapter explains why—and explores what this change bodes for future efforts to regulate and expand infrastructure.

Why Are Network Utilities So Important?

NETWORK UTILITIES PROVIDE CRUCIAL SERVICES FOR MANUfacturing and commerce, and so significantly influence the growth of national production (World Bank 1994b; Newbery 2000a). Thus economic development depends on such infrastructure—and failure to reform and modernize it undermines national competitiveness and risks economic stagnation.

Deficient infrastructure—along with weak management and poor economic organization—accounts for a large share of low factor productivity in developing countries

This report's focus on the regulation of network utilities is also motivated by their unique economic characteristics, which make them a natural target for government intervention yet render them difficult to regulate in the public interest. These characteristics include (Spiller and Savedoff 1999):

- Extensive economies of scale and scope that generally lead to market concentration and inhibit competition. As a result regulation cannot be completely abolished.
- Large sunk costs relative to fixed and variable (avoidable) costs. Sunk costs are those that in the short- and medium-term cannot be eliminated even by ceasing production. Such costs impose considerable risks and so discourage entry by new service providers.
- Services deemed essential to a broad range of users, making their provision and pricing politically sensitive.

Extensive economies of scale and scope often lead to monopolistic organization of network utilities.[2] Large sunk costs exacerbate the problem of market power and ensure that private, unregulated pricing and investment decisions will not be socially optimal. The combination of large, durable assets with significant sunk costs and highly politicized consumption makes network utilities vulnerable to administrative expropriation—both directly and through uneconomic price controls. Because private investors feel vulnerable, they reduce their investments, demand high risk premiums, or both (Zelner and Henisz 2000). These basic features, common to varying degree to utilities across different sectors, create special challenges for effective regulation.

From State to Market—Changing Views on Utilities

AFTER WORLD WAR II THE VERTICALLY INTEGRATED, STATE-owned utility became the industry model for electricity, telecommunications, water, natural gas, and railways and other transportation services. In electricity, for example, the same publicly owned company was often responsible for generating power, transmitting it to local networks, and distributing it to retail consumers.

Unlike previously private utilities that were highly fragmented or too large to prevent monopolistic abuse, publicly owned entities seemed like a sensible way to secure the benefits of size—and the required large-scale financing—without suffering the drawbacks of monopoly pricing. Thus most countries opted for nationalization instead of regulation. An exception was the United States, where network utilities were privately owned but subject to comprehensive regulatory controls. Still, industrial structures were quite similar under these two forms of ownership and regulation (Newbery 2002).

At first, vertically integrated, state-owned utilities produced reasonably satisfactory results (Fare, Grosskopf, and Logan 1985). For example, French and U.K. public firms became leaders in efficient utility pricing starting in the 1950s (Turvey 1968). In the United States the Tennessee Valley Authority demonstrated the advantages of reaching down the demand curve by reducing prices (Scherer 1980, p. 487). And Brazil's state-owned telecommunications company, Telebras, grew impressively after it was consolidated and restructured in 1972 (World Bank 1992).

Since the early 1980s, however, the monolithic model has proven increasingly unsuited to dramatically changing conditions in both industrial and developing countries. As a result there has been a worldwide reassessment of public policies for network utilities.

This reassessment began in the late 1970s, when the United States initiated wide-ranging regulatory reforms (Joskow and Noll 1994; Noll 1999). Revolutionary changes in U.S. economic policies and network utilities were driven by a series of serious challenges—including stagflation, energy crises, double-digit inflation, increased environmental concerns, the bankruptcy of backbone industries (such as railways), and a perceived erosion in national productivity and international competitiveness (box 1.1). Proponents of deregulation argued that unleashing competition among service providers would lower inflation and restore productivity growth. At the same time, concerns about the energy crises and environmental protection facilitated the introduction of economically efficient pricing, which was expected to discourage wasteful consumption (Kahn 2001).

During the same period the United Kingdom began transforming major sectors of its economy. Large-scale privatization began in 1984, when 51 percent of British Telecom was sold to the private sector. The company's divestiture was driven by the government's desire to remove telecommunications investment from its balance sheet in order to meet its targets for public borrowing (Kay 2001). The subsequent privatiza-

---

Box 1.1   Milestones in Infrastructure Reform in the United States, the United Kingdom, and the European Union

U.S. deregulation

Airline Deregulation Act	1978
Staggers Act (rail deregulation)	1980
Motor Carrier Act (trucking deregulation)	1980
AT&T divestiture (telecommunications deregulation)	1984
Federal Energy Regulatory Commission Order 636 (gas deregulation)	1992
FERC Order 888 (electricity deregulation)	1996
Telecommunications Act	1996

U.K. privatization

British Telecom	1984
British Gas	1986
British Airways	1987
British Airports Authority	1987
Water and sewage companies	1989
Electricity companies	1990
British Rail	1995
British Energy (nuclear)	1996

EU liberalization directives

Telecommunications	1990
Railways	1991
Electricity	1996
Gas	1998

---

tion of other utility industries was accompanied by radical regulatory reforms (Newbery 2000a). Several new regulatory bodies were created, and new tasks were assigned to existing agencies such as the Monopolies and Mergers Commission (Armstrong, Cowan, and Vickers 1994).

Meanwhile, members of the European Union increasingly came to see state-owned monopolies as hindrances to international trade in goods and services. Thus in the 1990s a series of directives were issued to create a single market where goods, services, people, and capital could move freely. These directives spelled out rules for telecommunications,

Table 1.1 Private Investment in Infrastructure in Developing and Transition Economies, by Sector, 1990–2001

(billions of 2001 U.S. dollars)

Year	Telecommunications	Electricity	Transportation	Water	Gas	Total
1990	6.2	1.3	10.3	—	—	17.8
1991	13.5	1.3	3.3	0.1	—	18.2
1992	7.9	8.9	4.6	2.0	4.0	27.4
1993	10.9	11.1	5.7	7.9	4.6	40.2
1994	20.3	15.2	8.9	0.5	1.8	46.7
1995	20.1	20.9	12.0	1.8	4.1	58.9
1996	29.7	30.6	17.4	1.9	3.0	82.6
1997	45.4	48.7	21.7	9.3	3.3	128.4
1998	57.3	24.6	18.4	2.4	6.5	109.2
1999	43.3	14.4	8.9	6.9	3.7	77.2
2000	45.3	26.4	11.6	4.8	2.3	90.4
2001	31.7	10.0	12.4	2.2	1.2	57.5
Total	331.6	213.4	135.2	39.8	34.5	754.5

Source: World Bank, Private Participation in Infrastructure Project database.

railways, electricity, and natural gas markets across EU member states, mapping out a common regulatory framework and liberalizing these industries. But little thought was given to the challenges of industrial restructuring or the details of policy implementation, and there was no careful assessment of the costs and benefits of these reforms.

As the United States deregulated, the United Kingdom restructured and privatized, and the European Union issued directives calling for extensive liberalization (but staying silent on the issue of ownership) and building a single market, a powerful privatization movement began sweeping developing and transition economies. Between 1990 and 2001, 132 of these countries took substantive steps to introduce private participation in their infrastructure sectors. During this period these countries saw $750 billion in private investment in infrastructure through divestitures, greenfield projects, and management and operations contracts involving major capital spending (table 1.1).

For many developing countries the primary push for privatization came from the debt and fiscal crises of the early 1980s (Estache 2001). Another major impetus came from the extraordinarily weak performance of infrastructure in these countries relative to industrial countries.[3] Similar reasons motivated reforms in transition economies start-

Figure 1.1 Latin America and the Caribbean Has Led Developing Regions in Private Investment in Infrastructure, 1990–2001

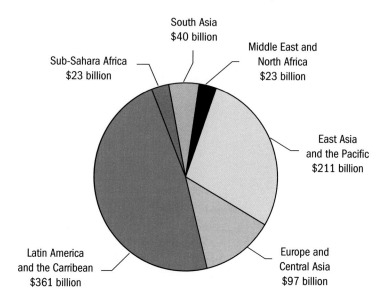

**Total Private Investment = US $754 billion
(in 2001 US $ billion)**

Source: Harris (2003).

ing in the early 1990s. Heavy debt burdens forced many countries to make fiscal adjustments that hit public investment in infrastructure especially hard. For example, in Latin America between 1980–84 and 1995–98 public infrastructure investment as a share of GDP dropped from 3.1 to 0.2 percent in Argentina, from 5.0 to 2.0 percent in Bolivia, from 3.7 to 0.6 percent in Brazil, from 3.1 to 1.7 percent in Chile, from 2.5 to 0.4 percent in Mexico, and from 2.0 to 0.6 percent in Peru (Calderon, Easterly, and Serven 2003). Yet in recent years Latin America and the Caribbean has led developing regions in infrastructure investment involving private participation (Roger 1999; Izaguirre 2002)—accounting for nearly half the total in 1990–2001, mainly through divestitures (figure 1.1).

Privatization was also spurred by the intolerable damage caused by mismanagement of public enterprises (Shirley and Walsh 2001). Most such entities pursued multiple, poorly defined, conflicting objectives, with managers often appointed based on their political loyalty, not competence. Investment funds were frequently squandered on poor projects.

Moreover, price controls were imposed without regard for their performance implications, subjecting enterprises to financial distress and impairing their ability to mobilize investments and provide reliable services (Kerf and Smith 1996).

Efforts to reform unproductive public enterprises had limited success, either failing to achieve or sustain desired improvements (World Bank 1995). Few governments were able to implement and maintain the many complex, demanding policies needed for efficient public enterprise performance. Moreover, in many countries inefficient public enterprises—especially in infrastructure—were draining state budgets, diverting resources from other social priorities (such as health and education), impairing the performance of banks, and impeding private sector development.

In a globalized economy, poorly performing state-owned infrastructure providers were increasingly seen as constraining economic growth and undermining international competitiveness. Developing countries simply could not continue to absorb the fiscal burden of these enterprises (Lieberman 1997). Around the world, it became evident to policymakers that the problems of public enterprises could be solved only by implementing radical structural changes and realigning the roles of the government and the private sector.

The Dawn of a New Utility Model

THE INFRASTRUCTURE LIBERALIZATION AND PRIVATIZATION that swept the globe in the 1990s were a significant departure from the previous economic consensus. This departure not only questioned the need for state ownership in these sectors, it also reexamined long-standing notions about natural monopolies and accompanying regulations.

Unbundling—Isolating Monopoly Parts

The historical model of network utilities was premised on the assumption that natural monopoly in some areas of their operations, combined with complementarities and coordination requirements between the natural monopoly and other components, meant that these industries were best served—and served best—when structured as vertically integrated monopolies. Moreover, monopoly franchises seemed to provide an assured base for financing long-term investments. This view was enshrined in the monolithic organization, where a single entity controlled all facilities, operations, and administrative functions and was obliged (in accordance with its public utility responsibilities) to serve on demand within its territory.

In recent years, however, there has been growing recognition that network utilities are not monolithic natural monopolies. Rather, they encompass several distinct activities with entirely different economic characteristics—entailing a mix of competition and monopoly elements in supply. Technological progress (which has proven a potent enemy of natural monopolies; Klein 1996a), along with the high costs of regulatory intervention, have been continuously undermining the public utility concept.[4] As a result it has become widely accepted that the vertically integrated monopoly model no longer applies to all network utilities.

Electricity, natural gas, telecommunications, railways, and water evolved as vertically integrated industries with transportation, transmission, and distribution networks linking upstream production to downstream supply. These networks consist of transmission links in electricity, national pipelines and regional distribution links in gas, transmission media and switching centers in telecommunications, earthworks, track, signals, and stations in railways, and pipes and sewers in water. Most network components involve substantial fixed costs that are largely sunk because their assets are of minimal value for other purposes.

But some components of these industries have cost conditions more conducive to competition, including activities related to upstream production and downstream supply (electricity, gas, water), certain parts of the network (interexchange services in telecommunications), and the operation of services on the physical network (railways; Gray and Klein 1997). Although these activities involve important economies of scale and some sunk costs, they are small relative to those in network infrastructure—and are constantly being shrunk by advances in technology. Thus substantial competition could emerge in many parts of these industries (table 1.2).

Reflecting these developments, a new paradigm has emerged for the organizational restructuring of network utilities. According to this model:

> The monopoly approach to supplying services, which dominated infrastructure markets for almost a century, is now in decline

Table 1.2 Noncompetitive and Competitive Components of Network Industries

Industry	Activities that are usually not competitive	Activities that can be and sometimes are competitive
Electricity	High-voltage transmission and local distribution	Generation and supply to final customers
Gas	High-pressure transmission and local distribution	Production, supply to final customers, and storage
Telecommunications	Local residential telephony or local loop	Long-distance, mobile, and value added services
Railways	Short-haul track and signaling infrastructure	Train operations and maintenance facilities
Water	Local distribution and local wastewater collection	Production, long-distance transportation, purification, and sewage treatment
Air services	Airport facilities	Aircraft operations, maintenance facilities, and commercial activities

Source: Gonenc, Maher, and Nicoletti (2001).

- Network utilities should be unbundled both horizontally and vertically, with different owners for potentially competitive components and natural monopoly components.
- For competitive or structurally contestable activities, government interference with market mechanisms and restrictions on ownership should be relaxed, and the scope for introducing competition through horizontal fragmentation should be fully exploited.
- Only components involving unavoidable natural monopolies or substantial sunk capital should be placed under regulation and perhaps even operated by the public sector (Guasch and Blitzer 1993).

Competition for the Market—A Promising Old Idea

Some analysts have questioned the need to regulate, at least extensively, the natural monopoly components of infrastructure industries by distinguishing between competition *in* the market and competition *for* the market. Proponents of this view have resurrected an old yet powerful idea: when a large number of firms submit noncollusive bids to become the supplier of a natural monopoly activity, the resulting price need not reflect exploitive market power (Demsetz 1968).

Thus, even when competition in the market is not feasible, some of its benefits can be achieved by introducing competition for the market. Under this approach monopoly franchises are awarded through competitive bidding and periodically rebid. This approach provides incentives for firms to perform well to retain their franchises (Klein and Roger 1994).

Still, franchising has some serious limitations. Bidding might be uncompetitive. Another difficulty involves contract specification and monitoring: complex products or services often lead to incomplete contracts and opportunistic renegotiations. Thus the idea that competition for the market can eliminate the need for regulation has been disputed. Moreover, case studies indicate that franchise bidding is beset with transactional difficulties—and the institutional infrastructure required to monitor contracts and avoid undesirable outcomes has many of the earmarks of regulation (Williamson 1976).

Technological Change—Breaking Down Monopoly Barriers

Technological innovation is increasingly driving the move toward competition in network utilities. Changes in production and distribution technologies have had especially dramatic effects on the market structure of the electricity and telecommunications industries.

In electricity new technologies have significantly reduced the minimum efficient scale of generating plants, the investment costs of new units, and the time needed to plan and build new plants (figure 1.2; for more details see chapter 3 and the references cited there). Generation could be structurally competitive in many developing and transition economies, especially those with access to natural gas. Smaller plants considerably increase the range of ownership options. Moreover, low-cost, small-scale generation units allow electric power to be produced closer to end users, reducing reliance on transmission and even distribution networks and undermining their natural monopoly characteristics as well. Small-scale, off-grid supply may ultimately prove a practical solution to the electricity problems of many low-income developing countries, especially in Africa.

Figure 1.2   The Optimal Size of Power Generating Plants Has Shrunk

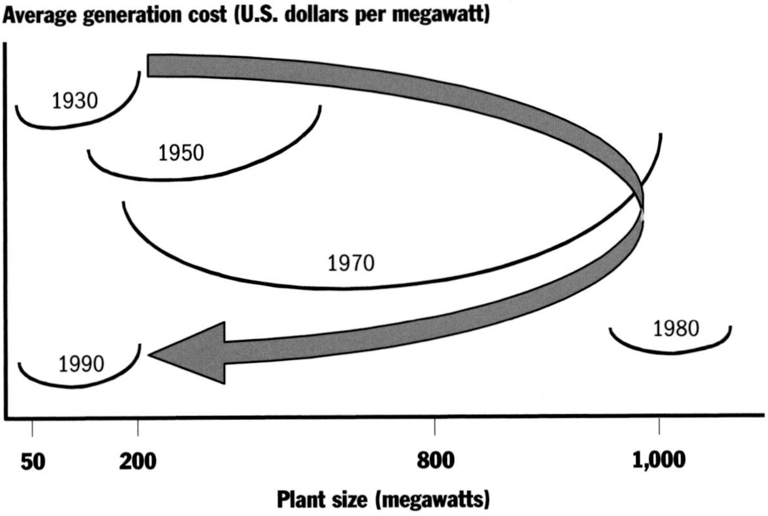

Average generation cost (U.S. dollars per megawatt)

1930

1950

1970

1980

1990

| 50 | 200 | 800 | 1,000 |

Plant size (megawatts)

Source: Bayless (1994).

The telecommunications industry has experienced revolutionary changes as a result of advances in microelectronics, optoelectronics, fixed and mobile Internet platforms, and a plethora of other new technologies (box 1.2). These innovations have radically altered the industry's cost structure and resulted in large, continuous increases in productivity.

Technology has intensified competition in many components of telecommunications networks. New entrants account for a growing share of global investment in telecommunications, rising from 24 percent in 1996 to 34 percent in 2000 (Siemens 2001). Technological change has almost eliminated natural monopoly in interexchange markets, as seen in several countries. Although the erosion of natural monopoly has been slower in local exchange service, significant competition has also emerged in this segment (Vogelsang and Mitchell 1997; Laffont and Tirole 2000; Woroch 2002).

The rapid growth of cellular telephones—which increasingly substitute for wireline services—has played a big role in reducing the importance of scale and natural monopoly associated with conventional local loops (figure 1.3). In its early stages, wireless technology was marketed as a premium product that delivered mobility and connectivity and was more expensive than wireline technology. As such, it mostly supplemented basic telephony.

Box 1.2   The Technological Revolution in Telecommunications

TECHNOLOGICAL CHANGE HAS HAD A MASSIVE but uneven effect on telecommunications. Costs have fallen sharply in the industry's long-distance and traffic-sensitive segments, reflecting advances in microwave, satellite, and optoelectronic technology. The impact of optoelectronics has been especially impressive: in just a decade, optical systems have vastly outperformed coaxial cables and fixed satellite links in long-distance, high-capacity transmission. Substantial cost reductions have also been achieved in switching, reflecting software innovations and lower costs for integrated circuits and computers. Lower costs and significant improvements in software have also facilitated a variety of data- and transmission-intensive services (see figure).

But technological change has not had nearly the same effect on costs in areas where use is not concentrated. Technological change has been limited for nontraffic-sensitive, customer-specific loops that connect every subscriber to a central office. For low-volume nodes, copper cable was until recently the lowest-cost technology. Still, fiber optic distribution and microwave bypass have become economically viable in large office buildings.

In recent years telephone networks have been substantially digitized. Digital bits traveling on these networks can be parts of voice, video, or computer applications. Voice is treated as data, blurring the boundary between voice telephony and data services. When regulation-imposed price discrimi-

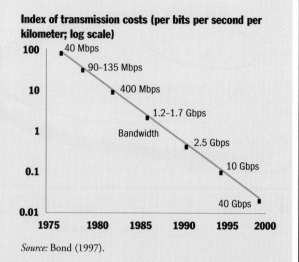

Index of transmission costs (per bits per second per kilometer; log scale)

Source: Bond (1997).

nation between voice and data is eliminated, arbitrage can dramatically reduce the cost of voice calls that use relatively few bits—with important implications for pricing and market structure. Internet-based telecommunications services already threaten traditional long-distance service providers. As bandwidth to customers' homes increases, placing voice calls over the Internet will likely become a viable alternative to wireline telephones. Thus advances in technology have made the old, monolithic structure of the telephone industry both inappropriate and unsustainable.

Source: Arnback 1997; Economides 1998; Noll 2000d.

But the costs of wireless technology have been declining, and in many cases (such as in areas with low subscriber density) it is now cheaper than wireline. As a result these services will increasingly substitute for one another. Moreover, the much flatter cost curves of wireless technology indicate that size does not confer significant cost advantages. It is now cost-effective to have several competing providers of

Figure 1.3 **There Are Now More Mobile Phone Users Than Fixed Phone Lines**

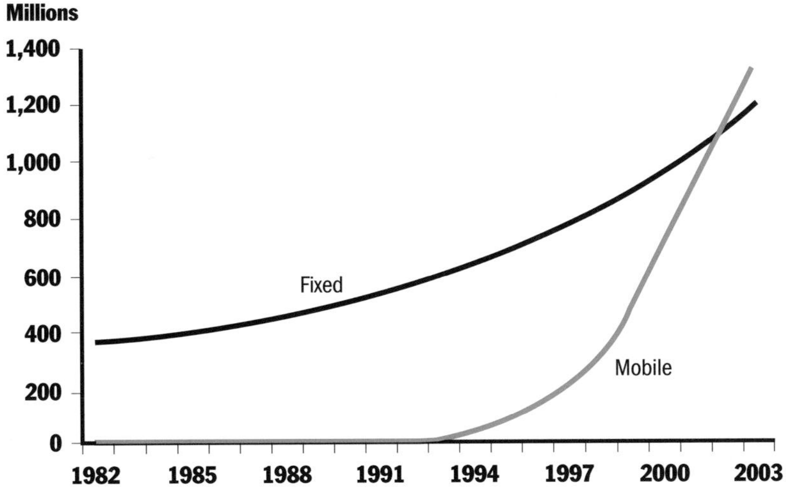

Millions

Source: ITU (2003).

local telecommunications services: a regulated monopoly is no longer the optimal market structure. These developments have enormous implications for developing countries with underdeveloped fixed networks, especially in low-density rural areas.

In contrast to electricity and telecommunications, technological changes in transportation have been evolutionary rather than revolutionary. The introduction of jet engines in the 1950s and the larger aircraft sizes and loads made possible by turbofan engines and improved airplane designs resulted in lower operating costs and dramatically changed the competitive landscape for long-distance passenger and freight transport. But in the early 1970s new engine, track, and signaling technologies made high-speed trains possible, restoring some of rail's competitive advantage—though the introduction of multiple-axle trucks and better road engineering significantly altered competition between trucking and railways in freight transport. The organization and conduct of transportation markets have also been profoundly changed by containerization, intermodalism, and advances in freight logistics and information technology (such as real-time tracking of freight containers). In the water sector, advances in telemetry and satellite imaging show considerable promise for the efficient management of scarce resources.

A new form of radio technology is challenging local loops—the traditional bastion of monopoly power

41

Framework for Assessing Reforms and Regulations

I N RECENT YEARS INFRASTRUCTURE IN DEVELOPING AND TRAN-
sition economies has been plagued by three related problems:

- Chronic underinvestment—causing significant deterioration in service quality and seriously undermining providers' ability to respond to new demands and expand service. As a result large portions of rural and poor urban populations lack access to basic services.[5]
- Underpricing—with both the level and structure of prices conflicting with the dictates of economic efficiency and arguably with social equity as well.
- Extraordinarily low operating and financial performance—with inefficient public utilities draining state budgets, diverting resources from other essential services (such as health and education), and impeding domestic economic growth and international competitiveness.

The performance of each infrastructure sector is multifaceted and not amenable to definitive evaluations. But given the common problems facing these sectors in developing and transition economies, reforms are evaluated in this report using three broad criteria: resulting investment levels (and thus service expansion), operating (technical) efficiency, and allocative efficiency (as indicated by the rebalancing of tariffs).

Given the high poverty in these economies, careful attention must also be paid to whether infrastructure reforms help reduce it. Poor people often lack access to basic infrastructure services, which forces them to pay high costs for low-quality substitutes—further undermining their economic opportunities (Brook and Irwin 2003).

One Model Does Not Fit All—Choosing among Imperfect Systems

The restructuring of network utilities over the past two decades has shown that there is no universally appropriate model for reform (Laffont 2003). Every restructuring and privatization program must take explicit account of each sector's features (its underlying economic attributes and the technological conditions of its production) and the country's economic, institutional, social, and political characteristics. A cookie-cutter approach to reform is unlikely to succeed and leads to problems for the public interest.

The limits of state ownership are numerous and widely accepted. But that does not imply that private enterprise is a superior organizational form for all infrastructure activities and in every country. Before state ownership is replaced, the properties and requirements of the proposed alternative must be carefully assessed—not just generally but also specifically for the activity and country in question (box 1.3).

The vertically integrated, state-owned utility model is largely a straw man from today's perspective

---

Box 1.3   Power Generation in Brazil Shows That Privatization Is Not Always the Best Approach

ADVICE ON PRIVATIZATION NEEDS TO REFLECT A thorough understanding of the sector and country concerned. Power generation in Brazil shows how even policy recommendations that make sense in most contexts can be inadvisable in others.

Hydropower accounts for 95 percent of Brazil's electricity system, relying on large, multiyear storage dams. Unlike in most countries, the long-run marginal cost of additional hydropower investment is probably lower than that of combined cycle gas turbines. But Brazil's dams have multiple uses, and managing them for irrigation and other purposes requires close basinwide coordination between water management authorities and power dispatchers.

These conditions provide a strong argument for public ownership and operation of the dams, while being the least propitious for a competitive, privately owned generation market. Investing in multiuse hydroelectric projects that require coordinated regulation would entail considerable risk for private investors. Dams are entirely front-end loaded, with massive investment costs but negligible operating costs. Thus the gains from private operation are likely to be small, while there are large risks that prices will be held down during periods of tight demand.

Investing in combined cycle gas turbines is equally unattractive to private investors. Though flexible plants with small capital costs may be desirable for low-cost system expansion, the thermal capacity would operate only in drought years—resulting in a likely overall load factor of less than 35 percent. Power prices would be determined by hydro units and would likely be unremunerative for combined cycle gas turbines unless special payments were made for their role in providing emergency or reserve capacity.

Thus it is unlikely that private ownership is an efficient way to plan, develop, and finance power generation in Brazil. And it remains an open question whether private ownership would ever be efficient in countries requiring large-scale, multiuse river basin management. The most favorable circumstances would be for dams used solely for hydroelectricity where the price of electricity is set by thermal plants, as in Argentina and Chile. Private involvement in generation has a comparative advantage when timely construction and maintenance are required to achieve efficiency benefits—but it is unlikely to work well in predominantly hydropower systems.

Source: Newbery (2001).

The benefits of privatization come from the changed incentives for privatized firms. But those incentives also depend on the competition and regulation facing such firms (Vickers and Yarrow 1991). In many developing and transition economies, small markets appear to limit opportunities for introducing competition among utilities. Efforts to establish effective regulation, especially in such naturally monopolistic small markets, will likely be impeded by a lack of technical expertise, insufficient institutional preconditions (such as well-developed accounting systems), and a resistant political and administrative culture. Thus the relationships between privatization, incentives, and efficiency are complex—and the difference between public and private ownership in developing and transition economies is often much less distinct than in countries with stronger institutions and better-developed private sectors.

Different sectors demand different reforms.   Among network utilities, telecommunications offers the most compelling case for privatization and liberalization in developing and transition economies, because:

- Revolutionary technological change has almost eliminated natural monopoly.
- In most developing countries coverage is very low and the gains from easing restrictions on entry could be substantial.
- The cross-subsidies embedded in monopoly pricing structures cannot be defended on equity grounds because most people with telephone connections are relatively well-off.
- There is significant scope for flexible pricing to alleviate supply shortages, because consumers are willing to pay for new and better services and the sector is suited to competition.
- The financial, technical, and managerial resources of private entities may give them an advantage in keeping abreast of this increasingly complex industry.

In many segments of the transportation sector—railways, trucking, ports, airlines, interurban busing—the pressures of inter- and intramodal competition justify substantial liberalization and privatization in most countries. It is difficult for regulators and service providers to predict efficient, market-responsive vertical relationships and combinations of logistical roles among rail entities, truckers, barge operators, port operators, air carriers, warehouses, and the like. But experiences from both advanced industrial economies and developing and transition economies confirm what theory predicts: decentralized, market-oriented decisionmaking—freed from excessive regulation and energized by market incentives—is the surest way to achieve efficient, innovative solutions to the needs of these transport modes.

It is important, however, to distinguish between transport services—which are generally competitive or contestable—and transport facilities—which may have natural monopoly characteristics. The case for privatizing transport facilities is much less compelling than that for services operating on the network. For rail track, basic and access port infrastructure, and portions of airport facilities—where monopoly is unavoidable or substantial sunk capital is involved—public regulation or even operation is essential.

Electricity restructuring and privatization are more problematic in developing and transition economies. Wholesale competition has worked well in industrial economies because of excess capacity, modest demand growth, and the availability of gas that enabled the entry of gas-fired plants at modest scale and relatively low cost. In contrast, electricity markets in many developing and transition economies face capacity shortages, excess demand, and periodic blackouts. The recent experience in the U.S. state of California shows how market liberalization under conditions of tight demand can create serious problems—market clearing prices are politically unacceptable and will likely derail attempts at radical liberalization.

In most developing and transition economies electricity prices have historically been low, and their realignment with underlying costs has been prevented by politicians. (In several developing countries attempts to raise tariffs during severe power shortages have led to riots.) Private entrants facing significant sunk costs would naturally demand credible commitments that future prices would provide adequate revenue. But most of these countries have not implemented the regulatory mechanisms needed to provide such commitments.

Moreover, electricity markets are relatively small in many developing and transition economies: in 60 developing countries peak system loads are less than 150 megawatts, in 30 between 150 and 500 megawatts, and in 20 between 501 and 1,000 megawatts (Bacon 1994). Opportunities for introducing competition in such small systems will be limited even under the most favorable circumstances. And even in a large market—such as Brazil's—sector conditions can make privatization of electricity generation nonviable (see box 1.3). Thus the suitability of privatizing electricity needs to be carefully assessed based on the circumstances in each case.

The scope for introducing competition in water and sewerage services is much more limited than for other network utilities. Local networks of pipes and sewers remain quintessential natural monopolies. Moreover, unbundling is not especially attractive because the benefits from increased competition in supply are likely to be considerably less than in other network utilities—the costs of producing water are low relative to the value added at the transportation stage, though this may vary across countries (Armstrong, Cowan, and Vickers 1994). On the other hand, there are greater opportunities for introducing competition in sewage treatment. Overall, franchising is likely the most effective way of increasing competition in this sector.

Unbundling is no panacea. In recent years policymakers have taken two broad approaches to restructuring utilities (Newbery 2000a, 2002). The radical approach has been to vertically separate the monopoly segments (transportation and distribution) of these industries from the structurally competitive segments (upstream production and downstream marketing). The second approach, called *competitive access*, allows integrated operations by the dominant incumbent utility on the condition that it make its bottleneck network facilities available to other entities on a fair and equal basis. These two options have different implications for efficiency, competition, coordination economies, scope economies, transaction costs, investment structures, regulatory complexity, and overall performance. Thus the choice between them is not clear-cut.

The basic tradeoff between vertically integrated and unbundled forms of organization is between potential losses of coordination and scope economies and possible increases in transaction costs, relative to potential efficiency gains from competition and increased transparency (Brennan 1995; Klass and Salinger 1995; Joskow 2003b). But in many cases these tradeoffs have not been carefully assessed. Instead, simplistic approaches to competition and restructuring have ignored economies of vertical integration and challenges of replicating vertical relationships with market mechanisms—leading to many problems in utility restructuring and privatization.

Lately, considerable attention has focused on vertical unbundling, where the ownership of infrastructure networks is separated from the provision of services—with the infrastructure assets held by the "infrastructure entity," whether it be the government, a consortium of operators, or a regulated private entity. This approach has considerable appeal because it can facilitate active or potential competition among service providers (operators) with equal access to network facilities. Thus unbundling can mitigate the problems associated with network infrastructure costs, which can block comprehensive deregulation and create significant entry barriers because such costs are large, fixed, and mostly sunk.

With vertical unbundling, operators need not be subject to detailed regulatory scrutiny. Moreover, competition encourages them to be more efficient, entrepreneurial, and responsive to consumer needs. But several links in this chain of policy reasoning may be inapplicable or incorrect in real-world circumstances, especially in developing and transition economies. Unbundling can cause serious coordination problems, reduce economies of scope, and impose other unnecessary transaction costs (box 1.4). So, separating operations from infrastructure networks is not a universal panacea for restructuring problems.

Unbundling is likely to be most attractive when market size and density would allow many infrastructure entities to function and compete. But in many developing countries, markets may be too small for substantial competition to emerge. Unbundling is also aided by well-developed fixed facilities, which minimize the need for new infrastructure investments and so the likelihood of incentive and coordination problems. Where such facilities do not exist—as is likely in most developing countries—regulation should permit the infrastructure entity to enter into medium- and long-term contracts with operators and end users. Doing so allows the risks and rewards of infrastructure investments to be efficiently shared by operators, users, and the infrastructure entity. Such efforts require coordination among parties whose investment interests are not necessarily in harmony.

Unbundling is also no panacea for regulatory challenges. Although separation creates incentives to give competing operators equal access to infrastructure facilities, it does not resolve the difficulties of regulating access to bottleneck facilities. Prices for end users will be at least the sum of operators' competitive prices for services and infrastructure entities' regulated prices. But because it is difficult to set prices that reflect users' varying needs, regulated prices are unlikely to cover replacement costs (see box 1.4).

Box 1.4   Disadvantages of Vertical Separation

- Providing innovative, market-responsive infrastructure services may require specific investments in infrastructure such as maintaining or upgrading fixed facilities. It may be difficult and inefficient for service providers to coordinate with monopoly owners of network facilities—especially if their incentives for investment are not in harmony. The investment incentives of any monopolist will depend on whether it is state-owned or, if in private hands, on the nature of its regulation.

- Efficient use of infrastructure facilities requires close coordination among service providers driven by their needs and sensitivities as well as those of their customers. Competing providers will battle over scarce or congested infrastructure facilities, and sorting out their claims is crucial to a utility system's efficiency and responsiveness. This task is hard enough for an unintegrated system with a monopoly infrastructure entity, but it seems almost impossible where there are rules against discrimination and infrastructure pricing is either tightly regulated or (for a state enterprise) politicized.

- It is plausible, especially in small countries, that upstream production or service activities on all

or part of a utility system are a natural monopoly—even when they have been split apart from network infrastructure. Thus a separated service provider may be a monopoly, and it may have considerable market power unless there is powerful potential competition.

- Separation makes it difficult to develop pricing that covers replacement costs for network infrastructure. Where economies of scale are important, efficient pricing for such costs requires that different network services have different prices relative to marginal costs. If service providers can evade price discrimination by the infrastructure entity—so that it cannot collect different prices from operators offering different services—it will be difficult if not impossible to efficiently defray the costs of the infrastructure. At the extreme, a regulated infrastructure entity charging competing service providers the same price for each unit of use of its facilities is essentially recreating a system in which prices are based on fully allocated costs. Such pricing can be a prescription for inefficiency and financial disaster.

Source: Kessides and Willig (1995).

Thus, while unbundling can reduce the scope for regulatory intervention by isolating monopoly segments and containing their damaging effects, it can also make performance much more sensitive to regulatory efficacy. Achieving the benefits of unbundling requires harmonizing regulatory oversight of monopoly activities and increased competition. Otherwise, inappropriate regulation of the interface between bottleneck components and competitive segments can create severe distortions that make the mixed system the worst of both worlds.

The primary virtue of the second restructuring option, competitive access, is that it exploits potentially important coordination and scope economies. Competitive access might be preferable when:

- Market size and density inhibit active and potential competition.
- Significant new infrastructure investment is needed.
- The industry's technical and economic characteristics render co-ordination among its segments critical.
- The country lacks well-developed contract law and dispute resolution mechanisms to facilitate flexible, reliable commercial agreements.
- Nonpayment issues are a serious concern.

But this option can be fraught with problems if the integrated utility is adverse to efficiency and competition. Competitive access generally requires that the integrated utility make its facilities available to other entities on a fair and equal basis. But if the utility has strong incentives to keep out other entities, it is unclear how effective equal access mandates will be. Despite such rules, several countries have seen potential competitors file disputes claiming unfair and unreasonable exclusion from a regulated utility's facilities (Estache and Rodriguez-Pardina 1999; Saavedra 2001).[6]

It may be extremely difficult to guard against such discrimination, especially in developing and transition economies with weak regulatory institutions. So, if an entrenched management and business culture make it impossible to convert a monolithic utility into one with competitive access, the more revolutionary approach to restructuring—vertical separation—may be a better option. Separation can lead to productive changes in the business culture and increase transparency by forcing a reassignment of responsibilities, roles, incentives, and information flows. Thus any assessment of competitive access must analyze the integrated utility's willingness to accommodate other potential service providers.

Goals for Regulation in Developing and Transition Economies

The general goals of regulation are to promote efficient markets and correct for market failures. In newly liberalized and privatized infrastructure sectors, regulation should focus on:

- Pursuing social fairness and promoting universal service—through pricing that balances economic efficiency and social equity.

- Ensuring incentives for investment—so that reforms draw resources into the sector to expand, modernize, and improve infrastructure facilities and services.
- Promoting fair competition—by lowering entry barriers and giving entrants access to network infrastructure.
- Facilitating innovation—by focusing on goals to be achieved and giving operators and investors leeway to introduce more efficient technologies and innovative service arrangements.
- Protecting public health and safety, and avoiding harm to the environment.
- Ensuring that even where the private sector takes the lead, services are reliable and networks interoperable.

Although these principles apply to all countries, developing and transition economies pose four special challenges that realign the priorities and tighten the institutional constraints facing regulators (Laffont 2000; Smith 2000a).

Expanding access.   In industrial countries (and better-off transition economies) most residents have access to electricity, telephone service, household water connections, sewerage, and a variety of transportation. Thus regulation can focus on maintaining overall incentives for efficiency and modernization. But in developing countries most people do not have access to these services at even a basic standard, and transportation and communication networks are sparse and of low quality. Large portions of the population—billions of people—live in urban slums and low-density rural areas that traditional utilities do not reach. The effectiveness of any regulatory strategy must be judged by its ability to expand access to basic services, rather than just increase convenience for people who already have services.

Increasing affordability.   Although people and firms in industrial countries are sensitive to the prices of infrastructure services, affordability is not a major constraint for most. But among poor people in developing and transition economies the costs of connecting to infrastructure networks can be significant relative to incomes, and past policies have discouraged a large-scale search for cheaper alternatives. Still, many poor people would be willing and able to pay for efficient services if they were offered. In countries that have introduced reforms, poor people have ended up with more services—though sometimes at higher prices. Any regulatory strategy must seek to promote affordability by encouraging lower service costs and providing manageable, effective subsidies where needed.

Strengthening administrative and regulatory capacity.   Many if not most developing and transition economies have few administrators and technical workers with sufficient training and experience to be effective regulators. Even the most dedicated professionals are handicapped by difficulties in communications, inadequate access to information, shortages of mid-level personnel, and institutional norms that tolerate corruption and impede oversight by civil society. These capacity constraints create extra burdens in proving that regulatory reforms will be feasible and generate social benefits.

Mitigating political and regulatory risk.   Most industrial countries have relatively stable political systems and independent judiciaries, and private investors have assurances that their rights will be protected without undue risk. But many developing and transition economies are undergoing political and institutional transformations. As a result private actors face less security and more political risk in making long-term investments, and so are wary of regulatory discretion. Without adequate safeguards against the misuse of regulation, investment will be discouraged and prices higher than needed.

Recent Experiences with Privatization and Reform—Promises and Perils

FOR MUCH OF THE 1990S PRIVATIZATION WAS HERALDED AS the elixir that would transform ailing, lethargic state enterprises into sources of creative productivity and dynamism serving the public interest.[7] National leaders burdened by large budget deficits and stagnating economies were outspoken on the need to foster private initiative as a means of promoting growth and prosperity and enhancing the economic opportunities of all citizens. International financial insti-

Figure 1.4   Latin Americans Increasingly Disapprove of Privatization

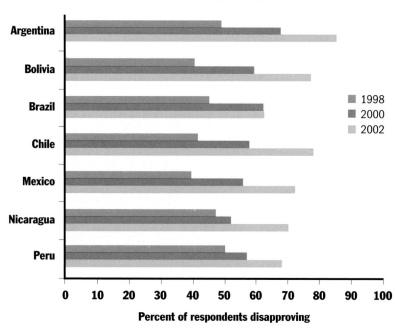

Source: Latinobarometro (2002).

tutions offered advice and promoted this movement in countries that received their aid. The global media provided a near-harmony of voices praising this development in policy thinking (Shapiro and Willig 1990; Willig 1994b).

But as with all economic elixirs, privatization was oversimplified, oversold, and ultimately disappointing—delivering less than was promised. Recently, the alleged failures of privatization, improper restructuring, and overly rapid deregulation have led to street riots, skeptical press coverage, and mounting criticism of international financial institutions. This hostility is not limited to a few radical protesters. Public opinion polls in several developing and transition economies, especially in Latin America, reveal growing disenchantment with privatization (figure 1.4). Disapproval ratings were higher in 2002 than in 2000, and those in 2000 were higher than in 1998. In 2002 nearly 90 percent of Argentines and 80 percent of Chileans polled disapproved of privatization despite demonstrable improvements in the performance of privatized firms. This disillusionment has been driven by employee layoffs, price increases, perceived long delays in benefits, and the distributional impacts of privatization.

Effects on Efficiency—Grounds for Optimism

Future privatization and regulatory reform in developing and transition economies will be determined not just by prevailing economic and political philosophies and macroeconomic conditions, but also by assessments of experiences to date. Although some outcomes have been disappointing, there have also been substantial—but not always obvious—gains.

Reviewing the evidence. It is difficult to get a clear picture of reform results because every network utility's performance is multifaceted, and different observers place different weights on different aspects of performance. It is even harder to reach an unequivocal verdict on the effects that privatization and regulatory reform have had on the diverse industries and countries that have experienced them in varying ways and degrees. Assessment is further complicated by the brief history of privatization, restructuring, and regulatory reform in most developing and transition economies, by the severe measurement problems for crucial economic variables, and by the fact that privatization and regulatory reform have usually been implemented simultaneously—making it almost impossible to econometrically identify their separate effects. (Only in the United States, where the structure of ownership remained constant, can changes in performance be confidently traced to changes in regulation.[8])

These difficulties notwithstanding, most empirical evaluations of privatization and restructuring seem favorable (Gray 2001; Megginson and Netter 2001). At the microeconomic level, evidence indicates that privatization improves the efficiency (in terms of labor and total factor productivity) and financial performance of utilities and leads to service expansion. This information comes from a variety of studies that have analyzed the pre- and post-privatization performance of individual firms, cross-sections of firms from different industries in the same countries, and cross-sections of firms from different countries (Galal and others 1994; Boubakri and Cosset 1998; Sheshinski and Lopez-Calva 2000; Delfino and Casarin 2001; Dewenter and Malatesta 2001; Torero and Pasco-Font 2001).

Other studies are more equivocal about the economic gains from privatization alone, and find that its success or failure depends on post-privatization regulation (Levy and Spiller 1996; Bortolotti, Siniscalco, and Fantini 2000; Torp and Revke 1998; Jamasb and Pollitt 2000; Villalonga 2000; Arocena and Price 2002) and the extent of competition introduced in the market (Bouin and Michalet 1991; Kwoka 1996; Kleit and Terrell 2001; Zhang, Parker, and Kirkpatrick 2002).

Assessing outcomes in telecommunications. A detailed assessment of post-reform performance in the electricity, transportation, and water sectors is provided in chapters 3, 4, and 5. This section analyzes experiences with privatizing and liberalizing telecommunications—the clearest example of changing public policy toward infrastructure, and the sector that has undergone the most reform in developing and transition economies.[9]

Several studies have shown that privatization contributes to network expansion. A study in Argentina, Jamaica, and Mexico found that telecommunications networks expanded significantly after privatization. Jamaica's telecommunications firm increased its annual network expansion rate from 4.5 percent in the 11 years before privatization to 18 percent in the 4 years immediately following (figure 1.5). Entel, the Ar-

Figure 1.5 Privatization Has Led to Rapid Growth in Telecommunications Networks

Increase in annual expansion rates after privatization (percent)

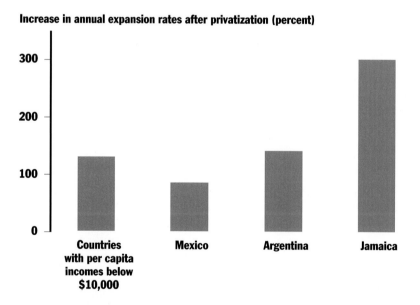

Source: Ramamurti (1996), Ros (1999).

gentine telecommunications firm, increased annual network expansion from about 6 percent in the decade before privatization to more than 14 percent afterward. In both cases increased network expansion resulted from a tripling or quadrupling in capital spending (Ramamurti 1996).

Analysis of both developing and industrial countries has found that privatization has similar effects on the performance of telecommunications firms. Holding other factors constant, privatization is associated with both a larger number of and higher growth in main lines per capita. Among countries with per capita incomes below $10,000, those that allowed majority private ownership in their incumbent operators had 31 percent more main lines per capita and 129 percent higher growth in main lines per capita during 1986–95 (Ros 1999). Moreover, privatization is associated with higher operating efficiency and labor productivity (as measured by main lines per employee). Efficiency gains seem to have resulted from better incentives and increased productivity, rather than from firing employees (Bortolotti and others 2001).

Though these results are encouraging, their incidence and magnitude depend on the extent to which the privatized telecommunications market is liberalized and on the effectiveness of regulatory regime. A study of 86 developing countries in Africa, Asia, the Middle East, and Latin America and the Caribbean over 1985–99 found that a combination of reforms—privatization, competition, and support for an independent regulator—produced the largest performance gains. On average, productivity was 21 percent higher than in countries with partial or no reform (Fink, Mattoo, and Rathindran 2002). Competition can have an especially powerful effect: Ros (1999) found that introducing both competition and privatization in telecommunications increased efficiency more than did either policy alone. In addition, an analysis of 30 telecommunications industries in Africa and Latin America reveals that privatization significantly improves performance only when it is accompanied by an independent regulator (Wallsten 2001).

In Latin American countries that granted 6- to 10-year monopoly licenses to privatized telecommunications operators, the average network growth rate was 45 percent higher than under state ownership—but only about half the rate in Chile, where the government retained the right to issue competing licenses at any time (figure 1.6). The complementarity between privatization and competition in spurring telecommunications capacity expansion is confirmed by an analysis of wireline performance in a large number of developing countries (Laffont

The efficiency benefits from private participation largely depend on the incentives created by competition and regulation

Figure 1.6 Private Competition Generated the Fastest Growth in Telecommunications Lines in Latin America

	Annual growth rate (percent)	
	1984–89	**1989–94**
Brazil, Colombia, Ecuador, Peru, Uruguay	7.0	7.8
Argentina, Mexico, RB de Venezuela	6.7	11.3
Chile	6.6	20.5

☐ State monopolies
☐ Privatized monopolies
☐ Privatized open markets

Source: Wellenius (1997b).

and N'Guessan 2002; Li and Xu 2001). The benefits of liberalization are also confirmed by an analysis of wireless markets in several small and medium-size emerging economies (Chile, Côte d'Ivoire, Ghana, Malaysia, Mexico, Philippines, Romania). In most cases the introduction of a competing cellular operator lowered prices, increased service options, and resulted in service innovations. Moreover, the lower prices and service enhancements stimulated demand, leading to more subscribers for all competitors—including the incumbent wireline operator (Rohlfs and others 2000).

Distributive Impacts—Need for Caution

Empirical evidence increasingly shows that concerns about privatization and market liberalization's adverse effects on poor people have been largely exaggerated. There is no evidence that such reforms hurt poor or rural consumers—at least in terms of access to service. Even when service prices increase, the share of poor and rural households with connections does not decrease. And in many cases coverage increases, possibly because connection fees fall once service is no longer rationed. Indeed, case studies show that allowing entry and competition in infrastructure services can dramatically increase services for poor people. Competition introduces a range of price and quality options, making service possible in regions and at income levels that monopoly providers would never have considered (Clarke and Wallsten 2002).

The discrepancy between scholarly assessments and public perceptions of privatization may reflect the use of different yardsticks and time horizons. Consumers dislike higher prices even if they result in better service. Similarly, the public dislikes layoffs even when overstaffing was obvious. And needed tariff adjustments can hurt poor people. Thus more comprehensive welfare assessments of privatization are required, incorporating its effects on workers, on households in different spending categories, and on company profits and other elements of industry performance.

Recent empirical work offers insights on the distributive effects of privatizing and regulating network utilities. Argentina began privatizing its utilities in 1990, and post-privatization changes in utility prices and access led to varying changes in welfare (as measured by consumer surplus) among sectors and income groups. Welfare gains were achieved in telecommunications and electricity, while losses were experienced in gas and sanitation. Moreover, changes in the level and structure of prices seemed to hit poor households harder—or provided them with the least benefit (Delfino and Casarin 2001).

But studies using computable general equilibrium models have found that all income groups in Argentina benefited from the efficiency, quality, and access improvements resulting from the privatization of utilities (Chisari, Estache, and Romero 1999; Navajas 2000). The provision of more efficient infrastructure services affects most other sectors of the economy and promotes economic growth, enhancing poor people's economic opportunities (Kraay and Dollar 2000). When these general equilibrium effects are taken into account, the poorest groups seemed to benefit the most from the increased productivity and access that resulted from privatization (Benitez, Chisari, and Estache 2003).

Recent research in four Latin American countries (Argentina, Bolivia, Mexico, Nicaragua) indicates that privatization has no clear effect on prices—prices fell in about half the cases. But privatization did have adverse distributive impacts on the poorer half of the population because of large layoffs in privatized utilities. Still, the negative effects of

In low-income countries most rural and many urban poor people do not have basic infrastructure services, so higher tariffs will primarily affect the middle and upper classes; but in middle-income countries higher tariffs will affect many poor people—especially in urban areas

layoffs and higher prices were more than offset by increased access for poor consumers, enhanced service quality, and changes in public financing that benefited poor people more (McKenzie and Mookherjee 2003).

Thus there is a discrepancy between the statistical evidence on and public perceptions of privatization, and none of the studies reviewed here adequately explain the growing popular disenchantment with such reforms.[10] It is possible that due to data limitations and perhaps even methodological flaws, statistical models do not accurately measure the true welfare impact of these reforms. It is also possible that public perceptions are subject to systematic biases. The benefits of reforms are generally shared by a large number of consumers with relatively modest individual gains—certainly not the topic of newspaper headlines.

On the other hand, firing a significant portion of the employees of a large utility is more likely to lead to protests and attract media attention, even if the employment contraction is small relative to a country's total labor force. Psychologists have found that individuals exhibit loss aversion: they react more strongly to losses than to gains relative to the status quo. They also tend to have short time horizons—focusing much more on the immediate effects of policy reforms that might require painful adjustments, while discounting heavily the gains flowing in the future.

Effective Design—Crucial to Success

Privatization's bad reputation is not fully deserved. Some of the difficulties experienced have resulted from disillusionment and misunderstanding by the general public and poor communication by political leaders. Impatience with the time required for some of the benefits of privatization to emerge reveals a lack of awareness that even in today's rich industrial countries, it often took decades for major institutional reforms to achieve their intended outcomes (Baumol 1993). But public policies are largely determined by public support. Thus it is not enough to show that privatization generally improves things: policies must be designed to ensure that it does—and is widely seen to have done so.

Negative popular perceptions might also reflect a process that has at times been deeply flawed. For privatization to achieve its public interest objectives, several institutional preconditions must be met (box 1.5;

Guislain 1992). In developing and transition economies where privatization was pushed in the absence of such institutional safeguards, it was often oversold as the solution to all the problems facing these economies. Advocates of privatization may have overestimated its benefits and underestimated its costs and institutional requirements. Changing the structure of ownership involves making tradeoffs between different costs (Laffont and Tirole 1991).

Every infrastructure reform program has three main elements: privatization, competitive restructuring, and regulatory reform. Achieving the public interest goals of infrastructure reform requires strong policy attention to all three. In practice, however, governments and their financial advisers have focused on privatization transactions.

The first trap: privatization without competitive restructuring. To generate more revenue, some fiscally strapped governments have sold utilities as monopolies—accompanied by regulation that ensures this outcome instead of promoting competition (table 1.3). This tendency toward exclusivity has been encouraged by prospective investors and underwriting investment banks (whose fees are generally calculated as a percentage of the sales price). International financial institutions have

Table 1.3 Exclusivity Periods for Incumbent Telecommunications Operators in Latin America

Country	Year exclusivity started	Length of exclusivity (years)
Argentina	1990	10
Bolivia	1995	6
Ecuador	1995	5
Honduras	1995	10
Mexico	1990	6
Nicaragua	1995	4
Panama	1997	5
Peru	1994	5
Venezuela	1991	9

Note: Exclusivity agreements cover local calls, national long distance, and international long distance (except for Mexico, where local calls are not covered).
Source: ITU (1999).

also supported such arrangements, on the presumption that even poorly designed privatization is better than continued state ownership (Noll 2000a).

Several rationales are used to support exclusivity for privatized utilities. It is argued that high profit margins are needed to finance substantial new investment; that competition would undermine universal service goals (because new entrants would only want to serve low-cost, high-demand customers, undermining existing cross-subsidies); and that domestic markets are too weak and uncertain to attract foreign investors without the assurances offered by exclusivity (Laffont and N'Gbo 2000).

Creating private monopolies involves clear tradeoffs. Longer exclusivity secures a higher bid price and so higher immediate proceeds from privatization, while shorter exclusivity stimulates the economy through competition and generates higher recurrent tax revenue. But the basic argument for exclusivity is economically flawed, and such arrangements have led to problems after privatization.

Longer exclusivity elicits higher bid prices because a stream of monopoly profits is more valuable than a stream of competitive returns. But without large public subsidies for customers with limited ability to pay, high monopoly prices reduce the demand for services—leading to less private investment. By contrast, lower competitive prices—as long as they provide enough revenue for the network utility to compete with other firms in the economy for financing to maintain, replace, modernize, and expand its facilities and services—increase demand and so lead to more private investment. This argument is especially powerful in developing countries, where much of the population has a limited ability to pay (Noll 2001). Recent empirical analysis of telecommunications in developing and transition economies found that exclusivity periods are associated with a substantial reduction in investment and up to 40 percent lower growth in the number of telephone mainlines (Wallsten 2000).

One of the main arguments against liberalization is that it undermines network expansion and universal service goals, under the logic that profit-maximizing firms will not find it attractive to extend service to marginal subscribers. But emerging evidence casts doubt on this argument, especially in telecommunications. Several studies analyzing telecommunications in developing and transition economies indicate that market liberalization spurs, and exclusivity agreements retard, network development (see above).

Countries are learning from their mistakes and those of others. In the early 1990s early movers in Latin America (Argentina, Mexico, Venezuela) offered 6- to 10-year exclusivity periods in their telecommunications sectors. In the mid-1990s the second wave of reformers (Bolivia, Panama, Peru) offered exclusivity for 5–6 years. By 1998 small and poor countries (El Salvador, Guatemala) were able to sell their telecommunications companies with no exclusivity. They were also able to attract large numbers of service providers.

Exclusivity is likely to be especially damaging in poor countries where the incumbent state-owned monopoly has not provided reliable nationwide service. People without connections to the monopoly network, especially the rural poor, could benefit from the availability of alternative suppliers who might make better use of technological advances and offer a wider range of prices and services than the incumbent monopolist. In the absence of competition, a privatized monopolist may remain lethargic and not innovate or expand coverage—especially if it is restricted by uniform pricing rules. Expanding access, especially to poor rural areas, requires a variety of approaches that exploit all technological opportunities and experiment with alternative forms of organizing supply. Exclusivity often undermines the potential for such service innovation.

Regulatory policing of exclusivity is also costly and difficult, especially in industries undergoing rapid technological change. For example, in telecommunications exclusivity has often been applied to traditional wireline services but not to wireless, satellite, and data services. But in recent years exclusive rights for a particular telecommunications technology have become a technological anachronism. Defining and enforcing the boundary between voice telephone service and data services are almost impossible. Although modern operators recognize this, they still complain that the exclusivity provisions of their licenses are being violated. Such complaints can seriously damage a country's reputation for foreign investment. Finally, exclusivity once granted can be very difficult or costly to reverse.[11]

The second trap: weak regulatory capacity. Especially during the early years of privatization, establishing appropriate regulation to curb the potential abuse of monopoly power was subordinated to the immediate goal of closing transactions. The limited attention paid to reg-

> When conditions make competition feasible, it would harm the public interest to privatize a monopoly using exclusivity arrangements

> The fiscal benefits from privatizing a monopoly are not worth the costs

ulation focused on creating regulatory entities and writing their charters to meet the formal requirements of the privatization process or the conditions of international organizations. Regulatory institutions were often created simply by replicating systems from advanced industrial countries, mainly the United Kingdom and the United States.

Chapter 2 provides a detailed analysis of the problems and the reality gap characterizing this "transfer" of regulatory policy to developing and transition economies. Regulators in these countries have a decidedly mixed record in achieving effectiveness. In some countries an unrealistically hopeful and incorrect presumption guided the creation of regulatory institutions: that if issues of funding, organizational design, and procedural safeguards were resolved, satisfactory regulatory performance would emerge—serving the public interest. This approach underestimated the probability that the same political interference that made public enterprises in these countries so effective in collecting and dispensing favors to special interests would seek to preserve these benefits by capturing or weakening regulation.

It should have been expected that fiscally constrained governments in constant search of tax revenue would be tempted to retain political control over regulation, leaving monopoly rents to the operators and then taxing them away rather than distributing the efficiency gains of privatization to consumers (Estache 2002a). Because of deliberate government actions and a lack of understanding of the importance of separation of powers, it has been exceedingly difficult to establish and maintain regulatory independence in developing and transition economies.

In most of these countries effective regulation is also undermined by scarce technical expertise (Stern 2000a). Although regulators may be strong in certain technical areas, they often lack staff experienced in accounting, economic policy analysis, finance, and law. Moreover, hiring decisions may be constrained by rules for civil service employment. As a result it takes time to change the skills mix of staff in line with the requirements of privatized and restructured infrastructure industries.

Insufficient regulatory capacity can make it difficult for infrastructure reforms to achieve their public interest objectives. Such capacity is required to manage the competitive restructuring of network utilities and subject them to market discipline. So, in developing and transition economies where such capacity is weak, it is one of the main reasons such tasks have not been fully achieved.

Given the central role that incumbent utilities have played in developing their industries, it is no surprise that they have remained powerful players after privatization. Many incumbents have been supervised by weak regulators lacking autonomy, authority, technical capacity, and a clear mandate to resolve post-privatization disputes between various market participants. Accordingly, such incumbents often have little incentive to negotiate with their competitors and comply with legislation.

Weak regulatory capacity has hampered privatization and other infrastructure reforms in a variety of countries. For example, in Mexico the local telephone market was opened to competition in the early 1990s, and many entrepreneurs were interested in entering the market (Casanueva and del Villar 2003). Yet no local competition emerged for several years because the incumbent operator, Telmex, engaged in a variety of anticompetitive practices. Weak enforcement by Cofetel, the sector's regulator, made it easy for Telmex to do so. Slow telecommunications liberalization in many other Latin American countries can also be attributed to weak regulatory agencies (Pyramid Research 2001).

Second Generation Reforms—Choices and Challenges

SINCE THE 1980S MANY DEVELOPING AND TRANSITION ECONOmies have implemented far-reaching restructuring, privatization, and regulatory reforms in key infrastructure sectors. Although experiences have varied considerably by country and sector, most of these first generation reforms have generated several of the expected social benefits of market liberalization and private enterprise, including enhanced productivity and cost-effectiveness, higher-quality output, greater responsiveness to consumer and business needs, and increased investment driven by market incentives rather than bureaucratic preferences. Policymakers in these countries deserve praise for their forthright privatization of utility industries and commitment to imposing market discipline.

Still, even in countries where reforms have been guided by state-of-the-art policy analysis, aspects of restructuring and privatization have had unintended consequences and are causing significant problems. Emerging second generation reform issues in the network utilities of developing and transition economies are endemic to infrastructure sectors everywhere and largely reflect problems that arise after privatization—especially when combined with unbundling. In fact, the asserted deficiencies of post-privatization regulation in these countries are similar to those experienced in advanced industrial countries. Still, developing and transition economies will see limited improvements in post-privatization performance unless they address these second generation issues.

This report seeks to refocus current policy debates on four second generation challenges that confront nearly all restructuring and privatization programs:

- Balancing economic efficiency and social equity.
- Fostering as much competition as possible given the changing technological and economic characteristics of these sectors.
- Adapting regulation to address emerging problems, changing circumstances, and new information in regulated infrastructure sectors.
- Protecting consumers, responding to their concerns, and soliciting their participation in the regulatory process.

Balancing Economic Efficiency and Social Equity

Two pressing tasks face policymakers in developing and transition economies that have introduced infrastructure reforms. First, they must redress long-standing underpricing of infrastructure, which in many cases has limited service availability, benefited the middle and upper classes, and left large portions of rural and poor urban populations without access to basic services (table 1.4). Second, policymakers must pursue social goals—such as universal service and access for poor people—efficiently and without distorting competition.

Political concerns have blocked cost-covering tariffs in developing and transition economies

Adjusting prices. Underinvestment was one of the main problems of the old utility model in developing and transition economies, and was largely caused by underpricing (figure 1.7). Prices for basic services were held below supply costs, subjecting infrastructure entities to financial distress and impairing their ability to maintain and expand services, especially in poor and rural areas. The failure of many governments to

Table 1.4 Access to Infrastructure Services in Urban and Rural Areas of Developing Regions, late 1990s

(percentage of households with access)

Region, income group	Electricity		Piped water		Telephone	
	Urban	Rural	Urban	Rural	Urban	Rural
Africa, low income	43.7	6.6	36.9	3.7	5.7	0.3
Europe and Central Asia, low income	100.0	99.5	87.4	32.7	52.0	13.3
Europe and Central Asia, middle income	99.4	93.9	79.9	28.3	67.8	44.7
Latin America, low income	84.5	20.7	60.2	13.5	16.5	1.1
Latin America, middle income	95.6	51.4	78.0	38.9	39.7	4.3

Source: Clarke and Wallsten (2002).

raise prices, especially during periods of high inflation, decapitalized their infrastructure systems. Government subsidies perpetuated the problem until fiscal crunches occurred.

The choice was either higher taxes or higher prices. Higher prices would generally affect people who already had services—the middle and upper classes—while higher taxes were likely to be felt partly through inflation taxes that hit poor people or other groups without protective assets. A sensible, and arguably less regressive, response was to realign prices with underlying costs. Privatization requires such adjustments to attract investors—arguably one of its more attractive features.

Even developing and transition economies that have acted—sometimes aggressively—to stimulate competition in infrastructure have made only minor changes in pricing policies. Old-style, centralized price setting by sector ministries remains prevalent. Yet major changes are required to realize the full benefits of competition, and infrastructure entities must be allowed to compete using flexible prices and terms.

Policy solutions consistent with both economic efficiency and social equity are not always available or politically feasible. Thus policymakers in developing and transition economies face no more challenging second generation task than designing and implementing pricing reforms that strike a better balance between these two goals. In the long run, pricing policies that lead to insufficient revenue, underinvestment, and inadequate maintenance obviously do not serve the public interest. Moreover, despite their purported focus on social equity, the historic pricing policies of these countries have not served poor people either, since many have not had access to basic infrastructure services.

Utility pricing is not the best mechanism for income redistribution, which is the responsibility of the tax system

65

Figure 1.7   Electricity Prices Often Fail to Cover Costs in Europe and Central Asia, 2000

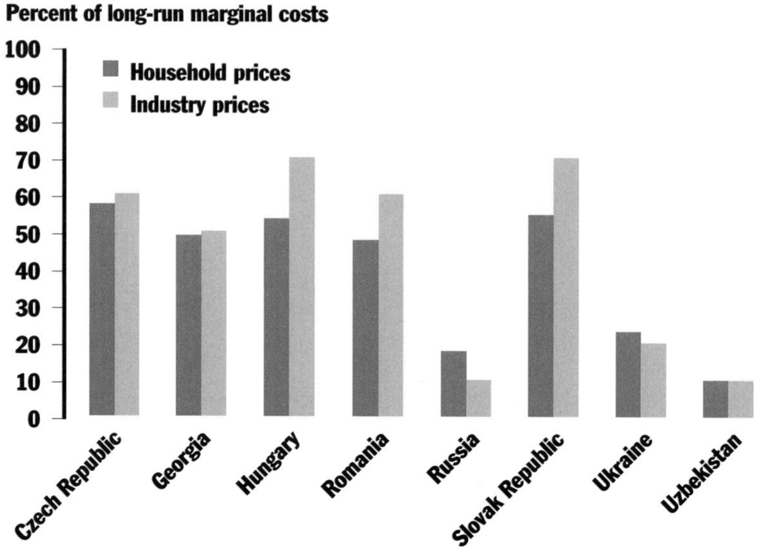

Percent of long-run marginal costs

Source: Stern (2002).

Still, even though rebalancing infrastructure prices is likely to benefit all affected groups and contribute to social welfare, there is reason to avoid too abrupt a transition to a new pricing regime. Rapid price changes impose large, often difficult adjustment costs on consumers and firms alike. Even optimal prices, if instituted too quickly, can lead to a costly and damaging transition that is far from optimal.

Caution on the speed of price adjustments is especially appropriate in transition economies that have been undergoing painful transformations from centralized to market-driven economic systems. In many countries these transformations initially led to significant contractions in economic activity and sizable reductions in income levels. By some estimates, if district heating prices in 2000 were realigned with underlying costs, prices in Sofia (Bulgaria) would have risen to $50 a month—unrealistically high for a large portion of the population in a country where pensions range from $28 to $56 a month (Newbery 2000c).

In many transition economies higher prices, no matter how justified, have caused hardships because they coincided with significant reductions in incomes. For example, in Ukraine the prices of electricity and natural gas were almost 6 times higher in 1998 than in 1992, and prices for district heating (in Kiev) were more than 16 times higher. Yet dur-

Table 1.5 **Average Household Incomes and Energy Tariffs in Ukraine, 1992–98**
(Index: 1992 = 100)

Year	Income	Electricity tariff	Natural gas tariff	District heating tariff (in Kiev)
1992	100	100	100	100
1993	65	47	27	69
1994	44	79	46	180
1995	41	376	448	1,270
1996	38	578	643	1,953
1997	43	617	613	1,973
1998	43	594	563	1,644

Note: Incomes and tariffs have been adjusted for inflation (based on the consumer price index).
Source: World Bank staff estimates based on data from Ukraine's State Statistical Committee and Ministry of Economy.

ing the same period average household incomes fell by more than half (table 1.5).[12] Thus price adjustments need to be appropriately phased and may need to be accompanied by other policies (such as social safety nets) to ease the burden on the most vulnerable consumers.

Finding effective alternatives to cross-subsidies.   Most countries aim to achieve universal access to certain basic infrastructure services. When services were provided by monopolies (typically state-owned, but occasionally private), these obligations were theoretically funded by subsidies and, more commonly, cross-subsidies: high-income and low-cost consumers were charged prices above costs to finance services to low-income and high-cost consumers, who paid prices below costs. In telecommunications, for example, rates for local calls and access tended to be low while rates for domestic and international long-distance tended to be high relative to underlying costs. Similarly, electricity service for households was often priced below its supply cost, while service for industrial users was priced above.

Subsidies have often been poorly targeted and failed to reach poor consumers. In India, for instance, state subsidies for water services totaled more than $1 billion a year (0.5 percent of GDP) in the late 1990s—but poor households captured only a quarter of these (Foster, Pattanayak, and Prokopy 2003). Although lower prices can increase demand for infrastructure services from rural and poor consumers, they also lead to supply-side distortions that reduce or negate their effects.

Moreover, the opaque nature of cross-subsidies makes it difficult to determine who pays for and who benefits from them. There is strong evidence that state-owned monopolies have failed to ensure access for rural and low-income urban consumers, especially in Africa (Clarke and Wallsten 2002; Brook and Irwin 2003). Indeed, wealthier consumers appear to have benefited far more from subsidies than have the poor.

Distorted prices impose significant economic costs by sending the wrong signals to consumers, suppliers, and investors. For example, low charges for telecommunications often exacerbate congestion by encouraging overuse of facilities. Moreover, prices based on cross-subsidies are unsustainable in a liberalized market. Indeed, policymakers overseeing restructured and privatized infrastructure industries in developing and transition economies will increasingly face a seemingly irreconcilable dilemma: it is generally impossible to impose cross-subsidies (to support favored groups of customers) while promoting competition (Baumol 1999). Competitive entry will destroy cross-subsidies. Moreover, generating adequate revenue—crucial to any rational privatization program—requires realigning prices with underlying costs. Thus market liberalization will require finding new sources of subsidies or raising rates that were below incremental costs.

Privatization and competition do not solve all the problems of providing infrastructure services. Competition limits the ability to cross-subsidize services. But entry and competition also allow entrepreneurs to test new ways of providing services to rural and poor areas, generating a wide range of service, price, and quality options. And given the near-failure of public monopolies to provide services to poor people, these reforms provide an opportunity to rethink how to fund social goals and ensure such access. If funding through general tax revenue is too difficult or costly, second generation reforms should focus on new methods to raise subsidies. Possible approaches include competitively neutral financing mechanisms such as universal service funds and subsidy auctions.

Fostering Competition after Privatization

In many developing and transition economies, developing free markets will require drastic changes in government regulations and business cultures, with radically different approaches to oversight and codes of

---

Box 1.6   Using Competition Policy to Avoid Regulatory Capture

TENSION ALWAYS EXISTS BETWEEN REGULATION and policies that seek to promote competition. As part of second generation infrastructure reforms, policymakers must strive to resolve this tension. Regulation typically pushes common rules for firms in the same industry—for example, by setting pricing formulas or even imposing common production technologies. Thus a regulator may have the statutory power to make decisions that in competitive markets would normally be made by firms. Regulatory capture occurs when market participants ex-

ploit this power at the expense of their competitors. Thus regulation often has significant unintended anticompetitive effects.

Competition policy can limit the extent and damage of regulatory capture. An antimonopoly agency can review important regulatory decisions, announce its views on the likely impacts of such decisions on competition, and take action against firms that use the regulatory process for anticompetitive purposes.

---

competitive conduct. Given the daunting policy challenges facing these countries in recent years, it is understandable that many governments have paid insufficient attention to competition policy during the early stages of infrastructure reform. But competition policy can provide an important complement to other policies aimed at fostering an efficient, dynamic economy—especially industry-specific regulatory reform and privatization (box 1.6).

The long structural legacy of infrastructure industries could make it extremely difficult to develop competitive markets. Nevertheless, the new model for network utilities offers considerable scope for competition. However, unbundling and relaxing rules on market entry will not be sufficient to develop and maintain such competition. Competition law has a potentially critical role to play and should be given maximum scope (Willig 1992; Newbery 2003). Thus an important second generation challenge is developing policies that promote competitive entry and prevent monopolies from leveraging their market power in competitive industry segments (box 1.7; Noll 1995).

Even when market conditions are favorable, government guidance is required for competition to work well (Willig 1999). This framework should not be limited to punishing anticompetitive conduct; there is also an urgent need to ensure that competition policy fosters entry and entrepreneurship by facilitating access to network facilities and other infrastructure.

Box 1.7   Telmex's Market Power in the Internet Market

DESPITE NUMEROUS CONCESSIONS GRANTED IN various segments, competition continues to be fairly limited in Mexico's telecommunications industry. The main obstacles to a competitive market are the overwhelming size of the incumbent, Telmex (Telefonos de Mexico), and the weakness of the regulatory agency, Cofetel (Comision Nacional de Telecomunicaciones). Through its extensive control of the industry's bottleneck facilities, Telmex enjoys considerable market power, which it has been leveraging into such competitive segments as the Internet and value added services. For example, Telmex is providing DSL technology to its Internet affiliate but not to competing Internet service providers. This refusal to deal is allowing Telmex's Internet affiliate to monopolize this important segment of the market.

Sources: Pyramid Research (2001); Casanueva and del Villar (2003).

Creating competition policy.   The first step in devising direct economic regulation—prescribing prices, entry conditions, service requirements, and the like—is to determine which markets and services should be subject to it and which are best left to market discipline. This determination is rarely easy: real-world competition is invariably imperfect, as is regulation. Conventional wisdom predicts that the benefits of even highly imperfect competition will typically exceed those of thoroughly regulated franchise monopoly. Still, it is usually necessary to directly regulate essential services supplied under natural monopoly—although here again, it is often impossible to be sure which markets and services are naturally monopolistic and which are perhaps only temporarily so, but sufficiently to justify imposing direct regulation.

For activities not subject to direct regulation, a purely laissez-faire approach will rarely be adequate to protect the public interest. Unregulated businesses can pursue their interests by colluding to suppress competition or excluding rivals from opportunities to compete. Thus most societies relying on open markets have felt it necessary, in the absence of comprehensive direct regulation, to enforce general antitrust or antimonopoly laws. Such laws vary by country. Some seek to remedy unacceptably monopolistic markets by subjecting them to restructuring or direct regulation. Others merely prohibit or correct attempts by firms to restrain competition among themselves or by market-dominating firms to exclude potential competitors.

Whereas direct regulation tends to be industry-specific—and administered by agencies specialized in controlling a particular industry—antitrust and antimonopoly enforcement is better vested in agencies that oversee the entire range of industries and markets. Such agencies tend to develop considerable expertise in appraising the structure, behavior, and performance of markets, identifying possibly excessive market power, and fashioning remedies that retain competition as the main governor of industry performance. These remedies include dissolving excessively monopolistic companies, requiring that dominant companies divest their assets, prohibiting tactics such as predatory pricing and exclusive dealing, and blocking mergers, acquisitions, and other business combinations deemed damaging to competition.

Many developing and transition economies, however, still lack strong antitrust enforcement. Some have not even implemented the basic elements of competition law—as in the Philippines—and have made uneven progress in establishing sector regulators and antitrust agencies. The creation of regulatory agencies has received more attention because they are required for privatization.

Regulatory agencies must strike a careful balance between monitoring restructured and privatized infrastructure industries and ensuring that they do not micromanage deregulation and hinder competition in these industries. This is a legitimate concern given the tendency of regulation to expand into areas where it was not intended, with undesirable consequences. Still, given the weakness of antitrust agencies in developing and transition economies, regulatory agencies will have to assume a greater monitoring role, at least in the short run.

Ensuring access to bottleneck facilities.   One of the most vexing tasks facing infrastructure regulators is designing the terms of access to bottleneck facilities for competing service providers. These facilities are essential in producing or delivering final products and are incapable of being economically duplicated. The best examples include the local loop ("final mile") in telecommunications, the transmission grid in electricity, the network of pipelines in natural gas, and the track in railways. Access policy is the cornerstone of the contemporary response to residual monopoly in infrastructure. Indeed, it is at the fore of discussions to facilitate competitive entry in activities traditionally run by franchised monopolies.

Without good access rules, efficient entry will not materialize in these industries and the benefits of market liberalization will not obtain.

Figure 1.8 Despite Liberalization, Entrants into the Local Exchange Account for a Small Share of Latin American Telecom Markets, 2001 Second Quarter

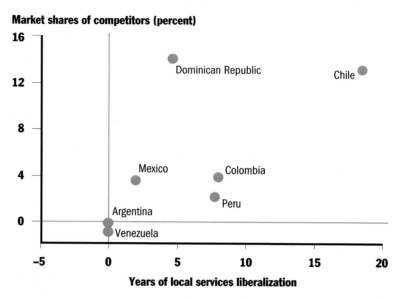

Source: Pyramid Research (2001).

In Latin America, for example, several countries—Argentina, Brazil, Chile, Colombia, Dominican Republic, El Salvador, Mexico, Peru, Venezuela—have opened their telecommunications markets to local-loop competition. But in none of these countries (including Chile, where local telecommunications services have been liberalized for more than 20 years) have new entrants been able to gain more than 15 percent of the market (figure 1.8). One of the main reasons is the lack of clear interconnection policies and the inability of regulators to enforce interconnection rates (Pyramid Research 2001). Local exchange carriers have not fared any better in Europe or the United States.

With the progressive introduction of competition in the public utility industries of developing and transition economies, more rival firms will seek to interconnect to their networks. At each interconnection point, an access price will have to be determined. Access terms should not distort how prices are adapted to consumer preferences and demands for services. Prices should be high enough to be compensatory (at least cover the long-run incremental cost of the use of the network by the entrant), yet not so high as to preclude efficient operations by entrants. Thus regulation should ensure that there is sufficient pressure on the owner of the infrastructure to operate in efficiently, but that no unnecessary duplication of network construction occurs.

A basic goal of access policy is ensuring competitive parity—meaning that competition in final service (product) markets is efficient and does not favor owners of bottleneck facilities or their actual and potential rivals. Rules consistent with competitive parity should minimize the costs of contested services by assigning responsibilities for them based on firms' efficiency, as indicated by their production costs and service prices. But achieving fair access rules has proven difficult, and is an area where developing and transition economies will require substantial technical assistance.

Adapting Regulation

Regulation must adapt to address emerging problems, changing circumstances, and new information in the infrastructure sectors. Regulatory adaptation is especially imperative in sectors undergoing rapid technological or market changes (or both).

Overcoming resistance to necessary change.   Inflexible privatization agreements are often a major obstacle to resolving post-privatization regulatory problems and disputes. Such inflexibilities were probably needed during privatization to create commitments to reform, protect consumers, and attract private investment. But they make it difficult to adapt regulation because many parties consider such changes a threat to the privatization commitments that protect their interests—as well as to the entire fabric of reform.

Methods are needed to make needed changes in regulation while honoring the interests embedded in privatization agreement. So, as part of second generation reforms, policymakers in developing and transition economies should develop frameworks for revising regulatory mandates and renegotiating concession contracts. Such frameworks must protect the public interest as well as interests of investors and consumers, and should promote efficient competition (Willig 1999).

Resolving disputes. Managing conflicts and resolving disputes are among the most important post-privatization tasks for regulators. Commercial disputes arise in almost every sector of an economy. But because infrastructure industries are so important, disputes between private parties often have significant public interest implications. Thus regulators of these sectors must actively ensure that such disputes are resolved in a way consistent with the public interest.

One area where disputes are arising with alarming frequency and intensity involves the renegotiation of concession contracts. Even well-designed infrastructure concessions require adjustment at some point (Klein 1998b). In Latin America nearly a third of all such contracts were renegotiated within about two years of being awarded (Estache, Guasch, and Trujillo 2003).

Many concession contracts do not have sufficient mechanisms to deal with such post-award adjustments. Moreover, concerns have been expressed about the relative bargaining power of regulators and operators. Due to the importance of basic infrastructure services and the political repercussions of interruptions in their provision, governments are reluctant to terminate concessions—raising the specter of collusion between regulators and regulated firms (Estache and Quesada 2001).

In many countries regulatory and dispute resolution arrangements suffer from serious drawbacks. In the United States, for example, they often entail too many contested administrative proceedings, overly rigid procedures for coping with increasingly complex issues, heavy involvement by courts lacking sufficient technical expertise, and too little flexibility for creative solutions.

Most developing and transition economies have newer, less developed regulatory institutions, enabling them to avoid the procedural complexities and other mistakes of U.S. mechanisms. Policymakers in these countries should explore different institutional approaches and innovative legal process that might be more appropriate given their institutional and legal characteristics.

Enhancing Consumer Participation in Regulation

Although infrastructure reforms in developing and transition economies have improved the performance of network utilities—sometimes significantly—many consumers remain dissatisfied with how the situation has evolved. This wariness may partly reflect consumers' perceptions that they were excluded from early decisionmaking and that even now they have limited opportunities to influence changes in regulation and policy. Thus enhancing consumer participation in the regulatory process is an important second generation reform.

Immediately after privatization, regulatory agencies focused on complex economic, financial, and technical issues such as tariffs, interconnection, technical standards, and licensing and market structure. It is understandable that specific consumer protection policies lagged behind these crucial issues. More recently, however, consumers (in Latin America and elsewhere) have complained about their lack of representation in regulatory processes, tariff decisions, and dispute resolutions (Apoyo Consultoria 2002). If their views continue to be neglected or given short shrift in policy deliberations, it could lead to costly policy reversals—and even threaten the entire reform process.

Consumer participation may be desirable for several reasons. Effective participation could provide a needed counterbalance to the strong influence typically exerted by well-heeled industry representatives. It might also provide regulators with political support and protect them from undue political interference in their rulemaking. Consumer participation in tariff rebalancing would enhance its credibility and might make it more acceptable to the public.

Consumers' lack of technical expertise often constrains their effective participation in the regulatory process. By contrast, regulated firms hire high-powered academic and other experts to argue in support of their views. But this imbalance is slowly being redressed. Consumer organizations in a variety of countries have forged innovative alliances with academic, labor, and other organizations to participate more effectively in the regulatory process (box 1.8).

One of the defining characteristics of state-owned monopolies, especially in transition economies, was their lack of customer orientation. Consumer opinions were rarely considered, and contracts between consumers and infrastructure service providers often did not include consumer protection clauses—meaning that consumers had no way to pursue legal action. As part of their reforms several of these countries have adopted consumer protection measures, mainly consisting of complaint resolution mechanisms and the power to fine operators.

Consumer protection policies can be justified by market failures, including the high transaction costs and asymmetric information problems for individual consumers dealing with large utilities, as well as the market dominance of some of these utilities. But competition and con-

---

Box 1.8   Consumer Participation in Colombia's Rulemaking

UNTIL RECENTLY CIVIL SOCIETY HAD ALMOST NO influence on Colombian regulation. Consumer organizations lacked the technical capacity to argue their positions, and regulatory authorities did not offer platforms for citizen participation. Regulatory bodies simply posted proposed rules on their Websites and required that all comments be submitted through the sites.

But in 2000 the consumer organization Consumidores Colombia forged partnerships with several of the country's universities to create an expert group for consumers. This move enhanced the credibility of the organization's participation, especially in debates of complex technical issues. As a result regulators began holding public hearings to learn the views of operators and consumers. Today regulators regularly invite Consumidores Colombia to discuss controversial issues.

Sources: Apoyo Consultoria (2002).

---

sumer protection policies complement each other. Competition enhances consumer choice and leads to more price and service options. Thus there is less need for consumer protection policies once robust competition is established.

Regulatory policy should not favor any particular group of stakeholders, including consumers, over others. Instead it should be neutral and focus on correcting market failures. And although consumer participation in the regulatory process should be encouraged, the temptation to put consumers on the boards of regulatory agencies and give them the power to vote should be resisted, because it will likely conflict with the requirements of regulatory due process and neutrality. Regulatory policy should seek to balance the interests of consumers and service providers—and such a balance would be disturbed if consumers could vote on regulatory decisions, in the same way as if service providers were given voting powers. Still, empowering consumers with information and making their voices heard on important policy issues would reduce regulatory capture and facilitate fair policies in regulated infrastructure sectors.

Notes

1. This mainly refers to the period after World War II. Until then private ownership in electricity was the norm in many countries in Europe and North

and South America. State ownership spread after World War II for ideological reasons (as in England and France) or because politically imposed price controls drove private firms into bankruptcy (as in Latin America). Similar situations prevailed for railways, trucking, and water in many countries. Telephone services became captive of state-owned post offices in Europe and Japan but not Canada, the United States, or, initially, Latin America.

2. The extent of scale economies in these industries is a matter of dispute. Research on cost structures finds that technical scale economies are weak and that the optimal market structure is often two or more firms. Moreover, network utilities encompass several distinct activities, many of which are structurally competitive or contestable. Thus concerns about market failure due to natural monopoly have been vastly exaggerated. In most countries government policy has been the real cause of monopoly (Joskow and Noll 1994).

3. The poor financial performance of state-owned utilities was a major cause of the fiscal crisis. Thus the cause and effect relationship between fiscal necessity and privatization is fairly complicated. Moreover, the loan and policy conditions imposed by international financial institutions provided a strong impetus for privatization.

4. The extent to which technological change has been undermining natural monopoly varies considerably by sector and by activity within sectors. Such change has been breathtaking in telecommunications (especially in interexchange services), impressive in electricity (in generation and to a much lesser extent transmission and local distribution), modest in transportation, and almost negligible in water.

5. Coverage has generally been much higher in transition economies than in developing countries.

6. The U.S. market for intrastate long-distance telephone services after the divestiture of regional Bell operating companies from AT&T provides a natural experiment for testing whether competition is hampered when an integrated utility is permitted to operate in a competitive market (competitive access option). The regional companies were restricted to telephone operations within the boundaries of local access and transport areas (LATAs). All inter-LATA traffic was to be carried by interexchange carriers such as AT&T, MCI, and Sprint. By 1996 more than 99 percent of lines were equipped for equal access in the inter-LATA market. In contrast, intra-LATA competition was available to only about 32 percent of the nation's lines. Thus the regional Bell companies were extremely effective at delaying the entry of competitors (Faulhaber 2003).

7. A package of policy reforms complemented privatization, including restructuring, regulatory reform, market rules, and competition.

8. Still, even in the United States there is ambiguity about the causal link between performance and regulation. For example, changes in telecommuni-

cations performance may be due to technology as much as liberalization. On the other hand, the sharp recovery in U.S. railways since the early 1980s can easily be traced to changes in regulation.

9. Because telecommunications reform has been extensively analyzed in the literature, this report does not devote a separate chapter to this important infrastructure industry. For recent studies assessing developments in telecommunications, see ITU (2002, 2003); Boylaud and Nicoletti (2002); Fink, Mattoo, and Rathindran (2002); Bortolotti and others (2001); Cave and Crandall (2001); Li and Xu (2001); Noll (2000c); Cowhey and Klimenko (1999).

10. Such popular opposition, possibly fueled by the global economic downturn, is being directed to economic reforms in general. Antiglobalization activists, however, have made privatization one of their main targets.

11. In 1994 Lattelekom was formed as a joint venture between the Republic of Latvia (51 percent) and Tilts Communications (49 percent) and was granted a 20-year exclusivity for fixed-line telecommunications services. Tilts Communications committed to invest $160 million in Lattelekom over a three-year period in return for the 49 percent equity stake. When in 1999 the government of Latvia shortened the Lattelekom exclusivity from 2013 to 2003, Tilts Communications demanded $380 million in compensation. A protracted legal battle ensued, impeding sector development.

12. These percentage changes exaggerate the magnitude of the problem because they reflect extremely low initial prices.

CHAPTER TWO

Crafting Regulation for Privatized Infrastructure

MANY INFRASTRUCTURE ACTIVITIES IN DEVELoping and transition economies already involve substantial competition. But others have little or none—though that may soon change (Klein 1996a; Gray and Klein 1997). For two main reasons, industries lacking competition require regulation. First, to ensure fair treatment of customers who lack the protection that comes with competition. Second, to ensure that competitors have fair access to bottleneck network facilities controlled by incumbent service providers. If incumbents do not face regulatory constraints, they can use these facilities to control—or destroy—their rivals.

Thus regulation plays a central role in subjecting network utilities to competition. Governments also have a permanent role in enforcing antimonopoly and antitrust policies, which ensure that competition is not suppressed by private monopoly power or by collusion among or combinations of competitors (Kahn 1996). So, one of the biggest challenges for policymakers in developing and transition economies is managing the shift from state ownership and control of infrastructure operations to more independent regulatory oversight.

The Emergence of Post-Privatization Regulation

WHEN PRIVATIZATION REFORMS WERE INTRODUCED, developing and transition economies had few precedents to guide the design of regulatory mechanisms. Until the 1980s the state owned and operated core infrastructure industries in most countries, usually as part of sector ministries. In the few countries that had private infrastructure, regulation was based on the principle that these industries were mostly natural monopolies. Accordingly, regulation sought to capture the efficiency benefits of size while protecting consumers from possible monopoly abuses.

The 1980s and 1990s saw a dramatic global reassessment of the state's role in infrastructure and of the view that such industries were mainly natural monopolies. As developing and transition economies began restructuring and privatizing their infrastructure, they looked to the countries that had first taken this approach: Canada, New Zealand, the United Kingdom, and the United States. But these advanced industrial countries have long traditions of market capitalism supported by strong legal institutions. They also have well-developed education programs that teach how to regulate private monopolies, facilitate entry by new service providers, and promote competition. Lacking these features, developing and transition economies have faced a huge challenge in developing effective regulation for infrastructure (Gray 1998; Noll 2000d).[1]

Under pressure from international agencies, investment banks, and financial advisers, many of these countries have hastily adopted regulatory templates from industrial countries, especially the United Kingdom and the United States. But these models have rarely been adapted to the political and institutional features common to poorer countries, including lack of checks and balances, low credibility, widespread corruption and regulatory capture, limited technical expertise, and weak auditing, accounting, and tax systems (Laffont 1996). As a result such efforts have had limited success—or been outright failures.[2]

Moreover, many government entities (especially sector ministries) have resisted giving up their regulatory functions. They have also been reluctant to limit their roles to policy oversight: assessing industry developments and adjusting policies accordingly (Criales and Smith 1997). Indeed, in Brazil the ministries of communications and of mines and energy have tried to recapture some activities assigned to regulatory agencies (Landau 2002). Morocco's telecommunications regulator, one of the world's best, continues to struggle with the sector ministry (Samarajiva, Mahan, and Barendse 2002). Most new regulatory agencies are not independent of government and insulated from political control—crucial conditions if privatization is to achieve its public interest goals.

Complicating matters further, state enterprises in developing and transition economies were often organized to achieve political objectives, not to solve market failures (Guasch and Hahn 1999). Many have been tools of special interest groups and corrupt officials. There is a danger that such rent-seeking coalitions, aiming to avoid financial losses from privatization and competition, will subvert the regulatory process (Noll 1999). Regulatory institutions and processes are exploited even in industrial countries. But social welfare is at much greater risk in developing and transition economies because the rule of law is often weak and cronyism and corruption are often endemic. Yet international donors and privatization advisers have largely ignored the substantial risks that political and regulatory capture pose to the public interest (Laffont 2003).

To contribute to social welfare, regulation must reflect local capacity. Almost all regulatory mechanisms have been developed by industrial countries and have substantial information requirements. Implementing them will be difficult in most developing and transition economies due to insufficient economic data and technical skills. For example, weak accounting systems hamper the use of long-run incremental costs—a key concept for public utility pricing in industrial countries (Laffont 1996). Until they develop economic and technical expertise, developing and transition economies will have to rely on simple, perhaps second-best regulatory mechanisms consistent with local capacity. There is also an urgent need for increased analytical and technical assistance from international agencies.

In addition, regulatory models from industrial countries should be carefully evaluated before being applied in developing and transition economies. For example, policymakers need to understand regulatory mistakes in the United States and elsewhere to avoid repeating them (box 2.1; Joskow and Noll 1994).

The Evolution and Elements of Effective Regulation

CREDIBLE, STABLE REGULATION IS REQUIRED TO ACHIEVE the benefits of privatizing and liberalizing infrastructure. The past two decades show the importance of planning such regulation before privatization, including its economic content and institutional architecture (Willig 1999). An inadequate focus on sector economics has been a serious weakness of privatization in many developing

---

Box 2.1   Regulation in Argentina—Repeating U.S. Mistakes

A 1995 REVIEW OF ELECTRICITY REGULATION IN ARGENTINA FOUND that the pricing of transmission services was based not on market demands or incremental transmission costs, but on economically meaningless accounting allocations. For example, charges for a new transmission line were based on a determination of the "energy benefits" for the line's beneficiaries. Such assessments were based on the fully distributed cost methodology of allocating common and fixed costs—a method that U.S. regulators abandoned in the 1980s because it was considered a major cause of the deteriorating performance and bankruptcy of the railway industry.

Source: Willig (1995).

---

and transition economies. It has also been a weakness of technical assistance provided by their international advisers, including the World Bank.

Moreover, many developing and transition economies lack the institutional prerequisites for effective regulation, including:

- Separation of powers, especially between the executive and the judiciary.
- Well-functioning, credible political and economic institutions—and an independent judiciary (Bergara, Henisz, and Spiller 1998).
- A legal system that safeguards private property from state or regulatory seizure without fair compensation and relies on judicial review to protect against regulatory abuse of basic principles of fairness.
- Norms and laws—supported by institutions—that delegate authority to a bureaucracy and enable it to act relatively independently.
- Strong contract laws and mechanisms for resolving contract disputes.
- Sound administrative procedures that provide broad access to the regulatory process and make it transparent.
- Sufficient professional staff trained in relevant economic, accounting, and legal principles.

Developing and transition economies cannot develop these crucial features overnight—achieving them will take time.[3]

Institutional Requirements

The structure and process of infrastructure regulation determine how effectively it supports reforms and promotes efficiency and other social objectives (Smith 1997c). In most developing and transition economies such regulation is at an early stage of implementation. Thus these countries can draw on recent findings for effective regulation of privatized utilities, including the importance of coherence, independence, accountability, transparency, predictability, and capacity (box 2.2; Noll 2000d).

Coherence.   Regulations for each infrastructure sector should be complementary and mutually supportive. The laws guiding regulation must be in agreement, and regulations must be consistent over time. New rules should take into account previous ones, with amendments made to eliminate significant inconsistencies.

Regulatory coherence requires that national regulators, ministries, and provincial and municipal regulators have clearly defined responsibilities—ensuring that the same agency always makes decisions involving specific aspects of regulation. Such arrangements imply continuity in the people and methods used to make decisions and make adherence to the rule of law more likely.

Similarly, the same agency should handle regulatory activities that require harmonization. For example, in Argentina's privatized telecommunications sector, service providers' access prices and cost reporting are the responsibility of the sector's regulatory agency, while end user (retail) prices are under the purview of the Secretariat of Energy and Communications (Kessides 1997). Regulation for access and user prices should be closely harmonized, however, and both institutions should base their decisions on cost data.

Regulators should be required to publish statements explaining their goals and reasons for decisions on entry, pricing, and other industry behavior subject to oversight. Doing so forces the government to think through its long-term policy objectives and regulatory principles. It also

Box 2.2   Recent Shortcomings and Achievements in Infrastructure Regulation

Romania—lacking coherence

IN ROMANIA RESPONSIBILITIES FOR OVERSEEING telecommunications prices are splintered among the National Agency for Communications and Informatics, the Office of Competition, the Cabinet, and the Competition Council. Moreover, unclear guidelines for determining which prices should be regulated produce strange anomalies, such as a lack of regulation for interconnections not involving Rom Telecom, the dominant carrier. In addition, regulators are not required to justify their policies, and they cannot request cost information from service providers. As a result pricing decisions are uncoordinated, and inconsistencies—such as different prices for local services, interconnections between Rom Telecom and mobile carriers, and interconnections between mobile carriers—are not explained.

Latvia—undermining independence

In 1999 Latvia's Telecommunications Rate Council approved large increases in telephone rates. But the sector ministry called the increases unfair and annulled the council's decision, a move not clearly allowed by the law. The Ministry of Justice evaluated the legality of the annulment and declared it legal—and was backed by Latvia's parliament, which argued that the council had failed to safeguard the interests of consumers. The government then announced that a new council would be formed and removed the original members.

Brazil—promoting accountability

Brazil's National Telecommunications Regulatory Agency has introduced a number of innovations. In 2000 it became the world's first telecommunications regulator to receive ISO-9001 certification, an international standard for meeting customers' technical needs. The agency's extensive Website enables Brazilians to comment on its activities and provides information such as telecommunications laws, service

prices for different providers, and annual updates on operator compliance. The Advisory Council, an entity with representatives from civil society, assesses the agency's annual reports and publishes its findings in the official gazette and on the agency's Website. In addition, the agency employs an ombudsperson who evaluates its performance every two years.

Peru—ensuring transparency

In Peru the Supervisory Authority for Private Investment in Telecommunications sets telecommunications prices, ensures a competitive market, and monitors compliance with concession contracts and quality standards. The agency uses transparent mechanisms to formulate norms—for instance, requiring that regulatory proposals be supported by assessments of welfare benefits and best practices. After being reviewed by the agency, each proposal is published in the official gazette and undergoes a 30-day consultation period. In addition, some proposals are subjected to public hearings. The agency has also created independent committees, supported by experts, to resolve disputes between service providers. If parties cannot reach an agreement, the committee can dictate a solution. Finally, the agency has created an internal tribunal to handle consumer complaints not satisfactorily managed by phone companies.

Argentina—undermining transparency and predictability

A 1996 review of Argentina's gas sector revealed investor concerns about the transparency and predictability of the National Gas Regulatory Authority. In one case the agency did not permit wholesale prices charged to distribution companies to be passed on to consumers. In addition, it used its authority over transportation and distribution activities to regulate field prices—changing the rules of the game since field prices were deregulated as part

---

Box 2.2 *(continued)*

of privatization. Moreover, the agency did not provide coherent or predictable principles for determining acceptable gas prices. There were also complaints about capricious penalties for violations of gas quality standards.

Ukraine—coming up short on capacity

Ukraine's National Electricity Regulatory Commission, established in 1994, was one of the first independent regulators in a transition economy. In 1997 the commission's specialists were about 70 percent engineers, 20 percent economists, and 10 percent lawyers. All but one of the economists had graduated from Soviet universities in 1965–81. The commission has no specialists in regulatory economics, and Ukraine offers no training in energy regulation. Moreover, key employees have left the electricity commission to join private companies regulated by it—increasing pro-industry bias and the potential for capture.

Source: Noll (2000d); East European Constitutional Review (1999); World Bank (2000); ITU (2001b,d); Kahn (1996); Tsaplin (2001).

---

enables firms and consumers to predict how they will be treated in the future, enhancing accountability (for more details see below, in the section on regulatory commitment).

Independence.   Effective regulation requires that regulators be largely free from political influence, especially on a day-to-day or decision-by-decision basis. Agencies must be objective, apolitical enforcers of policies set forth in controlling statutes.

Still, complete independence for regulators is not possible or even desirable (Kahn 1996). The executive branch should be able to ensure that the regulators it appoints are sympathetic to its reforms and to administration policies. But if regulators are not insulated from political intervention, the regulatory process may become politicized, decisions may be discredited, and policies may lack continuity.

Compromise is needed to ensure that regulators are both independent and responsive to an elected administration's policy goals. Safeguards that can help achieve such compromise include (Smith 1997c):

- Giving the regulator statutory authority, free of ministerial control.
- Setting clear professional criteria for appointing regulators.
- Requiring that both the executive and legislative branches participate in appointments.

- Appointing regulators for fixed periods and prohibiting their removal without clearly defined cause (subject to formal review).
- Staggering the terms of an agency's board members so that they can be replaced only gradually by successive administrations.
- Funding agency operations with user fees or levies on service providers, to insulate agencies from political interference through the budget process.
- Exempting agencies from civil service salary caps, to enable them to attract and retain well-qualified staff.
- Prohibiting the executive branch from overturning an agency's decisions except through new legislation or judicial appeals of existing laws.

Accountability.   A regulator's independence should be reconciled with its accountability. Allowing a regulator to set prices and quality standards gives it enormous power to redistribute rents. Without an accompanying obligation to respect previous decisions and the legal rights of all parties, a regulator has considerable leeway for opportunism. Thus checks and balances are required to ensure that regulators do not become capricious, corrupt, or grossly inefficient. Citizens and firms should be able to find out who makes regulatory decisions and what guides them, and to voice their concerns. In addition, affected parties should be able to easily and quickly obtain redress if a regulator acts arbitrarily or incompetently.

It is difficult to strike a proper balance between independence and accountability, but certain measures can help:

- Writing statutes that specify the rights and responsibilities of each regulatory agency and distinguish between primary and secondary objectives when there are multiple goals.
- Subjecting agency decisions to review by courts or another nonpolitical entity.
- Requiring regulators to produce annual reports on their activities and subjecting their performance to formal reviews by independent auditors or legislative committees.
- Removing regulators that act inappropriately or incompetently.
- Allowing stakeholders to submit their views on matters under review and requiring regulators to publish their decisions and the reasons behind them.

Transparency. Infrastructure regulation is an important policy issue, and in a democracy all citizens need transparent information about it to evaluate government performance. Thus all regulatory rules and agreements—and the principles guiding them (and future regulation)—should be a matter of public record. This record must be accessible to all market participants, not just service providers, to inform long-term business plans. Transparency helps induce investment by incumbents and new entrants—and avoid costly, time-consuming regulatory disputes.

Transparency also protects against corrupt regulation. In addition, it makes citizens (especially those adversely affected by regulatory decisions) less likely to believe that decisions are corrupt. When regulatory decisions and principles are clearly written, the reasons for them are apparent. Moreover, corrupt decisions are easier to detect and harder to defend.

Predictability. Regulatory agencies are predictable if they follow the rule of law, particularly respect for precedent and the principle of *stare decisis*. Respect for precedent means that regulators reverse past decisions only if they have created significant problems. *Stare decisis* requires that cases with the same underlying facts be decided the same way every time.

Thus regulatory decisions must be based on durable rules and procedures that will apply in future cases unless new information is obtained. Even then, regulators must prove that past decisions should be changed. Otherwise, market participants will lack confidence in regulation, undermining the size, scope, and quality of infrastructure and related investments.

Capacity. A regulatory agency's responsibilities should match its financial and human resources. Available financing reflects government willingness to support independent regulatory institutions. But with the possible exception of very small and poor countries, lack of financial capacity is unlikely to be a genuine constraint—though failure to provide adequate financing for regulation is a more common problem.

Inadequate expertise is a much bigger challenge in many developing and transition economies. Well-developed economic, accounting, engineering, and legal skills are required for regulatory functions such as monitoring industry performance, analyzing cost data, dealing with information asymmetries, and analyzing the behavior of regulated firms. But until recently infrastructure in these countries involved little private activity or assets. As a result there are few regulatory experts. To overcome these deficiencies, regulatory agencies need to be given complete freedom to hire specialized staff (Estache and Martimort 1999). This may require exempting such agencies from civil service salary and recruitment rules (Noll 2000c).

Moreover, most regulatory efforts have focused on institution building: writing enabling legislation, defining organizational architecture, determining administrative procedures, identifying sources of funding, and so on. Not enough attention has been paid to identifying issues that require regulatory resolution—ensuring access to bottleneck facilities, eliminating anticompetitive cross-subsidies, setting prices and rebalancing tariffs, developing mechanisms to fund universal service mandates—and to developing related expertise. The scarcity of such skills has been one of the main impediments to effective regulation in developing and transition economies (Petrazzini 1997; Stern 2000a).

In many of these countries staff and budget resources have not been allocated based on careful, rational planning. Because engineers dominate many infrastructure activities, high priority is often given to purely technical functions. Accounting and financial and economic analysis receive much less attention. Moreover, low budgets severely constrain hiring decisions, resulting in slow changes to the skill mix of regulatory staff.

A recent review of state and central electricity regulators in India shows the problems created by inadequate capacity (Prayas Energy Group 2003). One of the main issues identified was grossly inadequate staff resources. Requests for professional and technical staff are routinely delayed for months or years. Although state regulators were supposed to have 8–10 professional and technical staff, all but two had 3 or fewer. And 8 of the 12 state regulators studied had no permanent professional and technical staff, instead often relying on temporary staff from incumbent utilities.

Building regulatory capacity is one of the toughest tasks of infrastructure reform

Preliminary Appraisal of Regulatory Systems

THE MOVE FROM MONOLITHIC STATE-OWNED MONOPOLIES TO regulated private entities is still under way in most developing and transition economies. Thus few regulatory agencies have been around long enough to allow for a definitive assessment of their effectiveness and impact on industry performance. Still, several empirical findings provide insights on appropriate regulation for these countries.

One point is clear: effective regulation requires more than formal requirements for independence, accountability, and transparency. Many governments are unlikely to observe the spirit of the law and implement proper, consistent regulation—especially if their initial ownership of reforms was weak and their acceptance of reforms was influenced by external pressures and loan conditions. Regulatory frameworks and attendant institutions may not operate as expected if they fail to take into account a country's constitutional, legal, and public interest mechanisms (Stern 1997).

A sample of progress—and problems—by region.   On paper, developing and transition economies have made considerable progress in establishing the institutional requirements for effective, independent regulation. But in practice the record is mixed, with discouraging developments in many countries and sectors. Moreover, it is unclear how well these agencies will work in the future.

Around the world, lack of regulatory independence has been one of the clearest institutional shortcomings. Even some early Latin American reformers with regulation based on the U.S. model have failed to achieve independence. Power regulators have a fair degree of autonomy in El Salvador and Nicaragua and to a lesser extent in Ecuador and Honduras (IADB 1999). But in Chile and Colombia the independence of power regulators is uncertain because their boards include government ministers and they rely on budget allocations made by ministry officials (Fischer and Galetovic 2000). Lack of independence allegedly led the executive secretary of Chile's regulatory commission to resign in 1999. Political interference has also undermined the independence of electricity regulators in Guatemala and Peru (IADB 1999).

Argentina's two power regulators, the National Electricity Regulatory Authority and the National Gas Regulatory Authority, are reasonably independent. But there have been concerns about the lack of transparency and predictability in some of their decisions (see box 2.2) and the absence of external scrutiny of their administrative practices (Estache 1997). Transparency problems also initially plagued the country's water regulator. And during its first few years the telecommunications regulator lacked both independence and transparency. Mexico's telecommunications regulator suffers from similar shortcomings (Noll 2001).

In Jamaica the multisector Office of Utilities Regulation, which became operational in 1997, has been handicapped by defective legislation. It can only offer advice, because line ministries retain control over decisionmaking (Stirton and Lodge 2001). Similarly, in Costa Rica government interference, especially in tariff adjustments, has weakened the independence and effectiveness of the multisector Regulatory Authority of Public Services (IADB 1999).

In Hungary the energy regulator's independence is limited by a lack of autonomous revenue, fixed-term appointments for the board of directors, and well-defined criteria for appointing and dismissing directors. In addition, civil service salary caps make it difficult to attract qualified staff (Stern 1999; Newbery 2000e). In telecommunications the head of the sector's regulatory authority reports to the minister of transport and communications (Rosston 2000).

The Czech Republic also lacks independent regulators for energy and telecommunications—not surprising given the government's ambivalence toward specialized regulatory agencies in the early years of transition (Stern 1999). As a result the Ministry of Finance has the final say in regulating gas and electricity prices, while the energy regulator is part of the Ministry of Industry and Trade (Newbery 2000d). Similarly, the primary regulator for telecommunications is part of the Ministry of Transport and Communications (Kessides and Ordover 2000).

Poland's energy regulator, by contrast, meets most of the formal requirements for independence. And Latvia's multisector regulator enjoys financial independence from the state budget and has shown strong commitment to transparency and accountability (Vanags 2001). But its independence is compromised by the close affiliation between its board members and the political parties that nominate them.

In Romania telecommunications regulation lacks coherence (see box 2.2), while gas regulation lacks any semblance of independence (Newbery 2000b; Noll 2000d). The minister of industry and trade appoints the chair, vice chair, and three members of the gas regulator's board of directors, ensuring ministerial control over the agency. In electricity, however, Romania and Bulgaria have taken bold steps to create independent regulators. Romania's National Electricity and Heat Regulatory Authority is a U.K.-style independent entity, while Bulgaria's State Commission for Energy Regulation incorporates, at least on paper, elements of U.S.-style independent commissions (Stern 1999).

Table 2.1 Ranking of Infrastructure Regulation in Asia, by Sector and Institutional Criteria, 1998

Country/sector	Institutional criteria				
	Coherence	Independence	Accountability	Transparency	Predictability
Bangladesh					
Electricity	D	D	D	E	E
India					
Electricity, federal	D	C	D	C	E
Electricity, Orissa	B	A	B	A	D
Gas	E	E	E	C	E
Telecommunications	C	B	B	A	C
Indonesia					
Gas	E	E	E	E	E
Transport	E	E	E	E	E
Malaysia					
Telecommunications	C	C	D	E	E
Transport	C	C	D	E	D
Water	C	D	D	E	D
Pakistan					
Electricity	C	B	C	C	D
Philippines					
Electricity	C	C	D	D	C
Water	C	C	C	C	D

Note: Rankings are on a scale of A (best practice) to E (highly unfavorable for private investment).
Source: Stern and Holder (1999).

A 1998 study of infrastructure regulation in six Asian developing countries (Bangladesh, India, Indonesia, Malaysia, Pakistan, the Philippines) found significant weaknesses in coherence, independence, accountability, transparency, and predictability. On a scale from A (best practice) to E (highly unfavorable for private investment), only electricity regulation in the state of Orissa (India) ranked better than C in four of these areas (table 2.1). It was followed by telecommunications regulation in all of India, which did better than C in three areas. Elsewhere the results were dismal: only one other sector ranked better than C in any area (the independence of Pakistan's electricity regulator). The rankings were similar across sectors in each country, suggesting the importance of country characteristics in regulatory design.

Other Asian governments have also been reluctant to cede control to new independent regulators. For example, during the first phase of Sri Lanka's telecommunications reforms (1991–96) the government insisted on keeping the regulatory agency a government department—despite clear evidence that it was unable to attract needed expertise (Samarajiva 2001).

Many African countries have established regulatory agencies for their utilities. These agencies face serious challenges, including obtaining adequate expertise, financial resources, and statutory authority. Many are simply extensions of sector ministries, which maintain a tight grip on regulated sectors and still perform key oversight functions. A recent analysis of telecommunications regulation in 29 countries in the region indicates problems with independence and transparency (Pyramid Research 1999). On a scale of 1 (worst) to 4 (best), 23 of the countries received scores of 1 for autonomy, and only 2 received scores higher than 2. Rankings for transparency were better, though 10 countries still received scores of 1, and only 2 scored higher than 2. Scores for credibility and efficiency were similarly lackluster.

Insufficient statutory authority among telecommunications regulators has led to enforcement failures in several African countries. In Ghana the incumbent fixed line monopolist (Ghana Telecom) entered the cellular business despite being legally prohibited from doing so. It also inhibited entry by charging—with impunity from the regulator—very high interconnection fees (Ahortor 2003; Laffont 2003). In Tanzania the dominant mobile operator (Mobitel) entered a region in direct violation of the regulator's order. And in Côte d'Ivoire the regulator has been unable to force the incumbent fixed line operator, CItelecom, to comply with the service quality and network expansion terms of its concession contract (Laffont 2003).

There are, however, notable examples of effective regulation in Africa. The Uganda Communications Commission is independent, competent, and has strong statutory powers to demand information from and fine operators that do not comply with its regulations (Shirley and others 2002). The Botswana Telecommunications Authority was one of the first independent regulatory agencies in Africa (Bruce and Macmillan 2002). It establishes and finances its operational budget and exercises its licensing authority without government interference (ITU 2001a). Similarly, Morocco's National Telecommunications Regulatory Agency has gained credibility for its impartiality, transparent decisionmaking, re-

Figure 2.1   Results from a Survey of Telecommunications Regulators, 2001

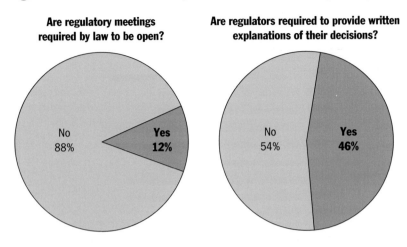

Source: World Bank (2001e).

spect for deadlines, and willingness to let all interested parties be heard on important policy issues (Wellenius 1999; ITU 2001c).

A recent survey of telecommunications regulators in 41 developing and transition economies found that only 5 are legally required to hold meetings open to the public—an important element of transparency (figure 2.1).[4] This finding suggests limited formal transparency among regulatory institutions and perhaps lack of appreciation of its enormous importance (World Bank 2001e). Still, two-thirds of the agencies surveyed hold at least some open meetings.

Less than half of these agencies, however, are required to publish explanations for their decisions—another important element of regulatory accountability and transparency (see figure 2.1). A similar survey of energy regulators in developing and transition economies uncovered even weaker commitment to transparency, with less than half opening their meetings to the public (World Bank 2002a).

Unrealistic expectations? Or just the first stage in an evolutionary process?   The label "independent" is somewhat exaggerated when applied to new regulators in developing and transition economies. Many of these agencies report to sector ministries and are mainly staffed by government representatives. Moreover, transparent regulatory practice remains limited in most of these countries.

Figure 2.2 Regulatory Indexes for Telecommunications in Latin America, 1980–97

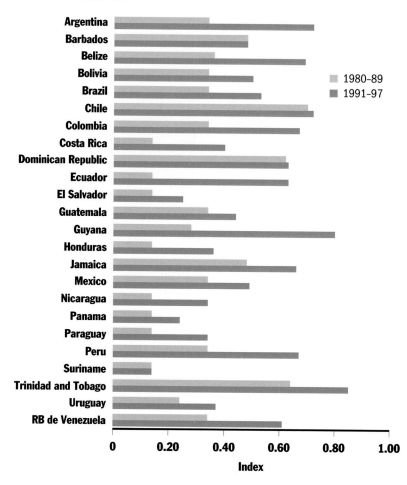

Note: Each index is the average of seven scores. Six scores for the country's regulatory agency, each with a value of 1 or 0, measure autonomy in funding and in potential for being removed from office, authority for regulating prices and assessing fines, accountability for decisions, and separation from the operator. In addition, the country's legal framework is given a score of 1 for a law, 0.5 for any other legislation, and 0 otherwise.
Source: Gutierrez (2002).

Still, assessments of regulation in the developing world are strongly influenced by attitudes toward regulation. Optimistic observers point out that regulatory regimes in developing and transition economies have been created from scratch, are still in early stages of development, and (at least in terms of formal arrangements) are moving in the right direction—toward greater independence, accountability, and transparency than under state ownership (figure 2.2). It is also worth remembering that it took many years for today's industrial countries to develop effective regulation, and that developing and transition economies face enormous economic, political, and social challenges.

Pessimistic observers, however, insist that the widespread reluctance of governments to give up regulatory control is more than a symptom of the early stages of an evolutionary process. Instead, they argue, it is a deliberate attempt to use the regulatory process to protect interest groups whose benefits under state ownership would be threatened by market liberalization and privatization (Noll 1999).

Pessimists could also argue that expectations of regulatory independence and transparency were unrealistic. Under pressure from international financial institutions, many countries—especially in Africa and Eastern Europe—adopted regulatory structures that were inconsistent with their political, institutional, and human capacities (Laffont 2003). One cannot reasonably expect strong regulatory independence to rapidly emerge in countries where the separation of powers and concomitant checks and balances are not prominent elements of political and legal structures. Thus it is uncertain whether these countries will honor commitments they have made (especially under pressure) to regulatory arrangements. For example, as a condition of a stabilization loan from the International Monetary Fund, in 1999 Bulgaria established a State Commission on Energy Regulation that was to start functioning as an independent regulator in mid-2000. But that goal was undermined when the government removed—without explanation—five of the commission's six members just as it began exercising its statutory authority.[5]

The truth probably lies between these two extremes. Moreover, some of the asserted deficiencies of regulation in developing and transition economies are similar to those observed in industrial countries (Kahn 1996).

The Structure of Regulatory Institutions

SEVERAL DECISIONS MUST BE MADE ABOUT THE ORGANIZATION of regulatory governance. How should regulatory responsibilities be assigned among national and subnational tiers of government? Should regulatory agencies focus on specific industries, or should they oversee multiple sectors? How should functional responsibilities— for prices, licensing, quality, and environmental considerations—be allocated? And what type of relationships should regulators have with sector ministries and with competition or antitrust authorities?

The economic and technological characteristics of a regulated industry, as well as a country's resources (including human resources), will affect the institutional architecture of regulatory governance. Moreover, effective regulation requires both an administrative body (to execute it) and a political institution (to ensure its legitimacy; Aubert and Laffont 2000). Formal regulatory structures that seem optimal in theory may be impossible to implement when political constraints are taken into account.

Centralized or Decentralized?

Designing regulation involves tradeoffs (Smith 2000b). For example, decentralization—making lower levels of government responsible for regulating utilities—offers several advantages. It:

- Allows local conditions and preferences to shape regulation.
- Moves regulators closer to services, allowing them to gather better information on users.
- Promotes competition among subnational regulators to attract private investment (Tiebout 1956; Oates 1999).
- May improve enforcement of regulatory decisions (Laffont and Zantman 1999).

But centralization also has advantages. A national regulatory structure makes the best use of scarce expertise and minimizes the fixed costs of regulation (such as those of maintaining regional offices). Centralization can also reduce the risks of a regulatory race to the bottom—as when jurisdictions competing for investment take on excessive financial risk or lower their environmental standards.[6] And centralization may be necessary if jurisdictions are too small to support an efficient scale or scope of operations for certain industries.

Regulatory decisions in some jurisdictions may have implications for others, as when effluents discharged into rivers affect downstream users. Moreover, subnational regulation can impede trade between jurisdictions (say, because of different technical standards), protect local monopolies, or create subsidies for local producers. These situations call for a higher-level regulatory authority to protect social welfare and ensure harmonization. Decentralized regulators also face a greater risk of being captured by industry interests or local politicians.

Thus the issues raised by centralizing or decentralizing regulatory oversight cut across a wide range of institutions and reflect a country's characteristics and constraints. Accordingly, analysis of the costs and benefits of either approach must reflect the country's institutional structure and the industry's technological features. Still, several general conclusions can be drawn.

First, small or poor countries may have only one effective tier of government. Large or rich countries have far greater potential for decentralization and more options in assigning different regulatory tasks to different tiers of government. But while multitiered approaches are the norm in large industrial countries, they increase the complexity of establishing new systems in developing and transition economies.

Second, spillovers across jurisdiction and industry boundaries depend on the industry:

- *Electricity*. Some distribution utilities operate solely within subnational boundaries. Most transmission grids are designed to operate nationally. And features of generation vary—serving one or multiple jurisdictions, sometimes with technological spillovers that affect much larger areas, and sometimes involving cross-border trade. Thus in most countries transmission and at least some aspects of generation may be best regulated at the national level, while in large countries it may be feasible to regulate distribution at the subnational level (Smith 2000b).
- *Water*. Most countries have decentralized responsibilities for water services. Many water utilities operate solely through local networks, with limited interconnection. But other utilities serve neighboring municipalities or draw on water resources that cross political boundaries. As a result municipal, state, and even national governments may dispute water regulation.
- *Telecommunications*. Of the three main utility industries, telecommunications involves the most competition. Networks have national (and international) reach, and major firms tend to operate nationally. Because firms in different jurisdictions should face consistent regulation, nearly all countries regulate telecommunications at the national level.

Box 2.3   Decentralized Water Services in Mexico and Morocco

ALTHOUGH MEXICO'S GOVERNMENT STRUCTURE is highly centralized, several water supply functions have been decentralized. First, public irrigation systems were transferred to user groups. By 1996 some 2.9 million hectares—87 percent of the area under medium- and high-level irrigation and 46 percent of the area under all irrigation—had been transferred to 386 water user associations. Water resource management remains the central government's responsibility, but local authorities manage many supply tasks.

Similarly, Morocco has a strongly centralized government but a highly decentralized regulatory structure for water, with considerable functional specialization. The Directorate General of Hydraulics (part of the Ministry of Equipment) plans and develops water resources. The National Office of Potable Water (under the same ministry) acquires and distributes water to households, firms, and local governments. The nine regional authorities for agricultural development (under the Ministry of Agriculture) develop and maintain water distribution networks and collect water charges. In smaller systems local governments and farmers play a larger role in distribution and maintenance.

Source: Saleth and Dinar (1999).

Finally, limited regulatory capacity bolsters arguments for centralized regulatory responsibility, at least initially. The potential benefits of decentralization can then be achieved using other strategies. For example, national regulators can tailor their efforts to local conditions and establish regional offices to be closer to firms and other stakeholders (box 2.3).

Multiple Agencies, or Just One?

If regulatory responsibilities are assigned to a single tier of government, should the government create industry-specific regulators? Or a single agency with a broader mandate? Establishing separate agencies has advantages. It recognizes the unique economic and technological characteristics of each infrastructure industry and enables regulators to develop deep, industry-specific expertise. It also mitigates the risk of institutional failure and encourages innovative responses to regulatory challenges.

But there are also benefits to using one regulator for several industries. Doing so makes it possible to share fixed costs, scarce talent, and other resources. Consolidation also builds expertise in cross-cutting regulatory issues: administering tariff adjustment rules, introducing competition in monopolistic industries, and managing relationships with stakeholders. In addition, the broader responsibilities of a multi-industry agency reduce its dependence on any one industry and so help protect against capture. And a multi-industry agency may be better able to resist political interference because its broader constituency gives it greater independence from sector ministers.

Moreover, the notion of distinct utility industries is under threat. Deregulation and changing business strategies have seen electricity, gas, rail, and water companies entering telecommunications, gas companies entering electricity, and water and electricity companies merging. A multi-industry regulator can address the issues emerging with these multi-utilities. In addition, a multi-industry regulator is in a better position to guard against distortions created by inconsistent regulation of utilities competing directly (such as electricity and gas) or for investment capital (Helm 1994).

So, deciding on the breadth of regulatory coverage involves numerous considerations—and no single approach will suit all circumstances. First, in economies with a small base of consumers (not necessarily population) and limited human and financial resources, there is a strong argument for merging regulatory responsibilities (box 2.4). For example, multi-industry regulators have been successful in Costa Rica, Jamaica, and Panama and in the states of Brazil. But in large economies the benefits of a multi-industry agency may be outweighed by concerns about insufficient industry focus and diseconomies of scale.

Box 2.4   Latvia's Public Utilities Regulation Commission

UNTIL 2001 PUBLIC UTILITIES IN LATVIA WERE REGULATED BY THE Ministry of Economy's Energy Regulation Council and the Ministry of Transportation's Telecommunications Tariffs Council, Railway Administration Department, and Communications Department (postal services). The government combined regulatory oversight of the four sectors in a single agency—the Public Utilities Regulation Commission—to ensure regulatory consistency and technological convergence and make better use of human and financial resources.

Source: http://www.sprk.gov.lv.

Second, regulators in developing and transition economies typically have less discretion than their counterparts in industrial countries. Multi-industry agencies with narrower responsibilities raise fewer concerns about inadequate industry focus or potential diseconomies of scale.

Third, if market substitution can occur between the output of regulated industries—especially between electricity and gas, but also between modes of transportation and telecommunications—economic distortions may arise from inconsistent regulation of common issues. Thus the case for consolidating regulatory responsibility may be stronger for some industries.

Fourth, the scarcity of expertise and vulnerability to political and industry capture in developing and transition economies also strengthen arguments for multi-industry regulation. The benefits of industry-specific agencies can then be gained through other strategies, including the creation of industry-specific departments.

Finally, different reform strategies place different demands on new regulatory agencies, affecting their ability to develop expertise and maintain focus. One common strategy is staggered reform, where the government reforms utility industries sequentially over time. This strategy allows a new regulatory agency to focus initially on one industry and build up experience. If things go as planned, the agency is better prepared to oversee additional industries as they undergo reform.

Under the other strategy, concurrent reform—also known as the big-bang approach—the government privatizes and reforms all or most utility industries more or less simultaneously. This strategy can place enormous demands on a new multi-industry agency. Governments intent on this strategy might consider the advantages of first creating industry-specific agencies and then merging them. Another approach, adopted in Bolivia, is to establish a hybrid structure that captures some of the benefits of both industry-specific and broader approaches (Criales and Smith 1997).

The Importance of Regulatory Commitment

REGULATION THAT ENCOURAGES SUSTAINED PRIVATE INvestment in infrastructure does more than serve the interests of investors—it also promotes competition and increases access to basic services. Such regulation must be clear and credible, ensuring investors that regulators are committed to fair, consistent, and sustainable policies and procedures. For two reasons, commitment and credibility are especially important in the restructured and privatized infrastructure industries of developing and transition economies. First, because of the economic characteristics of these industries. Second, because of the history of arbitrary administrative intervention and discretionary executive power in many of these countries.

Infrastructure industries are essential for the public and for the economy. When infrastructure service prices are based on costs, they can eat up a large portion of household budgets. Thus price changes can have a considerable impact on the level and distribution of real incomes. Cultural attitudes toward paying the full cost of these services change slowly, and price increases often encounter strong resistance. For example, in 2002 in Kerala, India, protestors ransacked utility offices and the political opposition called for a general strike in response to the state government's decision to raise electricity tariffs by 60–100 percent. The decision was quickly reversed (*Platts Power in Asia*, 19 September 2002).

Because infrastructure services are also essential for other economic activities, service levels and prices can significantly influence industrial costs and international competitiveness. Moreover, having only a few utility operators in each locality raises concerns about concentrated market power and excessive prices and profits.

Infrastructure characteristics also create opportunities for government manipulation (Spiller and Savedoff 1999). Because many infrastructure investments are fixed and sunk, private utilities will continue operating as long as prices cover short-run marginal costs. Thus once sunk investments have been made, bargaining power shifts from investors to regulators (Hart 1995). At that point governments may impose special taxes, require special investments, control procurement and employment practices, restrict the composition and movement of capital, or lower the regulated prices that utilities can charge for services (box 2.5). Recognizing these risks, private utilities will likely invest less than is optimal—especially in activities with large sunk costs—or demand high risk premiums unless governments can credibly commit to regulatory stability.

The extent of the commitment problem depends on the country's political institutions and the industry's production technology. In sectors like telecommunications, where technology is changing rapidly, assets depreciate quickly. Thus sunk costs and expropriation risks are low.

Development requires facilitating investment and growth and empowering poor people to participate in that growth

Box 2.5 Examples of Allegedly Opportunistic Government Behavior

Argentina's electricity regulator cuts the penalty for late payments

In 1999 Argentina's National Electricity Regulatory Authority ordered the country's three distribution companies—Edenor, Edesur, and Edelap—to reduce from 10.0 percent to 1.2 percent the penalty for paying electricity bills late. The distribution companies said that this order changed agreed rules, and they feared that the agency would try to change its other agreements with the industry.

Ghana imposes a new telecommunications tax

In January 2002 the Accra Metropolitan Assembly introduced a new tax of 50,000 cedis per mobile telephone subscriber and 20,000 cedis per fixed line subscriber. The dominant mobile operator, Scancom, estimated that the tax would cost it $1 million a year. In December 2002 the assembly closed the offices of Scancom and the other mobile operator, Millicom Ghana, for failing to pay the tax—leading both companies to file a writ challenging its legality.

Kazakhstan's government reverses a promised increase in energy prices

In 1996 Tractebel—a subsidiary of Suez Lyonnaise—acquired Almaty Power Consolidated, the producer and distributor of electricity and heat in Almaty, the former capital of Kazakhstan. The government promised to raise tariffs in exchange for a $300 million investment in distribution by Tractebel. But in 1997 a nationalist administration took office and refused to allow the tariff increases. When Tractebel claimed breach of contract, it became the target of demonstrations. The conflict contributed to Tractebel's withdrawal from the market and the return of assets to state ownership in 2000.

Ecuador's government is sued by the leading private utility

In 1992 Empresa Eléctrica del Ecuador (Emelec) was awarded $51.9 million in international arbitration because for a decade the government had refused to set rates that would allow Emelec to achieve the contractually guaranteed 9.5 percent rate of return on its investment. The government refused to pay the award, and in 1995 Emelec sued it to abide by the arbitration decision—prompting the government to agree to a settlement. But in a 1999 lawsuit Emelec sought substantial additional damages because it alleged that the government had failed to honor the 1995 settlement. Even though Emelec has had its position vindicated by several tribunals and Ecuadorian courts (including the supreme court), the government has refused to honor its obligations.

Source: NERA 1999; Haggarty, Shirley, and Wallsten 2002; *Balancing Act News Update,* 6 January 2003; Bayliss 2001; PR NEWSWIRE Reuters Textline, "Ecuador's Leading Private Utility Sues Government of Ecuador in the US Courts for Dollars 900,000,000," 14 July 1999.

But commitment can be a severe problem in the water sector, where assets depreciate slowly. The risk of expropriation is also high in countries where regulatory procedures are inadequate, the judiciary has little authority or capacity to review administrative decisions, and elections are frequent, highly contested, and dominated by well-organized constituencies (Spiller 1992). However, in small, poor countries the more likely scenario is that the regulator will be small and too weak to avoid capture by powerful interest groups, rather than that it will behave opportunistically and expropriate private assets (Noll 2000c).

Opportunistic behavior is not the exclusive domain of governments. Some regulated firms behave opportunistically, with outcomes dependent on their bargaining power relative to regulators. A major imbalance can occur when low-income countries deal with large foreign investors and multinational corporations. Private investors may demand post-privatization contract adjustments, and countries might agree because they need foreign investment and because legal action (regardless of its merit and outcome) might result in caution among all foreign investors.

Commitment through Administrative Procedures

In some countries utility regulation is based on well-defined administrative procedures. These procedures determine how regulatory agencies make substantive decisions and define mechanisms for appealing them (Spiller 1996). For example, U.S. regulators must:

- Announce that they will consider an issue and their intention to hold hearings on it.
- Solicit comments on major policy issues from interested parties.
- Facilitate participation in decisionmaking by allowing interested parties to offer testimony and evidence, and even to cross-examine other stakeholders.
- Set deadlines for reaching decisions.
- Justify their decisions.
- Provide arrangements for appealing decisions.

By specifying the institutional environment for decisionmaking, procedural requirements limit regulators' range of policy decisions and so their discretion (McCubbins, Noll, and Weingast 1987).

Ideally, such procedural requirements strike a balance between ensuring that all stakeholders receive both due process—meaning quasi-judicial procedures, hearings, written opinions, and avenues for appeal—and administrative efficiency—which aims to avoid an overly judicial regulatory process. Not all policies should be formulated and not all decisions made using a quasi-judicial approach. Wherever possible, procedures should rely on informal negotiations between regulatory staff and interested parties (though open to public scrutiny, review, and possible appeal) or other informal dispute resolution procedures (such as negotiations between interested parties, with the regulator intervening only to arbitrate unresolved issues).

A mandate to rely as much as possible on market-like solutions—such as auctions and negotiated settlements—is one aspect of the quest to achieve administrative efficiency and minimize the need for direct regulatory determinations of results. Another example is a preference for price caps over cost-plus, rate base, or rate of return regulation. Price caps offer regulated companies market-like incentives for efficiency and innovation, and should enable efficient providers to recover costs, including a return on investments commensurate with risk.

At the same time, in many developing and transition economies there is a need to subject regulatory procedures and decisions to prescribed deadlines. In addition, decisionmaking processes and decisions themselves should be transparent, justified, apolitical, and accountable to an impartial nonpolitical arbiter—and should not be subject to alteration by officials from the executive branch.

There have been many claims that regulators in these countries abuse their powers, fail to meet deadlines, rigidly enforce rules even when the results are irrational, and fail to respond to requests to relax rules in such circumstances. Such controversies are inevitable even under the most enlightened regulation. Moreover, it is difficult to determine the merits of such complaints and of the often conflicting problems asserted by opposing parties.

One way to resolve such issues is to have external consultants conduct management audits of regulatory agencies to examine claims of excessive rigidity. Another way to resolve such disputes as they arise, rather than after the fact, is to create an ombudsperson for each regulatory agency or for all regulatory agencies. Although legislative committees could conduct such oversight, that approach could undermine regulatory independence—particularly if such committees tried to resolve specific disputes. Ombudspersons in the executive branch could combine the objectivity needed for prompt, apolitical resolution of controversies and the accountability of informal, impartial, external scrutiny.

Commitment through Concession Contracts

In some infrastructure sectors (telecommunications, electricity generation, gas production) ownership has been transferred to the private sector through outright divestiture. In others (water and sewerage, transportation, electricity transmission and distribution, gas transportation and distribution) legal, political, and constitutional restraints have hindered the transfer of ownership to the private sector. As a result many countries have used innovative strategies to facilitate private participation in those sectors. Concession, lease or affermage, and (to a much lesser extent) management contracts have emerged as attractive alternatives to outright privatization (Guasch, Kartacheva, and Quesada 2000).

A concession contract grants a private company, typically through competitive bidding, the exclusive right to provide a service for a specified period by using existing facilities and developing new ones. Thus a concession agreement entails only a temporary transfer of assets to the private sector. At the end of the concession period the assets are transferred back to the public authority. From a political perspective, concessions offer advantages over privatization. Continuing government ownership of infrastructure assets is perceived as providing some assurance that social obligations will be met and that, if service is inadequate, the government will intervene (Uribe 2000).

In an ideal environment—with well-developed technology, well-defined demand, homogeneous service, and low asset specificity—franchise bidding also has properties that make it superior to regulation. A concession contract typically defines the concessionaire's obligations (in terms of service coverage and performance standards), rights, incentives, and risks, including pricing arrangements (Klein 1998a). By establishing an explicit contractual relationship, concessions limit the government's discretionary powers and can reduce the risk of political expropriation. Contracts that contain certain guidelines—say, for revising tariffs and settling disputes—can help minimize regulatory discretion and opportunism (Crampes and Estache 1998; Stern and Holder 1999). Moreover, concessions granted through competitive bidding contribute to allocative and productive efficiency by resulting in average cost pricing and the selection of the most efficient firm.[7] In addition, periodic rebidding of concessions creates competition for the market, potentially solving the problem of natural monopoly (Demsetz 1968; Klein 1998b). Thus franchise bidding can achieve allocative and productive efficiency at lower costs than regulation because it requires less information. In essence there is no need for a regulator, because rivalry in the open market imposes the needed discipline.

But in a more real-world setting—with substantial technological and demand uncertainty, incumbents who acquire particularized knowledge, and specialized long-lived assets—franchise bidding differs mainly in degree than in kind from the regulation it is supposed to supplant. The convergence of franchise bidding and regulation becomes evident when one considers the challenges of contract execution and renewal under these less than ideal conditions. Fixed price bids become problematic in the face of uncertainty and rapid technological change. Cost-plus contracts are more appropriate, but they require auditing—the standard requirement of regulation (Williamson 1976). Thus regulation and concession contracts are complements, not supplements, in the context of network industries (Stern 2003).

The main challenge of infrastructure concessions is writing enforceable contracts that cover all the contingencies that might arise over time. Contractual incompleteness is inevitable given the technical complexity and economic uncertainty involved in such activities. Allowing for renegotiation and adjustment is appropriate and even desirable in the face of new information and experiences. But incomplete contracts can also lead to opportunistic renegotiation by both regulators and concessionaires. If concessions are governed by credible regulation that defines the criteria for contract revisions, dynamic and socially desirable adjustments are feasible and less likely to place significant strain on contracts involving uncertain economic conditions. In industrial countries renegotiation is not a big concern because high-quality institutions enforce adherence to contracts and can guide the renegotiation process (Laffont and Tirole 1993).[8] But in developing and transition economies the limited supply of credible institutions makes opportunistic renegotiation an important public policy issue—and one of serious concern to private investors. Without an independent and credible mediating regulator, adjustments have to be renegotiated with the government, increasing the risk of political interference.

Early or frequent renegotiation hurts sector performance if there is uncertainty about the institutional environment.[9] It can also undermine the credibility of the concession process and the reputation of the country. A bidder who knows that early renegotiation is possible may submit an unrealistically low bid with a view to renegotiating better terms (without competition) shortly after securing the concession (Dnes 1995).[10] And that bid might be accepted, regardless of its implications for efficiency and value. Thus the way that private enterprise is introduced has important implications for performance.

For political and economic reasons, renegotiation often favors operators. After a concession has been awarded, the government typically

Table 2.2 Example of Infrastructure Concessions in Developing and Transition Economies

Telecommunications (wireline voice)	Electricity generation	Natural gas transportation and distribution	Railways (mainly franchises)	Water distribution
China, Cook Islands, Guinea-Bissau, Hungary, Indonesia, Madagascar, Mexico	China, Côte d'Ivoire, Guinea, Hungary, Mexico	Argentina	Argentina, Brazil, Burkina Faso, Chile, Côte d'Ivoire, Mexico	Argentina, Brazil, Chile, China, Colombia, Côte d'Ivoire, Guinea, Hungary, Macao, Malaysia, Mexico, Senegal

claims that it is a great success and points to the large amounts of promised investment. Rejecting a request from an operator to renegotiate soon after a concession has been awarded may result in its abandonment or suspension, which could be seen as a failure and might require issuing a new concession at a potentially high transaction cost. Faced with this dilemma, governments usually agree to renegotiate, demonstrating the leverage of the operator. But in cases where the original contract shifts too much of the risk of uncertain initial conditions to the concessionaire (as has been the tendency in some water concessions), renegotiation that favors the operator may simply be an effort to make the contract more realistic.

Since the late 1980s thousands of concession contracts have been awarded to private infrastructure operators around the world (table 2.2); in Latin America and the Caribbean alone more than a thousand concessions have been signed. Yet despite their early promise, concessions have had mixed results.[11] There have been serious doubts about their efficacy, acrimonious disputes over contract compliance, numerous bankruptcy claims by concessionaires, and frequent complaints about excessive tariffs, poor services, and opportunistic renegotiation. Excluding telecommunications, more than 40 percent of concessions have been renegotiated—and 60 percent of those were renegotiated within their first 3 years, despite contract periods of 15–20 years (Guasch 2001). As noted, some renegotiation can be for the good. But the excessive share of renegotiated contracts (including more than 80 percent in the water and transportation sectors) and extent of early renegotiation strongly suggest opportunistic behavior and flawed contract design.

Many concessions have had problems because they lacked mechanisms for resolving disputes

Recent empirical work suggests that the high incidence of concession renegotiation can be attributed to political interference, weak regulation, and flawed contract design (Guasch, Laffont, and Straub 2003).[12] Setting up a separate regulatory body to govern concessions appears to significantly reduce the incidence of renegotiation. Contingencies that occur during the concession can then be dealt with through the revision process stipulated by the regulator, reducing the need for disruptive renegotiation and the consequent transaction costs—though whether the regulator's decisions contribute more or less to social welfare than do renegotiations is an empirical question. Having a separate regulator can also signal a commitment to enforcement and may signify experience in dealing with complex contract issues.

Commitment through Substantive Economic Restraints

Government discretion can be limited by having regulators publicly articulate the basic economic principles that guide their policy decisions (Willig 1999). Before utilities are privatized and private investments made, regulators should commit to the transparent application of these principles to reach decisions and resolve disputes.

To enhance government credibility, these principles should be embedded in privatization and concession contracts. Alternatively, they could be contained in an overarching statute and so have the force of law. They would not, however, rigidly micromanage the terms of privatization. Instead these principles would allow space for regulation to adapt to changing market conditions and require regulators to:

- Refrain from unilaterally imposing policy or rule changes that undercut promised investment value.
- Refrain from intervening in activities of regulated firms that relate to competitive markets, or at least markets not identified as protected natural monopolies.
- Avoid expanding regulatory interventions without demonstrating that the benefits outweigh the costs.
- Ensure competitive service quality and prices by avoiding privatization deals that result in higher prices than necessary, allowing consumers to challenge deals that result in higher prices in return for higher government revenue, using price cap mechanisms to

control regulated monopoly prices (see below), and allowing consumers to seek rate adjustments if service quality falls far short of that promised in a privatization agreement.

- Provide consumers, suppliers of complementary and substitute services, suppliers of inputs, and investors with signals and incentives for efficient actions by ensuring that prices reflect the value and marginal costs of services and by giving service providers pricing flexibility.

- Require infrastructure monopolists to give rivals open access to their bottleneck facilities at prices with the same markups as the competing services sold by these monopolists.

- Pay competitively neutral attention to social goals pertinent to each infrastructure sector by targeting subsidies as much as possible and requiring that any surcharges or taxes imposed have equal effects on the prices charged by competing suppliers (Willig 1999).

Balancing Commitment and Flexibility

To encourage efficient performance, a regulatory system must be able to adapt its mandate and rules in response to new challenges, circumstances, information, and experiences. Such flexibility is especially imperative in sectors experiencing rapid technological and market changes.

The goal of dynamic regulation argues in favor of granting discretion to skilled, well-intentioned regulators. But discretion can be abused, whether by governments (to advance short-term political goals) or regulators (to benefit themselves). Thus the owners of sunk assets subject to regulation may see discretion as a mortal threat—because the value of investments in such assets can be destroyed if aggressive regulation disallows revenue beyond that needed to recover short-run variable costs. Accordingly, the fear of regulatory discretion can override incentives to invest.

If there is significant concern about the abuse of regulatory flexibility, discretion can be reduced by introducing rigid, specific rules. For example, in the early 1980s Chile introduced a law that significantly reduced the scope for regulatory opportunism in the electricity sector (Spiller and Martorell 1996). But the resulting rigidity undermined the regulator's ability to adapt to market changes (box 2.6). Thus this approach creates substantial risks for the public interest. Actual or per-

---

Box 2.6   Regulatory Rigidity in Chile

IN 1981–82 CHILE INTRODUCED A NEW ELECTRIC-ity law to assure potential investors that the regulator would not expropriate their investments. The power to make decisions was taken away from the regulator and embedded in the law, which made it comprehensive and complex. Still, at the time this seemed like a good approach: in the early 1980s Chile needed to convince investors that the rules of the game would not change based on regulatory whim. But although this mechanism attracted investment when electricity was eventually privatized, it made the regulatory regime excessively rigid.

The system's inflexibility became quite costly during the 1998–99 drought. During the crisis the entire regulatory system collapsed, and the country suffered prolonged blackouts without any compensation to users—causing $300 million in damage to the economy. The failure of regulation during the crisis was partly due to the lack of flexibility embedded in the law, which limited the regulator's ability to respond quickly to the drought.

Source: Fischer and Serra (2000).

---

ceived regulatory risk can also be curtailed by including detailed regulations in privatization and concession agreements. Indeed, tight privatization contracts have become common in many developing and transition economies. Again, though, a careful balance is needed between limiting regulatory discretion and avoiding micromanaged privatization and concessions.

Getting the Economics Right

MUCH OF THE DISCUSSION OF INFRASTRUCTURE REFORM has focused on the institutional foundations of effective regulation and nondiscretionary governance. Institutional mechanisms that restrain arbitrary intervention signal to potential investors that the value they add to infrastructure will not be expropriated. This type of commitment reduces investment risk and so the discount rate applied to net present value and cash-flow calculations.

But effective regulation requires more than just building institutions and ensuring regulatory independence. To create an attractive investment environment, policymakers must also focus on regulation's substantive content. That includes sector economics, which must be attractive for any investment plan to be feasible.

For example, in 2000 household electricity prices covered less than 50 percent of long-run marginal costs and industrial prices less than 70 percent in almost all the countries that form the Commonwealth of Independent States (von Hirschhausen and Opitz 2001). Even with independent, transparent regulation, such a pricing policy would make it impossible to attract private investment. Similarly, regulation that forbids flexible prices or imposes social service obligations on only some competitors will not promote efficient investment—even if institutional mechanisms provide a credible commitment to stable policies.

Thus pricing reform is perhaps the most important element of investment-oriented regulation. For prices to encourage efficient actions by consumers, suppliers, and investors, their structure and level will require substantial adjustment in most developing and transition economies. Cost-reflective tariffs enable infrastructure operators to maintain, replace, modernize, and expand their facilities and services, benefiting consumers and the economy.

Financial viability is crucial to any program of price regulation. But how should financial viability be gauged? And what information is required to determine when a utility's revenues are adequate to cover its pertinent costs? Though the answer seems obvious, the history of regulation shows that this issue is widely misunderstood. Among the costs that must always be included in these calculations is the cost of the firm's capital, including internally generated capital.

The logic of this criterion is straightforward. Revenues are adequate if they enable a firm to maintain, replace, modernize, and (if needed) expand facilities and services. If revenues are lower, services will deteriorate (and possibly disappear) and utilities will have a harder time obtaining new capital. The market for funds simply offers no room to those who cannot face competition from others seeking capital.

The following principles determine whether a firm's revenues are adequate (Kessides and Willig 1995):

- Its rate of return must equal the returns being earned by a typical firm with similar risks elsewhere in the economy. Otherwise it will be denied required funds.
- The adequacy of a firm's revenues can be judged only by comparing them with the earnings of other firms, not with the market value of the firm's equity. That market value will automatically fall to match any regulatory action that lowers the firm's earnings below

a compensatory rate of return, so such a comparison would appear to justify any earnings restriction—no matter how inappropriate.

- In determining the revenue required for financial viability, the rate of return obtained by comparison with other firms must be applied to a rate base that covers the replacement cost of all facilities.
- With the rate base determined in this way and the rate of return on that base equal to the cost of capital—as indicated by earnings elsewhere in the economy—one has determined the net earnings by the utility considered adequate for it to compete in the capital market.
- This earnings figure must not be applied as a rigid ceiling. Otherwise utilities will not be able to earn this figure over the long run, because they will be precluded from making up for revenue shortfalls that may result from temporary ebbs in the demand for their services.

For prices to make sense economically, they must always be compatible with this earnings level. Of course, no prices can guarantee that regulated utilities will earn adequate returns overall. If demand for their services is insufficient, their operations are conducted wastefully, or their services are poor, even appropriate prices cannot be expected to lead to profitable operations. But once utilities are permitted to charge appropriate prices in a competitive environment, regulatory impediments to financial viability will have been eliminated. It is then up to the utilities to take advantage of this opportunity through efficient operations, high-quality services, and effective marketing.

Mechanisms to Regulate Prices

FIVE BASIC GOALS SHOULD GUIDE THE DESIGN OF PRICE regulation:

- Rent extraction—setting rates that strike a socially acceptable compromise between the interests of investors and consumers.
- Supply-side efficiency—providing signals and incentives for suppliers and investors to increase efficiency.
- Demand-side efficiency—providing signals and incentives for efficient consumption of regulated utility services.
- Revenue adequacy—allowing regulated firms to earn sufficient revenue to attract needed capital.

- Fairness—ensuring that prices are just and reasonable, and contribute to universal service goals without creating significant distortions (Joskow 1998b).

These goals cannot all be achieved simultaneously. Indeed, practical regulation entails tradeoffs among them. For example, a regulatory mechanism that passes on to consumers (through lower prices) all the cost reductions achieved by a firm will meet the rent extraction goal. But it will likely do a poor job of promoting supply-side efficiency and attracting investment.

On the other hand, a regime under which the firm is the residual claimant on all cost savings will provide strong incentives for cost-reducing innovations (supply-side efficiency). But it will do poorly in achieving the rent extraction goal (Laffont and Tirole 1993; Joskow 1999). Two alternative mechanisms for regulating prices are cost-plus and price caps. This section analyzes these approaches and their likely implications for pricing policies.

Cost-Plus Regulation

Until recently cost-plus regulation dominated utility industries in the United States and several other countries (box 2.7). Policymakers have been attracted to this mode of controlling utility behavior because it

---

Box 2.7   Cost-Plus Mechanisms

- *Pure cost-plus.* The regulated firm simply submits a bill for its operating expenses and capital costs (depreciation plus an after-tax return on its investment that equals or exceeds its cost of capital), and the regulator passes on these costs in the prices charged to consumers. Prices are continuously tied to these accounting costs.
- *Rate of return.* The regulated firm's capital and operating costs are evaluated using a specific accounting system. Prices are then set to cover these audited costs plus a reasonable return on investment. Once these base prices are set, they are not adjusted automatically for changes in costs over time—they remain fixed until the subsequent regulatory review.

---

seems fair to both the regulated firm and its customers. It permits the firm to earn sufficient revenues, including a fair return on its investment, by passing its costs on to consumers through the prices charged. It is also designed to protect consumers from monopolistic pricing distortions.

One of the attractions of cost-plus systems is that they are likely to attract investment to a regulated sector because investors know they will recover their operating and investment costs, perhaps with a return that exceeds their cost of capital. These systems shift a variety of firm- and market-specific risks to consumers, satisfying the goal of revenue adequacy. Moreover, by holding revenues close to costs, cost-plus systems keep utility services reasonably affordable. These are important considerations given the socioeconomic characteristics of many developing and transition economies and their substantial requirements for infrastructure investment.

Still, cost-plus systems have shortcomings. The firm has an incentive to engage in accounting contrivances and to pad its costs to convince the regulator to approve higher prices. These systems allow considerable scope for such behavior: a range of estimates is possible due to conventions for calculating depreciation, procedures for allocating joint costs between regulated and unregulated outputs, and procedures for calculating capital costs. Unless the regulator has a well-developed cost accounting system to audit the firm's costs, the firm can misrepresent them. If that happens, the regulator will set prices too high, frustrating its rent extraction goal.

Moreover, in the presence of asymmetric information about the firm's capabilities and the level of managerial effort and other costs it must incur to realize a specified level of operating efficiency, a pure cost-plus regime distorts the firm's incentives to minimize its costs—even if the regulator has sophisticated auditing technology. Because the firm is not rewarded for reducing costs, it has no incentive to do so (Armstrong and Sappington 2003). In addition, the firm has incentives to expand its rate base by adopting excessively capital-intensive technology (the Averch-Johnson effect). So, although consumers pay prices that just cover the firm's costs, such costs may be too high. As a result rents may accrue to the firm's managers, employees, and input suppliers, undermining supply-side efficiency.

Few pure cost-plus systems (in which prices are continuously tied to accounting costs) are in place today, and no one would choose such a system to promote the public interest. Indeed, constant review of costs to keep prices equal to the cost-plus target has never been conducted anywhere. In practice, under rate of return regulation (a form of cost-plus), prices are set in public hearings that evaluate cost data using specific accounting criteria. Once set, prices remain fixed until the regulator reviews them again.

The tendency of prices to adjust slowly to changing costs, commonly referred to as regulatory lag, restores some of the incentives for efficiency lost under a pure cost-plus system. By partly decoupling prices from costs, the regulatory lag imposes penalties for inefficiency and incorrect guesses, and rewards efficiency by permitting the firm to keep the profits it earns from cutting costs and improving performance. Moreover, regulators normally have the authority to disallow operating and capital costs that they find imprudent or unnecessary. The threat of disallowing such costs encourages the firm to make efficient production decisions. Similar benefits are obtained if the regulator limits profits to a certain range (banded rate of return), allowing price adjustments only when returns fall outside that range (Joskow 1974; Joskow and Schmalensee 1986). Thus cost-plus has gotten a worse reputation than it deserves.

Price Cap (Incentive) Regulation

Given the weak incentives for productive efficiency under cost-plus regulation, many types of incentive-based regulation have been developed (Vogelsang 2002). These mechanisms encourage the regulated firm to achieve desired goals by granting it some—but not complete—discretion. In essence the regulator delegates certain performance-related decisions to the firm, and the firm's profits depend on its performance as measured by the regulator.

Price caps are the main incentive mechanism (Baron 1989; Laffont and Tirole 2000). Their key purpose is to control the prices, not the earnings, of the regulated firm (box 2.8). Thus this form of regulation does not make explicit use of accounting data. Under price caps the regulator:

- Defines a set of prices (or a weighted average of prices for different services) that the firm will be allowed to charge. The firm is free to price at or below these ceilings. (Price floors may also be set to prevent predatory behavior.)
- Estimates the ability of firms in the regulated industry to limit cost increases and compares that with firms in other industries.

Box 2.8 Price Constraints Imposed by Price Cap Plans

FOR A BASKET OF REGULATED GOODS OR SERVICES, THE TYPICAL price cap plan limits the weighted average (percentage) price increases to not exceed the difference between some measure of the general inflation rate and the specified productivity offset:

$$\sum_{i=1}^{n} w_i^t \left[\frac{p_i^t - p_i^{t\pm1}}{p_i^{t\pm1}} \right] \leq RPI^{t\pm1} - X,$$

where $w_i^t = \dfrac{p_i^{t\pm1} q_i^{t\pm1}}{\sum_{i=1}^{n} p_i^{t\pm1} q_i^{t\pm1}}$

n = the number of regulated goods or services,
t = year ($t=0$ at the start of the price cap plan),
p_i^t = the unit price of good or service i in year t,
q_i^t = the number of units of good or service i sold in year t,
RPI^{t-1} = the inflation rate in year $t-1$ (most recent 12-month period),
X = the specified productivity offset, and
w_i^t = is the proportion of the firm's total regulated revenue in period $t-1$ derived from product i.

Source: Sappington and Weisman (1996).

The estimated differential in productivity between the regulated industry and the rest of the economy is called the X factor.

- Specifies a formula for adjusting prices (or the weighted average price) over time to reflect input inflation (easily observable changes in costs beyond the firm's control) and the expected rate of productivity improvement (X factor). Thus price cap regulation severs the link between the firm's authorized prices and its realized costs.

In a typical price cap plan, related services and products are grouped into categories often referred to as baskets. Alternatively, all services may be bundled in a single basket. An overall price cap is set for each basket. This index ceiling is usually a weighted average price for all regulated services in the basket (box 2.8). The average price of each basket is allowed to rise at the economywide inflation rate less the productivity offset

(X factor), which may vary across baskets. Moreover, the firm can set the price of any service in a basket as long as it does not exceed the index ceiling (although restrictions are often imposed on the prices of individual services to protect specific groups of consumers or promote socially important services). Thus the firm can rebalance its prices over time.

In a pure price cap regime the firm's realized costs and profits do not enter into the regulatory contract: once the index ceiling and its path are set, they are not changed (infinite regulatory lag). Pure price cap regulation operates much like a fixed-price contract under which the firm is the residual claimant for all its cost savings (Laffont and Tirole 1993). The firm has strong incentives to pursue cost-reducing innovation, use the lowest-cost technology, operate with no waste, and report its costs truthfully (Weisman 2001). At the same time, consumers are protected because prices do not vary with the firm's reported costs.

Actual price cap regulation, however, is not as straightforward as the theoretical case. Price caps do not last indefinitely. It is standard for a price cap mechanism to be reviewed after a stipulated period, often three to five years. Such a review could lead to a revision of the basic parameters of the price cap formula (such as the X factor). If a firm realizes strong earnings under the initial regime, the review could also lead to more demanding standards being placed on the firm by raising the X factor (table 2.3).

Moreover, unless prohibited by law, the regulator could conduct a full earnings audit to recalibrate prices so that expected future earnings move toward a target rate of return. So, while the firm's earnings do not directly affect prices under a pure price cap regime, most price cap

Table 2.3   X factor Decisions in U.K. and U.S. Telecommunications Regulation, 1984–Present

(percent)

United Kingdom		United States	
Year	**X factor**	**Year**	**X factor**
1984–89	3.0	1991–94	3.3
1990–91	4.5	1995–97	3.3–5.3
1992–93	6.25	1998–2000	6.5
1994–97	7.5		
1998-present	4.5		

Source: Ros (2001).

plans include provisions for adjusting prices if the rate of return falls outside a given range (Braeutigam and Panzar 1993).

When strong efficiency gains cause an increase in future productivity offsets, it dulls the firm's incentives to cut costs and improve performance. This reduction in incentives becomes more pronounced if the price cap regime is reviewed more frequently. Still, the regulator is not supposed to intervene in the firm's pricing decisions during the review period—implying that the firm has an incentive to cut its costs faster than was envisaged when the X factor was set, because by doing so it can keep the resulting high profits.

It also implies that in setting the period between price reviews there is a tradeoff between providing incentives for efficiency (supply-side efficiency goal) and reducing excess profits (rent extraction goal). The longer is the period, the greater are the benefits for the firm. The shorter is the period, the greater are the benefits for consumers (because they do not benefit from cost reductions until the price cap is reset). Very short periods would make the price cap system look like rate of return regulation. There are grounds for expecting a ratcheting-up effect in the price cap system: as the end of the review period approaches, the firm will ease off its cost-reducing activities so that the reset caps will reflect its higher costs. Empirical evidence supports this conjecture. In Chile's electricity system, for example, the cost reductions of distribution companies (which operate under a price cap regime) are U-shaped. Strong initial cost reductions reverse every four years, coinciding with the timing of regulatory reviews (Di Tella and Dyck 2002).

Price caps offer regulators a variety of choices. Which services will be subject to a price cap? Which services will be used to construct the price index? Will certain cost increases be automatically passed on to consumers, and if so, to what extent? Different utilities will require different designs, so introducing price cap regulation can be costly in terms of information requirements and human capital. Still, this approach has sufficiently desirable properties—in terms of lowering prices and reducing regulatory costs—to be worth the setup costs.

Hybrid Regimes

Pure cost-plus and pure price cap mechanisms represent opposite regulatory extremes. Practical considerations and multiple regulatory objec-

---

Box 2.9   Hybrid Regulatory Mechanisms

MOST PRACTICAL REGULATORY SYSTEMS INVOLVE aspects of cost-plus and price cap mechanisms. Examples of these hybrids include:

- *Banded rate of return.* A range (band) of earnings is specified, and prices are set to generate earnings that fall within the range. Prices are not revised as long as earnings fall within the band.
- *Sliding scale profit- or cost-sharing.* Prices are automatically adjusted if the firm's rate of return differs from a preset target. But to encourage efficiency, the adjustment is only partial. Thus the firm and its customers share both risks and rewards. Alternatively, the rate of return can vary within a preset range without causing price adjustments. If the return falls outside the range, it can trigger profit (or cost) sharing.
- *Institutionalized regulatory lag.* Price reviews do not occur for a specified period, usually two to five years. During that time all investigations into the firm's earnings are suspended. Whereas the time between price reviews can vary significantly under traditional rate of return regulation, it is known and fixed under institutionalized regulatory lag.

---

tives imply that neither is likely to be the most feasible or desirable regulatory scheme. Each trades incentives for rent extraction (with weight placed on consumer surplus) against those for supply-side efficiency (with weight placed on producer surplus), with cost-plus regulation focused on rent extraction and price caps focused on supply efficiency. The optimal balance between these two goals depends, among other factors, on the cost of public funds. It is best to place the entire weight on supply efficiency only when the marginal social cost of taxation is zero—a condition that will never be met (Ergas and Small 2001).

Most practical regulatory regimes are hybrid schemes that involve tradeoffs between supply-side efficiency, capital attraction, rent extraction, and demand-side efficiency (box 2.9). These mechanisms aim to share cost benefits and burdens between the regulated firm and its customers. For example, under some profit sharing mechanisms the firm is allowed to keep all profits as long as the rate of return (revenue) falls within a specified range. That approach retains incentives for firms to achieve cost efficiency. But if the rate of return falls outside this range, consumers receive a portion of the gain or loss—weakening the firm's incentives. Overall, incentives for cost efficiency are stronger under such profit-sharing schemes than under rate of return regulation, but weaker than under price caps. Similarly, institutionalized regulatory lag restores some of the incentives for cost efficiency lost under rate of

Table 2.4 Features of Rate of Return and Price Cap Regulation

Feature	Rate of Return	Price Cap
Sensitivity of prices to costs	High	Low
Firm's flexibility to adjust prices	Low	High
Regulatory discretion	No	Yes
Regulatory lag	Short	Long

Source: Armstrong and Sappington 2003.

return regulation. But an institutionalized lag does not provide firms with ideal incentives for investment.

Choosing between Rate of Return and Price Cap Regulation

From a public policy perspective, the choice between rate of return and price cap regulation is an empirical question. Textbook models of pure cost-plus and pure price cap regulation differ substantially in terms of regulatory discretion, the links between prices and costs, the pricing flexibility granted to the regulated firm, and the frequency of regulatory review (table 2.4). But in practice there has been significant convergence between the two schemes. Thus the choice between them is not nearly as clear-cut as once thought.

Comparative linking of prices to costs.   One area where the difference between the two mechanisms has been exaggerated is the extent to which they link prices to costs—and hence their different implications for the tradeoff between incentives for supply-side efficiency and rent extraction. Under price cap regulation, prices are not linked to costs, and incentives for lowering costs are strongest if the cap is never reset. But that approach is politically untenable if the regulated firm earns extremely high profits at any point.

Moreover, nearly every price cap regime is periodically updated at preset intervals. Regulators typically use these updates to eliminate excessive returns and to pass on to consumers (through lower prices) a portion of the efficiency gains the firm made in the previous period (Cowan 2002). Even if political considerations are discounted, when setting a price cap the regulator has to forecast future costs and revenues to ensure that the firm will be financially viable. Otherwise, having no link between prices and costs could bankrupt the firm and disrupt service (Ergas and Small 2001). Price cap regulation with periodic updates is similar to rate of return regulation with regulatory lag.

Under a price cap the rate at which prices vary over time is fixed for several years. Thus the regulatory lag is supposed to be exogenous and long. But price cap reviews are often initiated ahead of schedule.

Cost-plus (rate of return) regulation, on the other hand, never involves ongoing hearings. The process typically involves periodic reporting of profits and other service measures. Hearings are initiated by firms, regulators, or interested third parties, with firms being the most common source of requests. Inflation is an important determinant of the frequency of reviews: when inflation is low, reviews are infrequent (Joskow 1974). Regulators can schedule automatic reviews every three to five years—for example, the rate of return regime established in 2000 for Bolivia's water sector uses a five-year regulatory lag (McKenzie and Mookherjee 2003).

Comparative pricing flexibility. In theory price cap regulation controls only the firm's average prices, leaving it free to change individual prices in each basket of services. By contrast, prices are rigid under rate of return regulation. But in practice the difference between the two schemes is not as pronounced. In addition to its overall price controls, price cap regulation often limits price changes for individual services. With separate baskets and basket-specific restrictions, price increases in one basket might not be allowed even if they are offset by reductions in another basket. These types of restrictions can severely limit a firm's pricing flexibility under price caps. Moreover, under cost-plus regulation firms have some flexibility in pricing noncore services (those not involved in universal service programs). They often also have the authority to cut prices and to raise them through automatic adjustment formulas.

Still, despite the convergence between the two regimes, important differences remain in terms of pricing flexibility. If all conditions are satisfied, proposed price changes are put into effect faster under price caps—an issue of crucial importance to regulated firms facing new competitors.

Cost-plus regulation is better for sectors with large investment requirements and countries with weak commitment capacity

Comparative regulatory discretion. Price cap reviews give regulators significant discretion over future policies. In infrastructure industries—where asset lives are much longer than the typical regulatory lag—concerns about regulatory credibility and uncertainty about future prices can inhibit investment. These problems can be especially serious if governments have limited capacity to commit to long-term regulatory rules.

By contrast, under a rate of return regime the regulator has a statutory obligation to ensure that the regulated firm earns a fair return (Armstrong and Sappington 2003). This commitment implies that rate of return regimes are less prone to renegotiation than price caps. Evidence supports this view: in Latin America 38 percent of price cap contracts were renegotiated before their scheduled reviews (which usually occur five years after a contract is awarded), compared with 13 percent for rate of return contracts and 24 percent for hybrid mechanisms (Estache, Guasch, and Trujillo 2003). Thus rate of return regulation can be preferable if significant new infrastructure investment is needed—as is usually the case in developing and transition economies. Moreover, in uncertain environments guaranteed returns are more attractive for potential investors.

Price caps might be preferable in countries with poor accounting and auditing, scarce expertise, and high inflation

Comparative information and human capital requirements. Most developing and transition economies do not have well-established cost accounting and auditing systems. And as noted, they often lack regulatory expertise. Thus the information and human capital requirements of different regulatory mechanisms are important. Given typical inflation rates in these countries, hearings could be common under rate of return regulation. At the end of each review period, price caps require similar information as rate of return systems. They also require forecasts of relevant variables through the next review. So, setting up and revising price caps requires the same type of professional skills as a rate of return system. But far less professional input is required between reviews: the regulator only has to verify compliance with the price cap by monitoring changes in a well-defined price index. Thus price caps will likely require much less information overall.

The choice in practice. The optimal choice among regulatory mechanisms depends on a variety of factors: the quality of accounting and auditing systems, the availability of economic and technical expertise, the efficacy of the tax system, the sector's investment requirements, the government's commitment powers, institutional checks and balances, and overall macroeconomic stability. Some of these will change over time. For example, auditing systems and expertise will likely improve if sufficient resources and independence are provided—making it possible to adopt more sophisticated regulation (Joskow 1998b).

Thus different stages of national development have implications for the choice of regulatory regimes. During the first stage of regulation, with scarce expertise and poor auditing and monitoring, price caps with provisions for adjustment are likely the best choice.[13] Initial prices might need to be high to attract capital and ensure firm viability, but increased investment and supply-side efficiency should compensate for them. This stage should be used to improve regulatory capacity and accounting and auditing systems.

Once these conditions have been met, the second stage can promote cost-plus mechanisms that facilitate large-scale, sustainable investment—especially if government credibility improves at a slower pace—and achieve the rent extraction goal in the face of continuing high costs of public funds. As development continues, with infrastructure system expansion nearly complete and enhanced commitment powers, the optimal solution is to move to hybrid regulation (Laffont 1996). Once infrastructure systems have been developed, firms can do better by being less efficient (padding their costs). Hence the need for more powerful incentive schemes.

Most evidence on performance under different regulatory mechanisms comes from industrial countries. In telecommunications, competition and incentive regulation together spur lower costs and prices, but incentive regulation alone often has limited effects (Sappington 2002). An international comparison found that price cap regulation exposes firms to much higher risk than rate of return regimes, increasing their cost of capital (Alexander, Mayer, and Weeds 1996). And in Latin America price caps have led to higher capital costs (and so tariffs) and reduced investment (Estache, Guasch, and Trujillo 2003).

> Price cap regulation is better for industries with excess capacity supported by institutions with strong commitment powers

Moving toward More Practical Regulation

DESIGNING EFFECTIVE REGULATION IN DEVELOPING AND transition economies is a daunting task for several reasons. Some are endemic to infrastructure regulation everywhere, while some are driven by the complexities of underdevelopment.

In the face of scarce technical expertise, severe information problems, weak accounting and auditing, limited separation of powers, lack of checks and balances, ineffective legal systems, widespread corruption, and poor commitment, adopting many aspects of U.K. and U.S. regulatory models will prove challenging for developing and transition economies. Most of these countries are poorly suited to the complex procedures required by quasi-judicial, command-and-control regulatory techniques.

Moreover, regulatory methods have very different implementation costs. Given the limited expertise in most developing and transition economies, it is crucial that these resources be allocated efficiently by:

- Exploiting all opportunities for competitive restructuring that might reduce the need for regulatory intervention.
- Isolating activities that require regulatory oversight from those that should be left to market forces.
- Identifying second- or even third-best regulatory instruments that demand less information but are better suited for countries with limited capacity.

International Benchmarking

Regulators in many developing and transition economies face severe problems measuring pertinent economic variables. The true economic costs of various infrastructure services are especially difficult to estimate, for several reasons. First, the costs reported by incumbents (former state-owned and often bloated monopolies) are unlikely to be efficient, and there are good reasons to believe that their technologies are not proper measures of forward-looking costs (that is, the costs of expanding services using currently available technologies).

Second, especially in economies undergoing a transition to a market economy, accounting costs are often largely fictitious because they reflect nonmarket valuations of inputs. Many firms do not know their efficient costs. And even when they do, regulators rarely have access to such information.

Although these measurement difficulties make it extremely difficult for regulators to assess the performance of utilities, they need not result in haphazard regulatory decisions. One way for regulators to ease information problems and determine efficient costs is by using international benchmarks, adjusted to country conditions. (Because the underlying technologies are available in international markets, certain costs should not vary much by country.)

For example, one of the most contentious issues in price cap regulation involves determining the productivity offset (X factor). A variety of benchmarking methods have been used to estimate the X factors (Jamasb and Pollitt 2000). Another vexing challenge for regulators is setting access and interconnection charges. In telecommunications several interconnection disputes have been resolved by benchmarking access fees against comparable international markets. For instance, in 2000 Morocco's telecommunications regulator resolved an interconnection dispute between Maroc Telecom (the fixed line incumbent) and Meditelecom (a mobile service provider) through international benchmarking and an analysis of the cost models used by the operators (ANRT 2000). International benchmarking was also used to settle an interconnection dispute in Botswana (Bruce and Macmillan 2002).

International benchmarking can be invaluable in assessing the scope for efficiency gains and the pace at which service providers in developing and transition economies could achieve those gains. In some countries it might be the only practical tool. Still, benchmarking raises methodological issues that must be considered before it is applied for regulatory purposes. First, utilities from different countries vary greatly in terms of size and operate under different regulations and ownership structures that affect incentives and distort production decisions. Thus the selection of countries included in a benchmark sample is of critical importance. Second, benchmarking makes companies "guilty until proven innocent" because it implicitly assumes that high costs are due to inefficiency (Shuttleworth 1999). Thus no matter how sophisticated its techniques, benchmarking can be subjective, lack transparency, foment disputes, and put utilities at financial risk (Ivastorza 2003).

Multinational Regulatory Authorities

The market areas of infrastructure industries often transcend national borders. For example, electricity, telecommunications, and transportation operate more efficiently if their networks are organized according to the patterns of their transactions. Thus regulation in these sectors rarely has purely domestic effects. International agreements about regulation and the creation of multinational regulatory authorities would help achieve regulatory harmonization and minimize distortions from national regulation (Noll 2000b).

Some regions contain many countries that are small or poor and lack formal institutions and technical expertise. A pragmatic response to this limited national capacity would be to increase policy and regulatory coordination and cooperation—and ultimately to create regional (multinational) regulatory authorities (Noll 2000c; Stern 2000). Furthermore, multilateral regulatory agreements could advance domestic reform, enhance credibility, and help countries overcome commitment problems.

In individual countries regulatory reform, especially when debated one issue at a time, is often blocked by well-organized interest groups. But if reform becomes part of a broader international policy that covers a range of issues, all stakeholders will likely participate—making it harder for a single group to block it. Moreover, regulatory credibility is often undermined by political interference and opportunistic behavior. It is much more difficult and costly for governments to behave opportunistically when regulatory policy is part of an international agreement, or to interfere in the decisionmaking of a supranational regulator. In addition, regional cooperation may generate large enough gains to discourage deviations from negotiated agreements.

Regional regulatory cooperation and the eventual creation of a regional regulator will be more feasible in countries that have had a fair amount of success in regional economic integration. For example, the Pacific Islands Forum Secretariat has helped harmonize economic policy among countries in the region (Fiji, Kiribati, Samoa, the Solomon Islands, Vanuatu), including consensus on the role of the private sector. A regional approach to infrastructure regulation might be a natural next step. Regional regulatory policy might also be a logical move in:

- Sub-Saharan Africa, where cooperation was achieved in the sensitive area of monetary policy through the creation of the West African Monetary Union.
- The Caribbean, building on the framework of the Caribbean Community.
- South America, based on the Southern Common Market (Mercosur).

Box 2.10   African Cooperation on Telecommunications Regulation

IN 2001, 21 NATIONAL TELECOMMUNICATIONS agencies formed the African Telecommunications Regulators Network to:

- Promote telecommunications modernization and regulatory reform as prerequisites for the development of Africa's information society.
- Increase cooperation on telecommunication regulation.
- Harmonize national regulation to foster economic integration.
- Coordinate national approaches to achieve greater efficiency in international forums.
- Exchange information and experiences among regulators and between regulators and other public and private entities engaged in information and communications technology activities in Africa

The network's activities include:

- Exchanging officials, technical staff, and experts between members.
- Organizing seminars and workshops on issues such as accounting, e-commerce, the Internet, and pricing.
- Conducting studies on telecommunications harmonization and economic integration.
- Maintaining a Website and promoting online discussions.
- Collecting, disseminating, and benchmarking data.

Source: ITU (2001e).

Regional regulatory initiatives are under way in several parts of the developing world; examples include the South Asia Forum for Infrastructure Regulation, Regional Electricity Regulators Association and Southern African Power Pool in Southern Africa, and African Telecommunications Regulators Network (box 2.10). The objectives of these initiatives range from designing training, building capacity, and sharing information to more ambitious goals of coordinating and harmonizing national regulatory policies and practices.

Obtaining consensus from all governments in a region for a regional regulator is problematic due to different attitudes and commitments toward reform, as well as concerns about national sovereignty. It requires considerable cooperation and trust between countries—more than now exists in most parts of the world. Thus regional regulatory cooperation might be a more realistic option for alleviating scarce regulatory expertise and resources, especially in small and low-income countries (Stern 2000). As a first step, regional regulatory advisers could be established to facilitate information exchange and offer nonbinding advice on procedural issues (such as dispute resolution) and matters such as standardization, interconnection, and pricing and costing methodologies. But consensus for multinational regulatory agencies could increase as more countries reform, gains from regional policy coordination and trade become more apparent, and countries (especially small ones) confront the costs and staffing challenges of creating and maintaining national regulators.

Decentralizing Decisions to Firms

In many developing and transition economies the pursuit of pricing and other regulations to elicit optimal industrial performance is hindered by a dearth of proper accounting systems and of information on marginal costs, demand elasticities, and other attributes of demand and cost relationships. Under the traditional command-and-control regulatory model, prices calculated without such information are apt to be inconsistent with economic efficiency and damaging to economic welfare. The information available to firms is also highly imperfect in many developing and transition economies. Still, firms will likely have better, more timely estimates of cost and demand conditions than will regulators (Baumol and Sidak 1994).

How can regulation in these countries have a realistic chance of becoming effective in the face of severe information problems? One approach would be to decentralize decisions on pricing and other key variables to firms that have the necessary information. Regulators' role would be limited to imposing floors and ceilings on prices, based on a rough analysis of costs or international benchmarks. Firms would be free to set prices within these ranges, with self-interest leading to prices that serve the public interest. Such a framework could enable infrastructure providers to earn adequate revenue while protecting consumers from monopolistic pricing.

Infrastructure entities can earn high profits if they are given considerable pricing flexibility and are not tightly regulated. They will have strong incentives to provide services to those who can afford to pay their prices—and so will resolve the problem of unavailable services for large portions of the population in developing countries. Moreover, to the extent that these firms enjoy large profits from increased usage, they will also have powerful incentives to eliminate the quality of service problems that plagued state-owned infrastructure monopolies (Noll 2000c).

Notes

1. The distinction between developing and transition economies is important here. Many developing countries have experience with legal institutions to support a market economy, though they may not have experience with regulating private utilities.

2. Notable examples of not getting the fit right include the Philippines, where in the face of a weak judiciary the adoption of the quasi-judicial U.S. model in the telecommunications and energy sectors led to significant regulatory failure (Smith and Wellenius 1999); and Jamaica, where the creation of a U.S.-style Public Utility Commission without the constitutional protections and well-developed rules of administrative due process prevalent in the United States led to regulatory instability that culminated in the nationalization of telecommunications in 1975 (Levy and Spiller 1996).

3. The most important features of U.S. regulatory institutions have been judicial review, constitutional protections against taking private property, and sound, transparent administrative procedures. Countries without these basic protections will have a hard time creating credible, durable regulatory institutions.

4. Open hearings are a U.S. regulatory tradition that is not widely practiced. Perhaps a more important issue is whether stakeholders have an opportunity to submit comments and the regulator responds to them.

5. Although the commission members refused to comment on their removal, one said that it was not his place to criticize the decisions of his superiors (East European Energy Report, June 2000).

6. In India in 1997, for example, lack of investor interest in the Haryana Power Project was exacerbated by the fact that other Indian states were competing for a small pool of international investors. As a result Haryana decided to provide an attractive regulatory environment, taking into account the privatization plans of other states. Part of Haryana's strategy was to reduce the financial exposure of the private sector by redesigning the privatization contract. Such an approach could have adverse long-term consequences if it transfers financial risk to the state government (World Bank 1997; Bayliss 2001).

7. Regulation could also achieve average cost pricing, but with much higher information requirements. To achieve average cost pricing, the regulator would need to have access to and analyze cost and demand data. Under franchise bidding no such information and analysis are required—competition, rather than a regulatory determination, leads to average cost pricing and the selection of the most efficient firm.

8. But if the contract is incomplete, there is uncertainty about how the adjudicator (even a high-quality one) will decide the case—and it is precisely this

leeway that permits opportunistic renegotiation. Still, this might be less of a problem in industrial countries because contracts are more fully specified, for some long-term supply contracts market prices act as a reservation value and so reduce the bargaining range, there may be less uncertainty about initial conditions, and the parties may be repeat players.

9. In a credible institutional environment, frequent renegotiation should not undermine performance any more than does frequent regulatory review.

10. There is some empirical evidence, however, that such underbidding is held in check by the desire of franchisees to maintain reputation (Zupan 1989).

11. A careful reading of history renders this finding unsurprising. After all, in many countries it was the failure of concessions that led to state ownership or regulated monopolies. In Europe, Japan, Latin America, and the United States many infrastructure services started as private concessions operating under contracts that ultimately failed. Moreover, the precise definition of renegotiation is important. If it includes any change to a contract that requires a contract amendment, frequent renegotiation in the early years is to be expected.

12. Poor regulation arguably has the same causes as frequent contract renegotiation. Thus there is a need for caution in drawing causal inferences from the observed correlation between the high incidence of concession renegotiation and weak regulatory governance.

13. Cost-plus mechanisms generally perform better than price caps in the presence of cost uncertainty and uncertainty about the capabilities of the regulated firms (Schmalensee 1989). However, during the first stage of regulation in many developing and transition economies, auditing and monitoring are likely to be so poor that a simple adjustment mechanism under price caps would still be the preferred option.

CHAPTER THREE

Restructuring Electricity Supply

ELECTRICITY IS ESSENTIAL TO THE PRODUCTION OF almost all goods and services and so is vital to the public interest.[1] In addition, reliable electricity systems have become more important because businesses and households rely on electronic devices to perform an enormous range of tasks, both basic and advanced. Thus adequate, reliable, competitively priced electricity is essential for modernization, domestic growth, and international competitiveness— and is among the most urgent challenges facing developing and transition economies.

Until recently most electricity industries were vertically integrated monopolies owned by national, state, or municipal governments (Joskow 2003a). But since the early 1980s, when Chile began a radical restructuring and privatization program, more than 70 countries have introduced electricity reforms (Bacon and Besant-Jones 2001). And especially over the past decade, views have changed dramatically on how electricity should be owned, organized, and regulated (Newbery 2000a, 2001). Accordingly, there are numerous perspectives and lessons on the most important reform issues and best policy options.

A clear-eyed assessment is especially important now given the crisis with electricity reform in California (United States), the recent blackouts in Europe (Bialek 2004), and the challenges confronting electricity systems in several developing and transition economies. Events in California have alarmed policymakers around the world, slowing reform and possibly impeding the development of competitive electricity markets (Besant-Jones and Tenenbaum 2001; Joskow 2001). Some developing and transition economies that had planned reforms might defer them. Others will not consider restructuring and deregulation until there is convincing evidence of their merits.

Background to Electricity Reform

AFTER DECADES OF STRUCTURAL IMMOBILITY IN THE ELEC-tricity industry, governments are allowing market forces to play a role in generation and supply. Structural change accelerated over the past decade and is now a global phenomenon. Although only a handful of countries have achieved substantive market liberalization, almost all have felt considerable domestic and international pressure to reform their electricity systems.

The Industry's Traditional Structure

The electricity industry has three components: generation, high-voltage transmission, and low-voltage distribution (figure 3.1). (In recent years, as a result of sector reforms, supply or retailing—power procurement, billing, and customer service—has increasingly been considered a fourth component.) A wide variety of technologies and primary energy sources are used to generate electricity. Nonrenewable sources include coal, petroleum, natural gas, and uranium; renewable sources include biomass and hydro, wind, solar, and geothermal power.

Historically, the electricity industry has had a monolithic structure, with a single entity owning generation and transmission capacity and performing all system operations. This entity transmits power to one or more distribution companies that hold exclusive rights to serve households and businesses in specific regions. In some countries distribution companies are independent entities with separate governance and legal structures, purchasing their power from the generation and transmission entity at regulated tariffs. In others there is common ownership of generation, transmission, and distribution systems. In most countries—except Germany, Japan, Spain, and the United States—these entities have been publicly owned (Joskow 1998a).

Electricity has unique physical and economic characteristics that limit the extent to which decentralized market mechanisms can replace vertical and horizontal integration (Joskow 2003a). Complementarities between generation and transmission result in significant economies of

Figure 3.1   Vertical Integration in Electricity

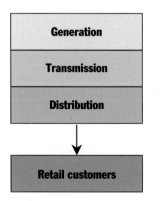

Box 3.1 Rationale for Structural Integration of the Electricity Industry

THE ECONOMIC RATIONALE FOR VERTICAL AND horizontal integration in electricity derives from characteristics of transmission networks and from operating and investment relationships between generation and transmission. A key attribute of a transmission grid is its ability to synchronize dispersed generating units into a stable network. This aggregation allows real-time substitution of production from facilities with lower marginal costs for production from facilities with higher marginal costs, increasing efficiency. It also improves reliability by providing multiple links between system loads and generating resources, and can economize on the reserve capacity required for a given level of system reliability.

Electricity generation and consumption need to be balanced continuously and almost instantly for a network to meet specific physical parameters (frequency, voltage, stability). Unlike other switched networks, such as railroads or telecommunications, where routing in the physical delivery of products can be specified, flows in electricity networks are hard to control. A transmission network is largely passive and has few "control valves" or "booster pumps" to regulate power flows on individual lines. Electrons follow the path of least resistance, and control actions are limited to adjusting generation output and removing or adding transmission lines. Moreover, every action can affect all other activities in the grid: if the failure of a single element in the system (such as the shutdown of a generation unit or transmission line) is not managed properly, it can destabilize the entire electricity grid. Similarly, large swings in load at one node affect conditions at other nodes. Thus electricity requires careful, deliberate, systemwide coordination to achieve real-time balancing of supply and demand.

Source: Joskow (2000a).

scale and scope, which are the main reason the industry evolved with a vertically integrated structure (box 3.1). In most countries dispersed generators are also horizontally integrated into a single firm. Transmission and distribution are quintessential natural monopolies (although technological change is weakening this characterization).[2] Because they entail substantial, largely sunk fixed costs, competition would lead to wasteful duplication of network resources. Thus in most countries a single entity governs the transmission network for all or most of the country. Although economies of scale are not pervasive in generation, vertical integration between generation and the network elements of the natural monopoly limits competition in generation—even when numerous generating plants are connected to the network.

Other features that distinguish electricity from other network utilities limit the scope for competition or reliance on market mechanisms. Electricity supply is rigid by nature. Electricity cannot be stored economically because storage technologies—such as batteries and hydro-

133

electric pumps—are extremely inefficient. Thus electricity is the ultimate real-time product, with production and consumption occurring at essentially the same time. But because of physical constraints on production and transmission, achieving real-time balancing of supply and demand is difficult and requires intensive system coordination. Network congestion constrains the ability of remote generators to respond to the supply needs of a given area. Moreover, generating units have capacity constraints that cannot be breached without risking costly damage. As a result the amount of electricity that can be delivered in an area at a given time is limited and supply is highly inelastic—especially at peak times (Borenstein 2000).

The challenges created by electricity supply are exacerbated by the lack of flexibility in demand. Although technologies are available to enable real-time pricing, no electricity market makes significant use of them. So, few if any electricity customers pay real-time prices. Because demand is almost completely inelastic in the short run, little or no supply and demand balancing can be conducted on the demand side. Inelastic short-run demand and supply (at peak times), combined with the real-time nature of the market, make the electricity industry highly vulnerable to the exercise of market power.

The physical properties of electricity transmission imply that an imbalance of demand and supply at any location on the grid can affect the stability of the entire system. Thus the matching between a supplier and a customer is effectively part of the overall system balancing. Any mismatch could disrupt the delivery of electricity for all suppliers and consumers (Borenstein and Bushnell 2001). Because of electricity's inability to be stored, the varying demand for it, random failures in generation and transmission, and the need to continuously match supply and demand at every point in the system to maintain frequency, voltage, and stability, there is a need for real-time "inventory" to keep the system in balance. In theory the inventory problem could be resolved by market mechanisms with standby generators providing ancillary services in response to changing demand and supply conditions. But in practice such systems are difficult to design (Joskow 2003a).

These features have important implications for the design of efficient electricity markets and regulatory institutions. Simplistic approaches that ignored these attributes have led to serious problems for the public interest.

Pressures for Reform

The forces driving structural changes in the electricity industry differ between countries—especially between industrial and developing countries. In mature industrial countries pressure for change has grown with the emergence of excess capacity and from disillusionment with capital-intensive generation projects triggered by the oil crises of the 1970s. In developing and transition countries reforms have been driven by the poor operating and financial performance of state-owned electricity systems (with low labor productivity, poor service quality, and high system losses), lack of public funds for badly needed investments, unavailability of service for large portions of the population, and government desires to raise revenue through privatization (IEA 1999; Bacon and Besant-Jones 2001; Joskow 2003a).[3] Reforms were also prompted—and facilitated—by technological innovation.

Excess capacity in industrial countries.
For about 30 years after World War II, industrial countries experienced remarkably high and steady growth in demand for electricity. But in the 1970s this growth was interrupted, and it has never returned to its previous level. In an understandable response to that decade's oil shocks, industrial countries tried to reduce their dependence on oil for power generation. This shift increased interest in options such as nuclear power and large, super-critical coal-fired generating stations.[4] At the same time, budget pressures, high inflation, and attempts by state enterprises to contain the prices of their goods (part of strategies to counter inflation) squeezed electricity profits, delayed investments, and undermined confidence in previously smooth-running planning systems.

Still, the resulting circumstances were fairly benign. The development of high-efficiency combined-cycle gas turbines weakened the case for closely integrated generation and transmission systems based on economies of scale. The rapid development of gas pipelines and increasing availability of cheap gas in Western Europe and the United States made combined-cycle gas turbines more attractive than existing technologies. Dense, well-integrated electricity grids, an abundance of power stations, and excess capacity made competition between generating companies feasible and attractive.

The United Kingdom began reforming and privatizing electricity in 1990, showing that it was possible to replace state-owned, vertically integrated monopolies with privately owned, unbundled, and regulated companies. The European Union soon started pressing for electricity liberalization in its member states, and its Electricity Directive required open access and liberalized markets starting in 1998.

Similar efforts were under way in North America. In the United States reform has been complicated by the need to ensure that stranded assets are compensated, though initially there was great confidence that a deal could be struck that would benefit all parties.[5] Then, just when the European Union was pressing for further reform, California's recent electricity crisis shook political confidence in the liberalization agenda.

Need for investment in developing countries. Many developing countries are at a stage of economic development where demand for electricity increases rapidly, requiring enormous investment. Between 1999 and 2020 global electricity consumption is projected to increase by 2.7 percent a year, but in the developing world the increase is projected to be 4.2 percent a year (table 3.1).

Table 3.1 Net Electricity Consumption in Industrial and Developing Countries, 1990–2020
(billions of kilowatt-hours)

Country group	1990	1999	2005	2010	2015	2020	Average annual change, 1999–2000 (percent)
Industrial countries	6,385	7,517	8,620	9,446	10,281	11,151	1.9
United States	2,817	3,236	3,793	4,170	4,556	4,916	2.0
Eastern Europe and former Soviet Union	1,906	1,452	1,651	1,807	2,006	2,173	1.9
Developing countries	2,258	3,863	4,912	6,127	7,548	9,082	4.2
Asia	1,258	2,319	3,092	3,900	4,819	5,858	4.5
China	551	1,084	1,523	2,031	2,631	3,349	5.5
India	257	424	537	649	784	923	3.8
Other	450	811	1,033	1,220	1,404	1,586	3.3
Central and South America	449	684	788	988	1,249	1,517	3.9
World total	10,549	12,832	15,183	17,380	19,835	22,406	2.7

Note: Data for 2005–20 are projections. Totals for industrial and developing countries include countries and regions other than those listed.
Source: EIA (1999, 2002b).

> ## Box 3.2   Power Shortages in the Philippines
>
> IN THE PHILIPPINES IN 1992, EXCESS DEMAND WAS EQUAL TO NEARLY half of system capacity. Brownouts lasted up to 10 hours a day. Shopping malls were ordered to reduce their hours of operation by 2 hours, and industrial areas faced 12-hour blackouts three times a week. Of 512 international firms that had or planned to open their Asian headquarters in Manila, 123 closed their operations and 226 cancelled their registrations.
>
> *Source:* Henisz and Zelner (2001).

Electricity systems are under stress in many developing countries. The balance between demand and supply is tight, and lack of spare capacity often leads to blackouts (box 3.2). Thus significant investments are needed in generation, transmission, and distribution. But the governance structure in the sector—typically vertically integrated, state-owned, and centrally planned—is poorly suited to mobilizing the long-term capital needed for adequate, reliable electricity supply.

In the early days of rapid growth and young plants, prices could be set at cost recovery levels and even allowed to fall due to the rapidly decreasing costs resulting from economies of scale and new technologies. Thus integrated, state-owned electricity systems performed reasonably well—but only at first.

Over time, especially as inflation and budget pressures increased, the margin between revenues and costs was squeezed. In most developing countries electricity prices stopped covering costs and were far below the long-run incremental costs of system expansion. Such pricing made it difficult to maintain facilities and finance new investments. As a result systems became inadequate and unreliable, and supply shortages increased. Moreover, underpricing for favored groups became more noticeable politically, yet harder to reverse. Political interference also led to management deterioration and extraordinarily high excess employment (figure 3.2). Lack of effective monitoring led to theft and losses that further undermined the sector's financial sustainability.

Technological innovation.   Recent technological advances have dramatically altered the cost structure of electricity generation. They are

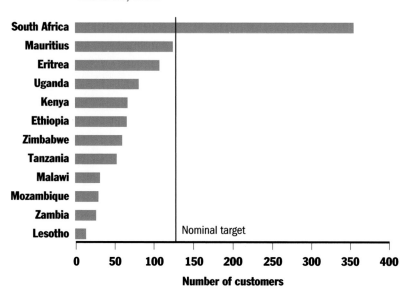

Figure 3.2 Customers per Electricity Employee in Selected African Countries, 1998

Source: Kerekezi and Kimani (2001).

also changing the network economics of the electricity grid in both industrial and developing countries.

From the start of the 20th century until the early 1980s, technological developments led to larger and more efficient fossil-fuel power plants built farther and farther from cities and factories. But in recent years technological improvements in gas turbines and the development of combined-cycle gas turbines have recast economies of scale in electricity, reversing a 50-year trend toward large, centralized power stations (Bayless 1994; Casten 1995). Combined-cycle gas turbines can be brought online faster (within 2 years) and at more modest scale (50–500 megawatts) than coal or nuclear plants (5–10 years and 1,000 megawatts). Aero-derivative gas turbines can be efficient at scales as small as 10 megawatts (Balzhiser 1996).

Although natural gas and light oil distillates are the preferred fuels for gas turbines, a wide variety of low-calorific fuels have also been used successfully. (For example, the Kot Addu plant in Pakistan has accumulated 60,000 hours of successful operation burning heavy oil and naphtha, and the Paguthan plant in India has accumulated 19,000 hours.) Thus gas turbine technology is of growing importance even for

Figure 3.3 Projected Costs of Small-Scale Electricity Generation Technologies, 2000–15

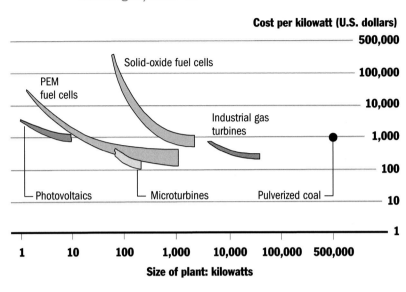

Source: "The Dawn of Micropower," *The Economist,* 5 August 2000.

developing and transition economies that lack natural gas resources (Taud, Karg, and O'Leary 1999).[6]

Electricity utilities are already using small-scale generators to meet peak demand and serve other purposes. But small generators can also be used to bypass utilities. And when demand is sufficient to realize economies of mass production, the capital costs of small-scale generating units will likely fall. In the 1980s wind generators cost $4,000 per kilowatt installed, but today cost just $1,250 per kilowatt. Thus it might soon be possible to add efficient capacity of 1–10 megawatts— the range needed for many factories, large housing developments, and other institutions (figure 3.3).

But while small-scale generation holds considerable promise, it is not yet competitive with centralized power systems. A number of factors affect the competitive balance between centralized and distributive generators, including differing regulations, efficiencies, fuel prices, capital costs, and environmental externalities.[7] Relative to large centralized generation, capital costs per kilowatt are about twice as high and efficiencies about half for distributive generation.[8] For example, gas-fired central plant generating facilities have efficiencies of 48–52 percent—

twice that of gas microturbines. Moreover, gas-fired distributive generators are likely to pay higher prices for inputs because large central stations can buy their gas in bulk at much lower rates. And because of their lower efficiency, small-scale technologies emit far more carbon dioxide than do efficient combined-cycle gas turbines. On the other hand, distributive generation leads to lower network costs (Lee 2003).

In most developing countries there is considerable uncertainty about the reliability of electricity systems. The proximate cause is the inadequate response to increased demand for electric power through generation, transmission, and distribution upgrades and expansions. What role (if any) distributive generation will play in the baseload electricity market—and thus in resolving the reliability problem—is hard to predict. If gas microturbines and other small-scale generation technologies significantly reduce their costs and improve their efficiencies, they might have a considerable impact on the structure of electricity markets.

Having many small generators operating at or close to load would reduce reliance on transmission and even distribution facilities. New electricity storage technologies would have the same effect (Thomas and Schneider 1997). Although small generators are not expected to displace large thermal plants, at least in the foreseeable future, new generation capacity will likely come from smaller units. Distributive generation can play an increasingly important role in providing ancillary services such as emergency backup power and voltage support, increasing system reliability. In developing countries—where centralized supply has yet to reach 1.8 billion people—small-scale, modular generation close to the point of consumption might be a more realistic and even economical option.

This new industry model would enhance the ability of gas pipelines to compete with electricity transmission networks. Having small generators delivering power at or near the point of consumption would cap the prices that other generators and transmitters could charge, especially to large industrial users. Indeed, the mere threat of bringing on-line gas turbine capacity would constrain the behavior of a transmission monopolist (Baumol, Panzar, and Willig 1988).

Small-scale generation is already changing the service landscape in several developing countries where there is no regulation or where entry to the sector is formally allowed. In Yemen small generators supply rural towns and villages not served by the public utility. Operations range from individual households generating power for themselves and a few neigh-

---

Box 3.3 Opening the Electricity Market—Photovoltaic Systems in Kenya

WHEN A UTILITY FAILS TO PROVIDE SERVICE TO many households, allowing entry by entrepreneurs can fill the gap. Kenya's electricity utility fails to provide connections to more than 98 percent of the rural population, so households have started turning to alternative systems. Between 1982 and 1999 the market for photovoltaic units grew into a $6 million a year industry.

In the 1980s the demand for photovoltaic systems came from nongovernmental organizations installing demonstration systems in schools and missions, and from off-grid community leaders and

middle-income households. Photovoltaic retailers realized that continued sales required expanding the market. The availability of smaller, cheaper systems helped on the supply side. Local marketing emphasized the technology's many uses—from lighting to television—raising demand. In the late 1990s local entrepreneurs sold more than 22,000 modules a year. Competition lowered the retail price from $100 a module in 1990 to $65 in 1998. The introduction of hire-purchase options has further extended the market. Since 1990, 60 percent of the 2.5 megawatts in photovoltaic sales has been to households.

Source: Hankins (2000).

---

bors to units supplying up to 200 households. Although these small electricity suppliers have been criticized for being inefficient and expensive, the alternative for Yemeni households is not service by the utility but no service at all—or far less efficient, even more costly alternatives such as dry cell batteries (Ehrhardt and Burdon 1999; Tynan 2002).

In Kenya, because the rural population is so sparse, expanding coverage from the national power grid would be extremely costly. So, some rural households are being served by private companies offering a different technology: photovoltaic systems (box 3.3). Since 1990 more than 2.5 megawatts of photovoltaic capacity have been sold, providing power to more than 1 percent of the country's 25 million rural inhabitants (Hankins 2000). Standalone photovoltaic systems are also being used in Brazil, India, Namibia, Senegal, South Africa, and Thailand—powering water pumps, streetlights, lanterns, and telecommunications relay stations.

Addressing the Problems of State Ownership

UNDER STATE OWNERSHIP, MANAGERS AND POLITICIANS favor underpricing to stimulate demand and secure political support. Excess demand signals a need for investment, which managers desire and politicians view as a sign of development. Before the reform era, international donor agencies were happy to fund investments in power because electricity utilities were a visible sign of technology transfer and had high social returns. Insufficient power had high costs even in developing countries. But inflationary pressures caused tariff agreements to be abandoned and further encouraged low prices for public electricity. As a result real electricity prices fell, as did profits—and hence utilities' ability to finance their investments. One problem with capital-intensive electricity utilities is that their operating costs (mainly fuel) are only about half their total costs, so if they underprice services they can still cover their operating costs.

A 1989 survey of 360 electricity utilities in 57 developing and transition economies found that the average annual return on revalued net fixed assets was less than 4 percent, well below the 10 percent target normally set by donors. In 1991 these utilities financed just 12 percent of their investment requirements, and revenue covered only 60 percent of power sector costs. Underpriced electricity imposed a fiscal burden of $90 billion a year in the early 1990s, or 7 percent of government revenues in developing countries—larger than required power investments of about $80 billion a year. Moreover, technical inefficiencies caused nearly $30 billion a year in economic losses (Besant-Jones 1993; World Bank 1994b; Newbery 2001).

These outcomes occurred despite several decades of studies on tariff reforms, agreements to improve pricing, and reports arguing that underpricing electricity was inefficient, fiscally harmful, and distributionally unjust. Underpricing was also the main cause of underinvestment in developing countries (box 3.4). Lacking an alternative source of investment, countries persuaded donors to continue support, reducing incentives to make politically unpopular pricing decisions. When Chile, followed by the United Kingdom and other countries, showed that privatization works, it seemed like the obvious solution to the problem—introducing financial prudence, competent management, and operational efficiency while relieving governments of heavy investment costs.

In competitive markets where private owners pursue profits, there are incentives for efficiency and mechanisms for adequate investment. The problem with electricity supply is that transmission and distribution are natural monopolies and cannot be operated competitively. The

> **Box 3.4 Underpricing Undermines Electricity Expansion in Zimbabwe**
>
> THE MAIN CASUALTY OF ZIMBABWE'S FAILURE TO RAISE ELEC-
> tricity tariffs to cost-reflective levels was the country's electricity de-
> velopment plan, which sought to expand existing power stations
> and add new ones. Frequent changes of ministers of energy and
> weak policy commitment to renumerative tariffs undermined efforts
> to privatize the Hwange power station and attract private participa-
> tion in a plant planned at Gokwe North. Foreign investors aban-
> doned privatization and expansion projects in 2000, mainly because
> of the government's failure to realign prices with long-run marginal
> costs.
>
> *Source:* Mangwengwende (2002).

logical solution is to separate potentially competitive generation and
supply (or retailing) from the natural monopoly networks. Generation
and supply can then operate in competitive markets, and the natural
monopolies regulated to imitate the effects of competition.

The crucial question is how to introduce competition into generation (and supply). The standard answer is that competition requires a
market, so generation needs a wholesale electricity market organized as
a power exchange or a pool. That model works well if there is adequate
generation and transmission capacity and enough independent generators to ensure competition. But such conditions are demanding and
may not be sustainable. Although many electricity industries have been
restructured successfully, they all started with substantial spare capacity.
As time passes, if prices remain low because of strong competition,
entry will be unattractive and capacity will become scarce. In addition,
generators may want to merge to increase their market power and deter
additional entrants.

Thus this approach should be pursued with caution. It may be sustainable if there is sophisticated regulation of competition and regulators can find a way to ensure adequate investment in transmission. But
California's recent experience is a reminder that sophisticated regulation is a scarce commodity even in advanced industrial countries.

Options for Restructuring Electricity Markets

Electricity markets can be structured in four ways, reflecting varying competition and customer choice:

- *Monopoly*—the traditional status quo, where a single entity generates all electricity and delivers it over a transmission network to distribution companies or costumers.
- *Single buyer*—where a single agency buys electricity from competing generators, has a monopoly on transmission, and sells electricity to distributors and large power users without competition from other suppliers.
- *Wholesale competition*—where multiple distributors buy electricity from competing generators, use the transmission network to deliver it to their service areas under open access arrangements, and maintain monopolies on sales in their service areas.
- *Retail competition*—where customers have access to competing generators, directly or through a retailer of their choice, and transmission and distribution networks operate under open access arrangements (table 3.2).[9]

Given the unique economic characteristics of the electricity industry—especially the need for coordination between generation and transmission, and the difficulty of replicating vertical relationships with market mechanisms—the monopoly option has some appeal. In theory an integrated company could minimize the cost of meeting demand at each point in time through optimal dispatch of its power stations, taking into account systemwide transmission constraints and losses. In the long run it could exploit the investment relationships between generation and transmission and undertake investments based on systemwide planning.

Table 3.2 Options for the Structure of Electricity Markets

Feature	Monopoly	Single buyer	Wholesale competition	Retail competition
Competing generators?	No	Yes	Yes	Yes
Choice for retailers?	No	No	Yes	Yes
Choice for customers?	No	No	No	Yes

Source: Hunt and Shuttleworth (1996).

But these benefits will likely be small relative to those that come from promoting competition in generation: lower construction and operating costs, incentives to close inefficient plants, and better pricing (Joskow 2000a). Because the monopoly option does not allow for competition in generation, it is largely a straw man today: no one would choose it to promote the public interest. The three other options progressively increase competition and market-oriented decisionmaking in the electricity industry and its vertical relationships. Most reform programs are designed to move from monopolies to wholesale and retail competition. Complex policy issues arise when determining whether the single-buyer option is a sensible transition to wholesale competition and the stage at which retail competition is appropriate and feasible. (The single-buyer option and wholesale competition are analyzed in more detail below.)

Though the options vary, there is wide agreement on the basic architecture for electricity restructuring. The standard reform model separates transmission, distribution, and system operations from the competitive activities of generation. Wholesale and retail competition is the standard prescription, with a regulatory agency setting tariffs for transmission and distribution (Joskow 2003a) and market entrants building new generation capacity with nondiscriminatory access to the grid and customers. There is less agreement on the sequencing of electricity reforms. In countries where underpricing is a serious problem, privatizing the distribution monopoly might be considered a necessary first step to promote the tariff adjustments required to revive sector performance (Newbery 2001). But the tight balance between demand and supply in many developing countries (and so the need to ensure adequate generation) and the dramatic technological changes that have made generation structurally competitive would argue for privatizing generation first.

Most of the downward pressure on prices from electricity restructuring comes from promoting efficiency at the firm level through wholesale competition. The issue of providing "customer choice" through retail competition has received considerable attention in the popular discussion of electricity reform. But there is considerable debate about the magnitude of the price benefits that electricity retailers are likely to bring, especially to residential and small commercial customers. Retailing costs are small and so reducing them by competition would lead to small customer savings. Also, the opportunities for price competition are likely to be limited and retail competition may be socially costly because of increases in marketing, advertising, settlement and transactions and other associated costs (Joskow 2000b). Thus it is asserted that only in very few cases have residential customers benefited much from retail competition. Still, others argue that retail competition can lead to better informed decisions by both suppliers and customers (what types of service to supply and what to consume) and help identify the best suppliers and (indirectly) the best generators. It can also provide better information about the relation of costs to prices, increase the political and economic pressure for improved cost allocation, and reduce the scope for government and/or regulators to favor particular interest groups (Littlechild 2000).

Privatizing Distribution

In the absence of reforms, most electricity systems suffer from unbalanced tariffs, inadequate revenues (often associated with failure to collect bills and reduce theft), excessive costs, and inefficient or insufficient investment. For example, cash collection (cash collected relative to the amount billed) averages just 46 percent in seven members of the Commonwealth of Independent States (Armenia, Azerbaijan, Georgia, Kyrgyz Republic, Moldova, Tajikistan, Uzbekistan), and commercial losses (unbilled consumption) exceed 20 percent. Power industries in southeastern Europe face similar problems (table 3.3).

The logical place to address revenue shortfalls is at the distribution and supply end (usually combined), which collects revenue from customers. The best way to start and sustain pricing and related reform is to separate the distribution monopoly from the rest of the industry, privatize it, and subject it to price or revenue cap regulation.

A related question is whether to separate the supply function from distribution, or at least signal that this will eventually happen. This partly depends on whether a supply franchise for small customers (those using less than 1 megawatt or possibly 100 kilowatts) is expected to continue. If so, the distribution company is the natural supplier to the franchise market, and the main requirement is to ensure that suppliers have nondiscriminatory access to the distribution network and meters. Still, the case for liberalizing supply is weak in industrial countries and even weaker in developing countries (see below).

Table 3.3 Cash Collection and Commercial Losses for Electricity Companies in Southeastern Europe, 2000

(percent)

Country	Cash collection	Commercial losses
Albania	60	40
Bosnia and Herzegovina	75	25
Bulgaria	85	10
Croatia	100	5
Macedonia, FYR	60	—
Moldova	55	35
Romania	45	5
Serbia and Montenegro	60	20

— Not available.

Source: Broadman and others 2003; Kennedy, Fankhauser, and Raiser (2003).

Private Participation in Generation

The private sector can become involved in generation in two ways. The most common way is for the government to sell a controlling share in generation companies, possibly retaining nuclear power stations, major multiuse hydroelectric dams, or both. If generation is to be privatized, the state electricity company must be split into a sufficient number of competing companies. The second way is for the government to invite tenders from independent power producers interested in supplying the (preferably restructured) state electricity company. This approach introduces new private investment into the industry yet requires only modest reform and restructuring. Private investors might be reluctant to enter such markets, however, unless the government gets out of the generation business.

In both cases the logical first step is to separate transmission from generation and create conditions for regulated third party access to transmission. Transmission will also need to be regulated, under principles similar to those for distribution. But fewer problems are likely if transmission remains publicly owned (at least for a transition period).

The arguments for separation (preferably ownership separation) of transmission from generation are standard. A transmission company with ownership stakes in generation will likely favor its generation over that of other owners. This may not be a serious problem if all new generation capacity is put up to auction and the transmission company acts as the single buyer. But far more serious problems arise if the intention is to create a competitive, less regulated wholesale market with free and contestable entry (see below for a discussion of such problems in Chile).

Two quite different approaches are used to introduce competition into generation. Under the single buyer approach the transmission company (which may be vertically integrated with generation and even distribution and supply) buys all publicly generated electricity.[10] Competition occurs through periodic tenders for new generation capacity, with the winners signing long-term power purchase agreements with the single buyer. The second approach creates a wholesale spot market (pool) or power exchange where generators sell directly to suppliers, final customers, or both.

Single buyer model. The single buyer model has evolved under a variety of organizational forms. It may simply comprise the state-owned, vertically integrated utility. Alternatively, the national utility might be split into generation, transmission, and distribution companies, with the transmission and dispatch facilities remaining under public ownership and the newly formed transmission and dispatch entity buying electricity from generators and selling it to distribution companies at regulated tariffs (figure 3.4; Lovei 2000). The model may further entail

Figure 3.4   The Single-Buyer Model for Electricity

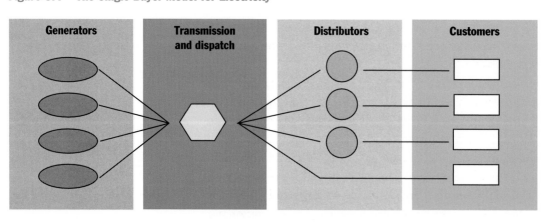

Source: Lovei (2000).

the dispatch company being unbundled from the single buyer entity. And in its completely unbundled form, the transmission company is also separate from the single buyer entity.

In the model's extreme form the single buyer buys all energy and capacity in the market, is the sole authorized seller of electricity (ruling out competitive supply), decides what, from whom, and how much to buy, and assumes most of the credit and market risk (active single buyer). Another form of the centralized buying model entails an entity acquiring a large part of the energy and capacity (and selling it to distribution companies at regulated tariffs) but not being the only buyer in the system (principal buyer). Finally, a relatively new model involves the buyer acting as an aggregator and procurement coordinator, responsible for the procurement of energy to distribution companies. But the buyer does not take the initiative on how much and from whom to buy, and assumes no credit or market risk (passive buyer; Barker, Mauer, and Storm van Leeuwen 2003).

The single buyer model provides a way for independent power producers to compete for long-term power purchase agreements—a precondition for private investment in generation in electricity sectors with few reforms. The model can also work if existing power stations are sold to private generation companies.

Since the early 1990s many countries in Asia, the Caribbean, Central America, and Eastern Europe—and to a less extent the Middle East and Africa—have adopted variations of the single buyer model. Competitive long-term power purchase agreements expedite private investment to meet growing electricity demand without the need for drastic industry restructuring. Indeed, the tendering process is sometimes just grafted onto a vertically integrated and otherwise unreformed electricity entity (as with Malaysia's Pusat Tenaga), which is probably a good model for small developing countries.

Efficient power purchase agreements specify availability payments (the amount charged for each kilowatt of capacity available for dispatch, possibly with different rates at different times of the year) and energy payments (linked to the fuel price, per megawatt generated). Given these and other technical parameters, the single buyer can determine which tender offers the best value or lowest cost. Thus competitive tendering can considerably cut the cost of generation. In Hungary, for example, tenders to build new power stations nearly halved average production costs.

Figure 3.5   The Wholesale Competition Model for Electricity

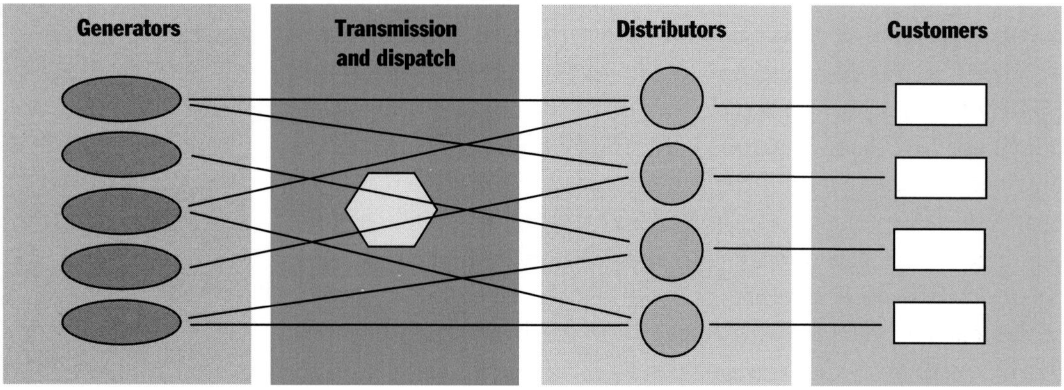

Source: Lovei (2000).

Wholesale competition.   With wholesale competition, local distribution companies retain their exclusive service territories and buy power from competing generators (figure 3.5). Customers cannot choose their suppliers, but users consuming more than a certain volume of power may be able to contract with generators. Though many countries have only a few hundred or few thousand high-volume users, they account for a large share of demand. By allowing wholesale customers to buy cheaper power from alternative suppliers and by providing more customers for independent power producers, this option makes the market more competitive and dynamic than does the single buyer model.

Several prerequisites must be met for wholesale electricity markets to succeed (Wolak 2003). First, buyers must have a spot market or power exchange (where buying and selling occurs) and a forward market (where market participants can negotiate contracts). Forward contracts mitigate the risk of volatile spot prices and encourage suppliers to bid aggressively in the spot market. California's recent electricity crisis shows the importance of load-serving entities purchasing a substantial portion of their energy needs in the forward market—at least a year before delivery.

Second, a competitive wholesale market requires a sufficient number of unaffiliated suppliers. Competitive entry will be inhibited if a single supplier dominates the market. Third, there is a need for active participation by as many customers as is economically feasible in both long-term and short-term markets. Allowing wholesale electricity buyers to enter long-term purchasing agreements with suppliers facilitates financing of new generation capacity. In the short-term market, suppliers will be much less likely to exercise market power if customers can alter their consumption in response to short-term price signals.

Fourth, wholesale electricity markets require an economically reliable transmission network—that is, one with adequate capacity so that each location on the network faces sufficient competition among distant generators, to preclude localized monopoly power. For transmission prices to encourage efficient use of generation and transmission resources, they must reflect generators' full impacts on transmission costs, including system congestion, stability, and reliability. In addition, the system operator should ensure the stability of the system's frequency and voltage.

Finally, there is a need for a credible, effective, fast-acting regulatory mechanism to deal with flaws in market design and encourage efficient behavior by market participants. This is especially imperative when wholesale electricity markets are established without all of the essential prerequisites just described.

Contrasting the single buyer model and wholesale competition.

The single buyer model is often the preferred approach for a variety of technical, economic, and institutional reasons:

- It promotes rapid investment and expansion by shielding the financiers of generation projects from market risk and retail-level regulatory risk.
- It facilitates system balancing (the balancing of differences between the planned and actual output of individual generators and between the planned and actual loads of individual distributors).[11]
- It provides the necessary scale and expertise to efficiently contract for energy, power, and ancillary services and improve system reliability.
- It can be implemented quickly because it does not require significant changes in the operating culture or in sector policy (Lovei 2000; Barker, Mauer, and Storm van Leeuwen 2003).

But the single buyer model also poses considerable risks, and in practice has experienced several problems. First, if the single buyer also owns generation, it may select bids from its generation subsidiary or bias competition in favor of it. Incumbent single buyers are loath to face the test of competition—which may reveal high operational costs—and well placed to impede entry by imposing unreasonable conditions. As a result potential generators may be reluctant to incur the costs of preparing a bid, reinforcing the power of the incumbent buyer and defeating the purpose of opening generation to outside investors.

Second, in its standard form (active single buyer) the model concentrates all financial risk in the hands of a single agent. If this state-owned agent is unable to meet its obligations to generators, the government is expected to step in (an expectation formalized in a guarantee agreement). Thus power purchase agreements under the single buyer model create a contingent liability for government that can affect its creditworthiness. Effectively, taxpayers or customers—not investors—bear all the risk.

Third, investments in generating capacity are not driven by market incentives, but rather by bureaucratic preference. Decisions about expanding capacity are made by government officials who do not face the financial consequences of their actions. In fact, governments have often abandoned least-cost expansion alternatives because of political reasons, expediency, and outright corruption.

Fourth, the single buyer model weakens the incentives of distributors for effective demand forecast and procurement, and for collecting payments from customers. The state-owned single buyer is often politically constrained and reluctant to take action against delinquent distribution companies. Thus the lack of direct contracts between generators and distributors inevitably undermines payment discipline. When paying and nonpaying distributors are treated alike, their incentives for efficient performance are clearly weakened. These distorted incentives are not easy to fix.

Fifth, the standard single buyer model involves a state-owned entity with weak incentives to minimize energy procurement costs, and it might be susceptible to political interference for the same reasons as the former state-owned electricity industry (Wolak 2003). Thus the single buyer model is likely to allow governments to influence the dispatch of generators and the allocation of revenues among them. In Poland and Ukraine coal miners were able to pressure governments to give special treatment to coal-fired generating plants (Lovei 2000).

Finally, the single buyer model tends to be self-perpetuating because of its excessively rigid contract structure. It risks stranding contracts that complicate further restructuring. Thus it increases the likelihood that under pressure from vested interests, governments will delay further electricity reforms.

Bid-based versus cost-based dispatch and pricing.   Many developing and transition economies lack some of the features required for competitive wholesale electricity markets. First, more than 100 countries have less than 1,000 megawatts of installed capacity—so unless there are strong connections to neighboring countries, the potential number of independent suppliers might be too small to support a competitive market (Besant-Jones and Tenenbaum 2001). Moreover, many medium-size and large countries have not undertaken sufficient horizontal restructuring in generation to mitigate problems of market power. Second, transmission networks are often poorly suited to wholesale competition. And third, most developing and transition economies have had a hard time establishing effective, credible regulation.

Under these circumstances a bid-based short-term (spot) market, where generators submit supply curves (indicating the quantity of energy they are willing to provide as a function of price) or multipart bids, might have disadvantages. The most obvious ones are the potential exercise of systemwide market power due to insufficient competition in generation or of local market power due to transmission bottlenecks in specific areas. If either outcome occurs, prices will likely be well above the marginal cost of the most expensive generator in the market (for systemwide market power) or in the specific area (for local market power). Thus potential market power problems must be carefully analyzed before a bid-based short-term market is introduced. If these problems are significant, the new market should be accompanied by strategies that mitigate them. Creating such strategies is a challenge even for experienced regulators.

Another disadvantage of a bid-based short-term market is the high start-up cost of the required real-time metering equipment, information technology, bidding protocols, and market-making and settlement software. For example, establishing California's spot market for electricity cost $250 million. Even a small bid-based real-time (or near-real-time) market entails significant up-front costs (Wolak 2000).

Thus in many if not most developing and transition economies it might be unwise to establish bid-based dispatch. A safer strategy might be to pursue, at least initially, a cost-based spot market where generators are dispatched based on their marginal production costs—so the marginal cost of the last unit called to meet demand determines the market clearing price. Almost every country in Latin America uses regulated unit-level costs to dispatch electricity and set prices (Colombia is an exception).

Cost-based spot markets offer several advantages. They:

- Ensure economically efficient dispatch (assuming generators are truthful in revealing their production costs).
- Make it harder for generators to exercise market power (because they must bid their regulated costs) and so avoid the time and expense of developing tools to mitigate it.
- Are easier to implement because they build on mechanisms that were in place prior to reforms and avoid the start-up costs of real-time bid-based systems.

By constraining the exercise of market power, cost-based mechanisms also reduce short-term variation in electricity prices. Lower volatility cuts costs for suppliers and load-serving entities because there is less uncertainty about prices over the duration of forward contracts (Wolak 2003).

But cost-based dispatch also has disadvantages. First, it does not eliminate the incentives or ability of suppliers to exercise market power (Arizu 2003). Suppliers may try to inflate their estimated or actual production costs, so the exercise of market power simply takes a different form. Thus an administrative procedure is needed to determine whether suppliers' input costs are prudent, which requires careful monitoring of fuel and other input markets. In many developing and transition economies, however, auditing is weak.

Second, cost-based dispatch offers a simulated spot market for electricity, not a real market. The price signals it provides to market participants are not as powerful as those in bid-based spot markets. For example, in a bid-based market the owners of hydroelectric units raise the price of their electricity if they anticipate water scarcity. In response, fossil fuel units will likely run more intensively much sooner, reducing the likelihood of electricity shortages.

Restructuring Generation and Transmission

Before the reform era, many countries had a number of separate distribution companies organized on a regional basis (except in very small countries), but it was common for transmission to be vertically integrated with generation. There are good reasons for this setup:

- The location of new generation needs to be coordinated with the construction of needed transmission lines.
- Central dispatch is standard, and also requires close coordination between the transmission operator and individual power stations. Stations need to be brought on line in merit order—with the cheapest stations providing base load, followed by stations with higher avoidable costs providing mid-merit and peaking power—but the transmission operator must ensure that transmission lines are not overloaded. These transmission constraints may require the operator to dispatch stations out of merit order.
- The transmission operator needs to obtain ancillary services to maintain system stability, and so needs to be able to call on or instruct stations to provide these services at short notice.

These coordination benefits can still be obtained when generation is unbundled from transmission, and any small loss in synergies should be more than offset by the increased efficiency that results from competition in generation. Moreover, the sharper focus that a separate business provides can foster considerable improvements in transmission companies.

Central dispatch can be maintained, and the transmission operator will still need to obtain and provide ancillary services through contracts, tenders, or spot purchases. The main problems to resolve involve planning new transmission lines and ensuring that new generation plants are located efficiently. A variety of models are available, and their lessons are being studied carefully (IEA 1999). Whichever one is chosen, charges for using the transmission system need to be set at a level that finances network expansion (if necessary not out of current cash flow, but out of borrowing secured on future revenues from the investment). Transmission charges may differ to encourage generators to locate efficiently, though this may also be achieved through the capital charge for connection to the system.

The difficulty of setting and regulating efficient transmission charges provides one of the strongest arguments for unbundling transmission from generation. Otherwise the incumbent transmission operator will devise charges (particularly connection charges) that favor incumbent generators and disfavor entrants, raising their costs and allowing existing generators to set higher wholesale prices. Thus this unbundling is among the most important steps in electricity restructuring and reform.

Restructuring generation.   When generation is unbundled from transmission, it needs to be restructured into independent companies—with revenue security if these are to be privatized. If the remaining transmission company is to become the single buyer, inheriting existing power purchase agreements with independent power producers, and if the generation companies are to be sold, they will need comparable and suitable power purchase agreements. This approach has been favored by transition economies in Central Europe as a means of financing refurbishment, and has both risks and benefits. If the aim is to create a fully liberalized wholesale market, additional steps are required.

In some cases the transmission company or its predecessor generation and transmission company may have power purchase agreements with recently created independent power producers. If the transmission company has been operating as a single buyer, it may acquire long-term purchase agreements even if the generation companies remain state-owned (box 3.5). In either case it is important to decide whether and

---

Box 3.5   Stranded Power Purchase Agreements in Poland

POLAND'S ELECTRICITY INDUSTRY WAS RESTRUCTURED AND UN-bundled in 1990, and by the end of 1993 consisted of 18 power plants, 24 combined heat and power stations, 33 distribution companies, and 1 transmission company, Polskie Sieci Elektroenerge-tyczne, which acts as a single buyer (and retains much of the expertise of the previously integrated power company). The generation companies had to borrow at high interest rates to finance refurbishment and pollution clean-up. This investment was secured against 24 long-term power purchase agreements with the transmission company, covering two-thirds of supply. These agreements, many of which are effectively stranded contracts, greatly complicated efforts to prepare the industry for privatization.

Source: Newbery (2001).

how to renegotiate these agreements and what contract arrangements should be put in place for new generation companies.

Ownership of the transmission grid.   The economic and technological characteristics of generation, as well as the need for significant new investment, make a strong case for its privatization. Similarly, privatizing and regulating distribution companies is important for establishing sensible electricity prices and hence allowing generators to be paid viable prices. But there is much less agreement about the importance of privatizing transmission and the speed at which the process should be completed (Bushnell and Soft 1997).

Many countries prefer to keep their transmission grids under public ownership (just as they often prefer to keep distribution companies under municipal or regional ownership). Some of these countries have mature networks that require little expansion and account for a small part of the final price of electricity. But in many developing countries strengthening the transmission grid may be a top priority, and efficient management of its expansion is critical to the costs of delivering power to final customers.

The wholesale electricity market's design and operation will determine the industry's success and the extent and speed at which efficiency improvements are passed through in lower prices. If the grid remains publicly owned, it is crucial that the commercial activities of systems operation and market management be placed in a commercial organization—whether nonprofit or for-profit (and subject to careful oversight).

One of the most persuasive arguments for delaying the privatization of a national grid is that it is hard to value the assets, because in most cases transmission was bundled with generation. Many of the transactions between generators and the transmission operator would previously have been internal transactions and canceled out. But under privatization they become revenues for the transmission operation and costs for the generation companies. There will be no history of accounts, let alone regulatory accounts, for the grid under its previous integrated form, so any revenue projections will have to be taken largely on trust. These projections will be strongly influenced by how regulation operates and the extent of cost reduction. The same is true for the distribution companies, but most will have been separate companies before and so have accounts setting out their costs. Thus there is less uncertainty in their case.

The absence of reliable accounts for the stand-alone grid business is a major problem—one that the passing of time will hopefully resolve. Another important issue under privatization is determining local transmission charges. Experiences from several countries indicate that it takes time to develop satisfactory regulated charges and incentives, and these may affect the reliability of revenue and cost forecasts. There is no obvious danger in delaying the privatization of transmission for several years after the privatization of distribution and generation, and there may be advantages.

Regulatory Challenges

GENERATION AND SUPPLY (RETAILING) ARE COMPETITIVE or contestable activities, and the normal policy conclusion would be that those activities should be deregulated. But given electricity's unique economic and technical characteristics (low elasticity of demand, nonstorability, significant short-run capacity constraints), electricity markets are highly vulnerable to the exercise of market power. Thus prices in wholesale electricity markets can remain well above competitive levels even when concentration is not especially high in the generating segment of the market (Newbery 2003). A policy of deregulation that does not explicitly address market power could seriously undermine the potential benefits of restructuring (Borenstein, Bushnell, and Wolak 2000). Moreover, distribution and transmission are prone to market failures (mainly due to their natural monopoly characteristics) and so also require regulatory oversight.

Regulation of Distribution

Restructuring and privatization are not feasible without a commitment to cost-reflective tariffs. The first step is to identify the efficient costs of distribution. These will include interest on and depreciation of the asset value (or regulatory asset base; Newbery 1997), as well as the efficient level of operating costs and distribution losses. The efficient operating costs may be substantially lower than what can realistically be achieved in the near term, raising questions about how best to motivate improvements without greatly increasing the risk placed on the company.

One appealing but risky strategy is to specify in detail how tariffs will be set over a realistic time horizon (four or five years) and how they will be revised periodically thereafter, then invite bids for the right to these revenue streams. This approach avoids one problem—that of determining the speed at which the company is able to drive costs down to the efficient level—but creates several others: the problem of determining the initial asset value, the bigger problem of how to reset the tariff, and the related risks of receiving a low privatization sales price or granting an unacceptably high return to buyers (or both).

All these problems will be better illuminated as experience accumulates. Chile has been commended and criticized for basing distribution tariffs on a hypothetical distribution company. One advantage of this approach is that it allows a determination of the total unit cost (including the return on capital) and provides strong incentives to outperform. But it suffers from high realized rates of return (the recent criticism) or from excessive risk or inadequate returns to investment (and to avoid this, tariffs may have to be set so high as to risk the first objection).

There is relatively little experience with resetting tariffs (apart from the unsatisfactory annual revisions in Orissa, India), so it remains to be seen whether experiences from advanced industrial countries (such as the United Kingdom) will translate to developing countries (or to which ones). Several issues have to be addressed in resetting tariffs—most obviously inflation but also sensitivity to various cost drivers.

Reviewing the tariff structure and setting the final price.   The distribution company will need to decide how to set various tariffs—distribution use of system (DUOS) charges—for its various customer classes (high-, medium-, and low-voltage). If the company operates under a revenue control formula designed to cover total costs, it will have an incentive to make these tariffs cost-reflective. That is because if one tariff is set above cost, some other tariff will be below cost, and an increase in sales under the latter tariff will generate losses.

Once the wholesale (or ex-power station) price is determined, the main elements are in place to determine the final prices of electricity delivered to franchise customers. This will be the wholesale price plus the transmission use of system (TUOS) and DUOS charges, and the amount needed to cover the costs of supply (billing, meter reading, contracting, and so on). The main mistake to avoid is regulating prices that contain volatile elements without some means of passing through or insuring against fluctuations in uncontrollable components, the most important of which is the wholesale price. If the final price is capped and the wholesale price is free to increase sharply, and if suppliers are not hedged with contracts, they will quickly go bankrupt, as in California.

As long as distribution companies are not prevented from rebalancing their tariffs and supply companies can pass through all the costs in the chain (wholesale electricity price, TUOS, ancillary services, DUOS) with an adequate margin, distribution companies can be privatized without waiting for a full restructuring of generation. The converse, of privatizing generation before implementing the full mechanism for sustainable pricing of the downstream elements, is unwise and may be very costly.

Rebalancing tariffs. Like industrial countries, developing and transition economies face political opposition to higher electricity prices and have found it difficult even to raise prices in line with inflation. Prices can be kept down by ignoring the capital embodied in transmission and distribution networks and by covering the average—rather than the marginal—cost of generation, again ignoring most of the capital value of the equipment.

The margin between wholesale and retail prices can be squeezed in the medium run by writing down the asset value and hence the regulatory asset base. But over time, as new investment is added, the capital cost element in transmission and distribution prices will gradually rise. This gradual adjustment will be less painful politically than a sudden increase, but at the cost of reduced proceeds from the sale of the transmission and distribution companies.

Better strategies are available to ease the transition to cost-reflective prices. Many countries offer lifeline rates, where customers pay a subsidized rate for a minimum level used each month (such as the first 50 kilowatts) and the marginal efficient rate for consumption beyond that. This approach selectively transfers to households the rents associated with past investment in the network while encouraging efficient con-

Figure 3.6   Average Ratios of Household to Industrial Electricity Prices, 1990–99

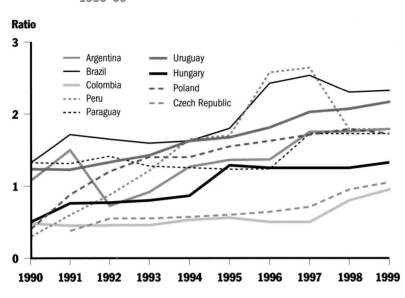

Ratio

Legend:
- Argentina
- Brazil
- Colombia
- Peru
- Paraguay
- Uruguay
- Hungary
- Poland
- Czech Republic

Source: Jamasb (2002).

sumption. Yet in some countries commercial, regulatory, and eventually political pressures conspire to eliminate lifeline pricing (Hungary is the most recent example, in 1999).

There seems to be no reason to subsidize industrial customers, who together usually account for about two-thirds of electricity demand. In some countries agricultural users pose a politically intractable problem—as in India, where underpricing creates serious inefficiencies, leading to the use of socially more expensive electric pumps for tubewells in place of perfectly adequate diesel pumps.

Historically, electricity prices in developing and transition economies included significant cross-subsidies from industrial customers to households. Open entry makes such subsidies unsustainable. Indeed, as these countries have begun to liberalize their electricity markets, cross-subsidies have been reduced and in some cases eliminated (figure 3.6).

Moreover, electricity underpricing cannot be defended on income distribution grounds. The main beneficiaries are invariably richer urban dwellers, and the costs are felt indirectly by poor people, who may be deprived of the chance to get electricity at all because of the country's inability to finance the extension of the system. Electric light is much

161

cheaper than kerosene and other alternatives, and customers are willing to pay high prices for a minimum level of consumption that provides light and allows the use of a television and small appliances. Political support may be concentrated in urban areas, where consumption is highest. But even there, improvements in quality (avoiding blackouts and brownouts) may more than compensate for higher prices.

Problems of Market Power

Most of the attention of the standard electricity reform model (entailing the separation of transmission, distribution, and system control from competitive generation and wholesale and retail marketing) has focused on issues of vertical market power. Thus considerable effort has been devoted to designing rules that ensure nondiscriminatory access to the transmission network by potential entrants in generation.

But one of the most important second generation issues in restructured electricity markets is the potential exercise of horizontal market power. Even in some large industrial countries that had an opportunity to create several private generators of approximately equal size, the market structure of generation tends to be highly concentrated. Market concentration in generation is even more pronounced in developing and transition economies (table 3.4).

Electricity markets are especially vulnerable to the exercise of market power because they are characterized by highly inelastic demand, significant short-run capacity constraints, and extremely high storage costs. These factors make traditional measures of market concentration somewhat inaccurate indicators of the potential for—or existence of—market power (Borenstein, Bushnell, and Wolak 2000). Moreover, an electricity market may sometimes involve very little market power, and other times suffer from a great deal. The shift between these states occurs when demand rises above the level that generators can supply. In addition, the distinction between these states is more pronounced in markets where small generators have limited production capacity and there is widespread potential for transmission congestion (Borenstein, Bushnell, and Knittel 1999).

These factors make the elasticity of demand for electricity a crucial factor in determining the potential effects of market power. Concentration measures do not incorporate information about the elasticity of

Table 3.4 Market Shares of the Three Largest Generation, Transmission, and Distribution Companies in Various Countries, 2000

(percent)

Country	Generation	Transmission	Distribution
Argentina	30	80	50
Bolivia	70	100	70
Brazil	40	60	40
Chile	67	100	50
Colombia	50	100	60
Czech Republic	71	100	49
El Salvador	83	100	88
Hungary	74	100	65
Indonesia	100	100	100
Malaysia	62	100	97
Pakistan	95	100	100
Panama	82	100	100
Peru	100	100	100
Poland	45	100	21
Thailand	100	100	100

Source: Jamasb (2002).

demand and so might be inaccurate indicators of market power. Indeed, electricity markets that are not overly concentrated could still be vulnerable to the exercise of market power. The dictum of confining regulation to the natural monopoly segments of the electricity industry has often been taken too literally—paying too little attention to the unnatural, or at least undesirable, monopolies in generation.

Thus there is a need for regulatory oversight to ensure that wholesale markets are not manipulated. A number of market power mitigation strategies are available to policymakers. Deciding on a suitable one requires careful analysis of where a country's market power problems are likely to occur. Strategies could include:

- Horizontal deconcentration of generation resources.
- Fixed-price supply contracts that encourage generators to expand rather than withhold supply.
- Investments in transmission capacity, to reduce the ability of large players to strategically congest transmission lines.
- Measures that promote long-term contracts (for example, requiring generators to offer a portion of their expected annual sales in the form of long-term forward contracts).

163

- Measures that make electricity producers and customers more responsive to short-run price fluctuations (Joskow 2000a; Wolak 2001).

Where wholesale markets have worked well in industrial countries, it has largely been because of excess generation capacity, modest demand growth, and the availability of cheap new technologies that allow independent power producers to enter at modest scale, putting downward pressure on prices. California has shown that tight demand, low contract coverage, and a liberalized wholesale market can quickly lead to high prices and bankruptcy (box 3.6). That raises the obvious question of whether competitive markets can work well in developing and transition economies with limited capacity, excess demand, and rapid projected growth in demand. The answer will depend on the existence of credit-

---

Box 3.6   Lessons from California's Experience

WHAT LESSONS DOES CALIFORNIA'S RECENT EXperience offer for electricity reform? First, tight electricity markets—those where the reserve margin falls below 10 percent—are likely to lead to high and volatile prices even if they are fairly competitive (meaning there are four or more generators competing at the margin of supply). As demand tightens relative to supply, inelastic and unresponsive demand means that large price rises have little effect on demand—but each supplier has growing and eventually considerable market power. The large price increase caused by any company withdrawing a small amount of capacity is more than sufficient to compensate for the loss of profit on that volume of sales, making such withdrawals highly profitable in tight markets.

Second, any transition from a vertically integrated utility to an unbundled structure introduces price risks between generators and suppliers that previously cancelled out. High wholesale prices for generators create profits that are matched by the losses of suppliers who must buy at those prices and sell at pre-

determined retail prices (unless purchases are hedged by contracts). Thus the transition to an unbundled industry requires contracts and hedging instruments to insure against unexpected events that can have dramatic effects on spot prices, particularly when suppliers sell at fixed prices. To reduce transitional risks, the U.K. privatization was accompanied by three-year contracts for sales of electricity and purchases of fuel.

Third, in an interconnected system operating under a variety of regulatory and operational jurisdictions, spare capacity is a public good that may not be adequately supplied unless care is taken to ensure that it is adequately remunerated. Fourth, it is even harder for a decentralized market under multiple jurisdictions to ensure adequate reserve capacity with a potentially energy-constrained hydroelectric system, particularly where reservoir storage is limited and annual water volume variations are high. Finally, uncoordinated and injudicious regulatory interventions in such an interconnected system can have perverse local effects and damaging impacts on interregional electricity trade

Source: Wolak, Nordhaus, and Shapiro (2000); Wolak and Nordhaus (2001).

worthy electricity buyers (ideally suppliers) willing to enter long-term contracts that can then finance new investment in generation. Such investment requires satisfactory pricing of transmission and distribution to ensure that power can be delivered from generators to customers.

If capacity is scarce, spot prices can rise to high levels in a competitive market. Provided that franchise customers are adequately covered by contracts—which can be imposed on state-owned generators when they are unbundled—high spot prices signal that entry is attractive and encourage customers to sign contracts that finance entry. High spot prices also ration scarce supply to customers most willing to pay them, and motivate such customers to seek more attractive long-term arrangements. Thus high spot prices provide finance at the margin, where it is needed, without necessarily raising prices for all customers. Markets, contracts, and well-regulated transmission and distribution charges therefore represent a significant improvement over a situation of power interruptions, underpriced electricity, and an inability to finance needed generation.

Nevertheless, although contracts may restrain market power in the short term, it will reappear when contracts are due for renegotiation—assuming that generators are privately owned and cannot be coerced to sign new contracts. Market power depends on the number of competing generators and overall market demand relative to capacity. If demand is inelastic and generators cannot meet it, those generators will have considerable market power. In a competitive wholesale market every generator will be aware of that power and will offer at least marginal output at a high price. Investment will reduce this market power only if there are enough independent generators.[12]

Relying on contracts alone may not be sufficient to address issues of market power, and it is important that a regulator has sufficient authority to implement a variety of market power mitigation mechanisms. In particular, the regulator should be given the authority to collect cost data and technical information from all generators.

Incentive Regulation for Transmission

One of the biggest policy challenges for a restructured electricity industry is developing regulations that encourage transmission owners and operators to operate efficiently and invest in increased capacity.[13]

The success of electricity restructuring, its reliance on competitive generation, and its ability to benefit customers depend on a robust transmission network—indeed, one more robust than during the era of vertically integrated monopolies.

Transmission regulation historically paid too much attention to transmission's direct costs (capital and operating costs) and too little to its indirect costs (congestion, ancillary services, local market power mitigation costs). The direct costs of transmission are a small fraction of the total costs of electricity supply: usually less than 10 percent of the average customer's bill. Any great effort to fine-tune the allowed return on transmission investments is unlikely to be greatly appreciated by customers. More important, regulators will not be doing customers any favor if a small price reduction in the short run destroys a transmission owner's incentives to invest. That is because in the long run, inadequate transmission investment increases congestion costs, market power problems, ancillary service costs, and the frequency and magnitude of energy price spikes.

The indirect costs of transmission include thermal losses, some of the costs of ancillary services, excessive costs and delays in connecting new generators, and the costs of local market power, market power mitigation mechanisms, and out-of-merit dispatch of generating plants to manage congestion and maintain network frequency, stability, and voltage criteria. The magnitude of these indirect costs depends on the incentives that transmission owners and operators have to minimize them through the choices they make about network operations and maintenance as well as when, how, and where they invest in network expansion.

Regulation for competitive wholesale electricity markets should encourage the efficient operation and expansion of the transmission networks on which these markets depend. In addition to providing financial incentives to transmission owners, regulation should lead them to view the pursuit of public interest goals as a business opportunity—not as a burden forced on them. The U.K. electricity sector has nearly a decade of experience with incentive-based mechanisms governing the revenues of the National Grid Company. Of particular interest is the transmission services scheme, which provides financial incentives for the company to reduce transmission uplift costs (the costs associated with thermal losses, ancillary services, and out-of-merit dispatch to manage congestion). The scheme does this by setting an uplift cost target, rewarding the company if it achieves the target, and penalizing the company if it exceeds it. This regulatory scheme combines a conventional price cap mechanism (covering the bulk of direct transmission system charges) with incentive schemes (applicable to transmission uplift costs and reactive power costs) and a separate mechanism governing cost recovery for connecting new generators to the system. Together these mechanisms have encouraged substantial new investment in the network, facilitated generator interconnections, reduced transmission uplift costs, and increased network reliability.

Reform Experiences and Lessons

IN MOST COUNTRIES ELECTRICITY REFORM IS STILL TOO RECENT to assess its effects on social welfare. Only a few countries have time-series data of sufficient length to permit meaningful empirical assessments. Still, several lessons can be gleaned from the experiences of countries that have the longest experience and that have gone the farthest with reforms.

Progress on Reform and Private Participation

Fiscal pressures, exacerbated by poor sector performance, have been the main drivers of electricity reform. Although these programs have generally sought increased private participation, reform strategies and success in attracting private investment have varied considerably across countries and regions. And while electricity restructuring is spreading, many countries have taken few or no steps toward reform.

By 1998, 15 countries had substantially liberalized their electricity systems, and 55 had some liberalization under way or planned—but many of these reformers were mature industrial countries. Of the 81 countries that had not taken any steps toward reform, many were developing and transition economies (Bacon and Besant-Jones 2001). Even in Latin America, the leading region for private participation in electricity, reforms are far from complete. In 2001 the state still controlled significant portions of electricity activities in many Latin American countries (Millan, Lora, and Micco 2001).

Table 3.5 Electricity Reforms by Region, 1998
(percentage of countries where reform has occurred)

Reform	East Asia and Pacific	Europe and Central Asia	Latin America and Caribbean	Middle East and North Africa	South Asia	Sub-Saharan Africa
State utility corporatized	44	63	61	25	40	31
Enabling legislation passed	33	41	78	13	40	15
Independent regulator at work	11	41	83	0	40	8
Private investment	78	33	83	13	100	19
State utility restructured	44	52	72	38	40	8
Generation privatized	22	37	39	13	40	4
Distribution privatized	11	30	44	13	20	4
All reforms taken	41	45	71	17	50	15
Reform score (scale of 1–6)	2.44	2.70	4.28	1.00	3.00	0.88

Source: Bacon and Besant-Jones (2001).

Table 3.5 presents a regional scorecard for electricity reform as of 1998, based on how many of the following steps had been taken by each country in a region:

- The state-owned electric utility has been commercialized and corporatized.
- Parliament has passed an energy law permitting partial or complete sector unbundling or privatization.
- A regulatory body, separate from the utility and the ministry, has started work.
- The private sector has invested in greenfield sites that are being built or operating.
- The state utility has been restructured or unbundled.
- The state utility has been privatized, whether through outright sale, voucher privatization, or a joint venture.

Out of a maximum reform score of 6.00 (where all reform steps were taken), the average score was 4.28 for Latin America and the Caribbean, 3.00 for South Asia, 2.70 for Central and Eastern Europe and Central Asia, 2.44 for East Asia and the Pacific, 1.00 for the Middle East and North Africa, and 0.88 for Sub-Saharan Africa.[14]

The level of private sector interest has been extremely mixed across countries and regions, reflecting differences in reform efforts. Between

Table 3.6 Private Investment in Electricity by Region, 1990–99
(billions of 2001 U.S. dollars)

Region	1990	1991	1992	1993	1994	1995	1996	1997	1998	1999	2000	2001	Total
East Asia and Pacific	0.1	0.5	5	6.2	7.8	7.9	12	15.1	5.6	1.6	3.9	2.9	68.6
Europe and Central Asia	0.1	—	1.1	—	1.4	3.7	3.5	2.3	0.6	0.7	4.6	1.1	19.1
Latin America and Caribbean	0.9	—	2.7	3.6	3.1	6.3	9.8	23.2	14.9	8.1	13.1	3.8	89.5
Middle East and North Africa	—	—	—	—	0.2	—	0.2	1.7	—	1	0.2	0.8	4.1
South Asia	0.2	0.8	0	1.3	2.5	3	4.6	1.7	1.6	2.5	3	0.9	22.1
Sub-Saharan Africa	0.1	—	—	—	0.1	0	0.5	0.5	0.8	0.5	0	0.7	3.2
Total	1.4	1.3	8.8	11.1	15.1	20.9	30.6	44.5	23.5	14.4	24.8	10.2	206.6

Source: World Bank, Private Participation in Infrastructure Project database.

1990 and 2001 developing and transition economies received approximately $207 billion in private investment in power projects (table 3.6). Over 43 percent went to Latin America and the Caribbean and about 33 percent to East Asia and the Pacific—while 2 percent went to the Middle East and North Africa and approximately 1.5 percent to Sub-Saharan Africa.

Private sector participation also varied considerably over the 1990s. Until 1997 electricity reforms and anticipated economic growth spurred enormous private investment in the sector. But investment then plummeted, reflecting financial problems in many countries in Asia, Eastern Europe, and Latin America (see table 3.6). It is difficult to predict whether this reversal will persist (Jamasb 2002).

Reform strategies have also differed significantly across countries and regions. Several Latin American countries (Argentina, Bolivia, Brazil, Chile, Colombia, Peru) restructured and unbundled their electricity systems and created wholesale electricity markets. This approach is also being adopted in Eastern Europe (Bulgaria, Hungary, Romania) and the former Soviet Union (Armenia, Estonia, Georgia, Latvia, Moldova). Other approaches involve:

- Limiting reform to the creation of independent power producers (Croatia, Slovak Republic).
- Providing third party access to a dominant utility (Czech Republic).

- Restructuring with plans for major divestitures (Poland, Russian Federation, Ukraine).

Many Asian countries have adopted variants of the single buyer model and invited private investment in generation through independent power producers, with negligible restructuring and reform (Bangladesh, China, India, Indonesia, Malaysia, Nepal, Pakistan, Philippines, Republic of Korea, Sri Lanka, Thailand, Vietnam). The model of independent power producers selling electricity to state-owned utilities has been adopted by countries in Central America and the Caribbean (Belize, Costa Rica, the Dominican Republic, Guatemala, Honduras, Jamaica, Mexico, Nicaragua, Panama); the Middle East and Africa (Algeria, Côte d'Ivoire, Egypt, Ghana, Jordan, Kenya, Morocco, Senegal, Tanzania); and South Asia. Almost 70 percent of private investment in electricity in Latin America and the Caribbean has been in divestiture projects, while more than 83 percent in East Asia and the Pacific and South Asia has been in greenfield projects (figure 3.7).

During the 1990s, 12 countries accounted for 83 percent of the private electricity investment in developing and transition economies (figure 3.8).[15] Some countries, such as Argentina and El Salvador, have attracted investment to all parts of the electricity industry. But

Figure 3.7   Types of Private Investment in Electricity, by Region, 1990–2001

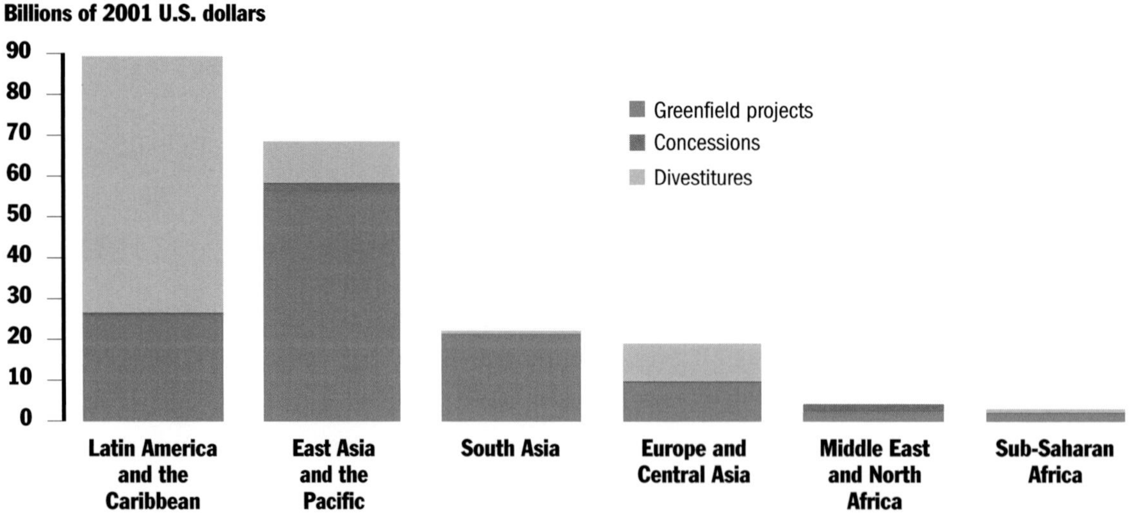

Billions of 2001 U.S. dollars

Legend:
- Greenfield projects
- Concessions
- Divestitures

Source: World Bank, Private Participation in Infrastructure Project database.

Figure 3.8 Top 20 Recipients of Private Investment in Electricity, 1990–99

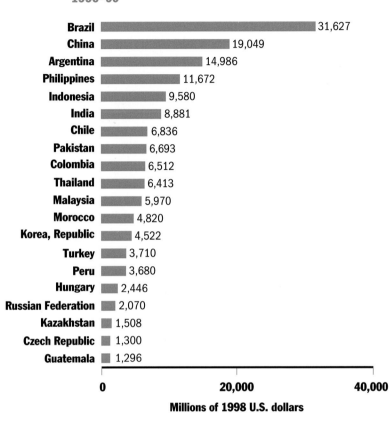

Country	Millions of 1998 U.S. dollars
Brazil	31,627
China	19,049
Argentina	14,986
Philippines	11,672
Indonesia	9,580
India	8,881
Chile	6,836
Pakistan	6,693
Colombia	6,512
Thailand	6,413
Malaysia	5,970
Morocco	4,820
Korea, Republic	4,522
Turkey	3,710
Peru	3,680
Hungary	2,446
Russian Federation	2,070
Kazakhstan	1,508
Czech Republic	1,300
Guatemala	1,296

Source: Jamasb (2002).

private investors have shown little interest in purchasing state enterprises or financing new infrastructure assets in Mexico, Turkey, and Ukraine, to name just a few examples. Indeed, some countries—including Hungary and Venezuela—have had to postpone privatization for lack of investor interest. Despite government efforts to attract private capital, these countries have been unable to reverse long periods of underfunding.

Reform Outcomes

Sector performance has improved dramatically in countries that have implemented electricity reforms such as competitive (vertical and hor-

171

izontal) restructuring, privatization, credible regulation that fosters efficient behavior by market participants, well-designed wholesale markets with enough independent suppliers to facilitate competition, and retail competition, at least for industrial customers (Joskow 2003a).

Achievements of privatization and liberalization in Latin America.

Latin America is not only where the first electricity reforms started—in Chile—but also where the standard reform model has been most influential and far-reaching (Suding 1996; Millan, Lora, and Micco 2001). Reforms in Chile (1982) were followed by reforms in Argentina (1992), Peru (1993), Bolivia and Colombia (1994), Costa Rica, El Salvador, Guatemala, Honduras, Nicaragua, and Panama (1997), and more recently Brazil, Ecuador, Mexico, and Venezuela (Rudnick and Zolezzi 2001). How well have these efforts worked?

The sequencing of Chile's reforms is instructive. The first steps involved creating regulation and restructuring the sector, to give reorganized enterprises experience with the regulation before privatization. To allay investors' fears about expropriation, the reform program paid special attention to clearly defining property rights in primary legislation that would be difficult to change. Privatization proceeded slowly, avoiding some of the risks of underpricing or large transfers to shareholders, while wide share ownership created political support for the new system (Bitran and Serra 1998; Newbery 2001). Progress under Chile's cautious approach showed the feasibility of private involvement in electricity in developing countries and provided valuable lessons for subsequent reforms around the world.

Chile's restructuring sought to achieve vertical and horizontal unbundling, competition in generation, a centralized power pool, open access to the transmission network, yardstick competition in distribution, and for large users freedom to purchase power from any generator or distributor. In 1986 Endesa, the state-owned vertically integrated electric utility, was split into six generating companies, six distribution companies, and two small isolated companies in southern Chile providing generation and distribution (Fischer, Gutierrez, and Serra 2003). Chilectra, which was nationalized in 1970 and controlled distribution in Santiago, was split into three companies: a generation entity and two distribution companies.

By 1991 Chile had 11 generation companies, 21 distribution companies, and 2 integrated companies. But these numbers are misleading in terms of the actual competition that emerged in generation. In 2000, 93 percent of installed generation capacity and 90 percent of generation were controlled by three companies: Endesa, Gener, and Colbun. The largest of these, Endesa, controls 58 percent of generation in Chile's large central region, which accounts for most of the country's electricity demand, and the company has most of the national water rights. Endesa also owns the country's largest distribution company, which provides more than 40 percent of distribution (Arellano 2003). And until 2000, when it was forced to divest, Endesa owned and operated the country's main high-voltage transmission grid.

Thus Chile's post-reform electricity market was not particularly competitive. Market power remains significant in generation. Moreover, Endesa's ownership of the largest distribution company (and until recently the main transmission company) gave it a competitive advantage over third party generators. It could handicap potential competitors through its control of bottleneck transmission facilities, self-dealing, and cross-subsidies. However, the ability of generators to exploit their market power was somewhat constrained by the adoption of a cost-based spot market.

Other reformers learned from Chile's mistakes, and most—such as Argentina, Bolivia, and Peru—restricted cross-ownership. They also sought to reduce horizontal market power, with Argentina limiting ownership of generation assets to 10 percent of the market and Bolivia limiting it to 30 percent. Argentina also developed one of the world's most competitive wholesale electricity sectors. By 1993 it had 70 firms trading in the bulk supply market. And by 1997 it had 40 generation and more than 20 distribution companies (Rudnick 1998).

Overall, privatization and the application of high-powered regulatory mechanisms have led to dramatic efficiency improvements in the electricity industry. In Chile labor productivity in Endesa's generation business increased from 6.3 gigawatt-hours generated per employee in 1991 to 34.3 in 2002. Similarly, labor productivity in Chilectra's distribution business improved from 1.4 gigawatt-hour sales per worker in 1987 to 13.8 in 2002 (Fischer, Gutierrez, and Serra 2003; Pollitt 2003).[16] In Argentina thermal plant unavailability fell from 52 percent in 1992—when most generation capacity was privatized—to 26 percent in 2000 (Rudnick and Zolezzi 2001). The improvements in Chile

Figure 3.9   Post-Privatization Labor Productivity in Electricity Distribution in Argentina, Chile, and the United Kingdom

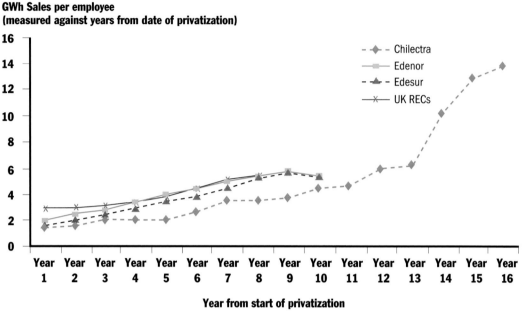

GWh Sales per employee
(measured against years from date of privatization)

Legend: Chilectra, Edenor, Edesur, UK RECs

X-axis: Year from start of privatization (Year 1 through Year 16)

Note: Measured in terms of gigawatt-hours of sales per employee.
Source: Pollitt (2003).

and Argentina are impressive even relative to the performance of privatized U.K. electricity companies (figure 3.9). Brazil's distribution and supply companies also saw labor productivity accelerate after privatization: between 1994 and 2000 the number of employees was halved and productivity jumped 147 percent (Mota 2003).

Reforms have had equally remarkable effects on the quality of supply. In Chile the average time for emergency repair service declined from 5 hours in 1988 to 2 hours in 1994. In addition, power outages due to transmission failures have fallen steadily since privatization (Rudnick and Zolezzi 2001). Energy losses, including theft, have also shrunk, dropping from 21 percent in 1986 to 9 percent in 1996 (Fischer and Serra 2000). Similarly, Argentina's privatized distribution companies have substantially cut their losses (figure 3.10). For example, in 1993 Edenor's losses equaled 26 percent of its distributed electricity; in 2000 its losses were just 10 percent (Edenor 2001). In the greater Buenos Aires area the number of hours of supply lost per year dropped

Figure 3.10 Energy Losses among Argentina's Distribution Companies, at Privatization and in 1999

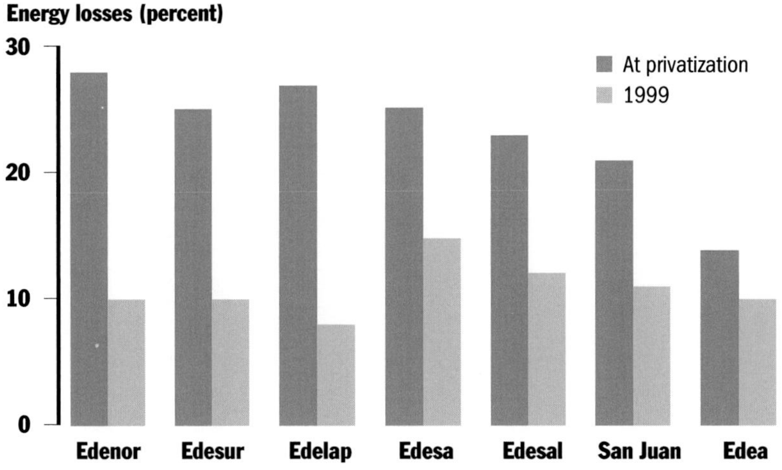

Energy losses (percent)

Source: Feler (2001).

from 16.8 in 1994 to 5.0 in 2001 (CAISE 2002). Technical losses in transmission also fell, from 6 percent in 1992 to 4 percent in 2000.

By relaxing the financial constraints facing state enterprises and establishing stable and fair regulation, electricity reforms have promoted investment and accelerated network expansion. In Argentina installed capacity grew from 13,267 megawatts in 1992 to 22,831 megawatts in 2002—an increase of nearly 5 percent a year. During the same period the route length of transmission lines rose from 16,958 to 22,140 kilometers (2.7 percent a year). Similarly, in Chile's main system installed capacity jumped from 2,713 megawatts in 1982 to 6,737 megawatts in 2002 (4.4 percent a year), while the route length of transmission lines went from 4,310 to 8,555 kilometers during the same period (3.7 percent a year). The impressive expansion of generating capacity in Argentina and Chile was achieved by private operators while keeping prices low (Fischer, Gutierrez, and Serra 2003; Pollitt 2003).

Before reforms, service coverage in Peru increased slowly—from 44 percent in 1986 to just 48 percent in 1992 (figure 3.11). But in the five years after reforms were introduced, service expansion accelerated considerably, and by 1997 coverage was more than 68 percent (Rudnick 1998). Moreover, network expansion has benefited poor people: among the poorest 10 percent of Chilean households the share without an elec-

Figure 3.11   Electricity Coverage in Peru, 1986–97

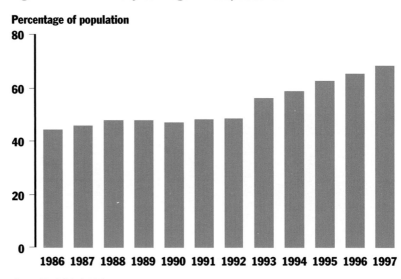

Source: Rudnick (1998).

tricity connection fell from 29 percent in 1988 to 7 percent in 1998. Among the second poorest 10 percent the share without a connection fell from 20 percent to 4 percent (Estache, Foster, and Wodon, 2002). An innovative rural electrification program—which relied on private investment, decentralized decisionmaking, and competition for project financing and implementation—had similarly impressive results. Coverage in rural areas increased from 53 percent in 1992 to 76 percent in 1999, exceeding the original target of 75 percent set for 2000.

Electricity reforms have better aligned prices with underlying costs to reflect resource scarcity, as efficiency requires. In many countries this has meant increasing prices that previously were too low (Joskow 2003a). But in some countries prices have been falling due to the efficient exploitation of regional natural gas networks and new production technologies (mainly combined cycle gas turbines). In Argentina the average monthly price per megawatt-hour in the wholesale electricity market fell from about $45 (with peaks of more than $70) in 1992 to about $15 in 2001. Similarly, in Chile the node price (including energy and capacity charges) of power delivered to Santiago fell from $30.1 per megawatt-hour in October 1982 to $23.3 per megawatt-hour in October 2002 (in October 2002 dollars), and for power delivered to Anto-faqasta fell from 102.4 per megawatt-hour in October 1984 to 24.8 per megawatt-hour in October 2002 (Fischer, Gutierrez, and Serra 2003; Pollitt 2003). Between 1986 and 1996 wholesale prices dropped 37 percent and final prices fell 17 percent.

The low prices of electricity and high rates of investment in Chile and Argentina have been accompanied by strong financial performance among the companies involved. In Chile, Chilectra's average nominal rate of return on equity during 1996–98 was 32 percent. Endesa's return on equity peaked at 16 percent in 1994 (Fischer, Gutierrez, and Serra 2003). In Argentina the financial performance of the largest state-owned company, Servicios Electricos del Gran Buenos Aires, was very poor before privatization. After, the average rate of return on equity in generation was 5.6 percent during 1994–99. The transmission company, Transener, earned a 5.1 percent rate of return on equity in 1998. Among distribution companies, during 1994–2000 Edenor and Edesur earned 8.3 percent and 7.2 percent pretax returns on net assets.

In Argentina, however, a severe macroeconomic crisis and a regulatory regime substantially weakened by political interference have undermined an otherwise spectacular sector transformation. In January 2002 the government scrapped an almost 11-year policy of pegging the peso one-to-one to the U.S. dollar. It also unilaterally modified the contracts under which it had privatized electric and other public utilities in the 1990s. For a year and a half after the devaluation, the regulated prices charged by public utilities remained essentially frozen (in pesos). Yet most of these contracts defined prices in dollars. Moreover, during the same period the cumulative inflation reached 45 percent at the retail level and 120 percent at the wholesale level (Urbiztondo 2003). As a result the revenues of the operating entities plummeted, while their debt and production costs (a significant portion of which were in dollars) soared. The generation, transmission, and distribution companies all posted big losses, and some saw their shareholders' equity get wiped out. Their condition was aggravated by delays in negotiations with the government. In May 2002 Transener suspended interest and principal payments on its $420 million in debt (Platts 2002). In October 2003 the electricity companies issued a grave warning of a power crisis in Argentina (Casey 2003).

The East Asian crisis and deficiencies of the single buyer model.

The East Asian financial crisis called into question the strategy of promoting rapid entry by private investors in an otherwise unchanged sector, with independent power producers selling to state utilities under long-term purchase agreements. Although this strategy seemed appropriate for East Asia given its power shortages in the late 1980s and early 1990s, the subsequent crisis highlighted the risks involved.

Several factors led to the region's power shortages, which were especially severe in Indonesia, Malaysia, the Philippines, and Thailand. These countries had experienced rapid economic growth, and so sharp increases in demand for electricity. But the public spending that fueled much of the growth left governments unable to finance expansions in electricity and other infrastructure. For example, during 1990–97 Thailand's electricity consumption rose 14 percent a year, but its installed capacity grew just 8 percent a year. In 1992 excess demand in the Philippines equaled 48 percent of system capacity, and in Malaysia the reserve margin fell to 19 percent, far below the 30–40 percent desired for rapidly industrializing economies. In 1990 it was estimated that Indonesia needed $20 billion to install 12 gigawatts of additional capacity by 2000—and a revised forecast in 1993 called for an additional 12 gigawatts within five years. Similarly, analysis in 1993 concluded that more than $40 billion was needed to meet Malaysia's peak demand, which was expected to skyrocket from 4.5 gigawatts in 1992 to 35.4 gigawatts in 2020 (Henisz and Zelner 2001).

Seeking relief from these supply shortages, these and other East Asian countries encouraged the entry of independent power producers by offering them long-term purchase agreements with state-owned, single buyer utilities. The agreements typically involved payments in dollars and required government guarantees (because default proceedings against state utilities are usually not allowed). This strategy was successful. Between 1990 and 1997 East Asia attracted $54.6 billion in private investment in electricity—more than 40 percent of the total for developing and transition economies. The other major recipient, Latin America, received $49.6 during this period (see table 3.6).

The financial crisis that started in East Asia in 1997 caused dramatic damage to the region's exchange rates, GDP growth rates, and electricity demand. The collapse in currencies doubled the cost of electricity under power purchase agreements—an increase that state-owned power companies were reluctant to pass on to customers. In the Philippines the foreign debt of the national power corporation rose to more than 20 percent of national debt (World Bank 1999a). Lower demand for electricity created strong pressures to renege on, delay, or renegotiate power purchase agreements, causing foreign investors to lose confidence.

It became painfully clear that this form of private investment in power generation is equivalent to expensive foreign debt. The terms of a power purchase agreement may conceal the true cost of the debt, but interest rates are inevitably high because of the source of finance and the risk involved. Even in stable markets private investors borrow at higher interest rates than institutions like the World Bank, and in corrupt economies foreign investors consider lending to state enterprises especially risky. During the crisis some East Asian governments tried to repudiate debts incurred by previous administrations, often claiming that the deals were corrupt, while others had to reschedule loans to avoid default. In the end this type of private involvement did not lead to much sector restructuring or address the problem of non-cost-reflective tariffs. If anything, the currency crisis worsened the problem of inadequate tariffs (Newbery 2001).

Lessons

During the 1990s many industrial, developing, and transition economies implemented significant institutional reforms in their electricity sectors. Although many of these efforts are still under way, experiences to date offer important insights on the reform process:

- When properly designed and implemented, a combination of institutional reforms—vertical and horizontal restructuring, privatization, and effective regulation—can significantly improve operating performance. In reformed electricity systems, labor productivity has increased in generation and distribution, in some countries dramatically. In addition, technical and nontechnical losses have been reduced and service quality has improved.
- Most reforms have attracted considerable private investment—one of the main goals of restructuring—in generation and distribution (though less in transmission). Thus a long history of underinvestment is being reversed in reforming countries.
- In several countries (such as in Latin America) electricity prices have fallen as wholesale markets have developed and entry by new generators has expanded supplies and increased competition.

- Retail prices have become more closely aligned with underlying costs, and cross-subsidies have been reduced and in some countries eliminated (Joskow 2003a).
- Substantial risks are created for the public interest when governments promote rapid investment in an unreformed electricity sector by offering independent power producers long-term power purchase agreements with state-owned, single buyer utilities.
- Many if not most developing and transition economies lack some of the initial conditions required to implement competitive wholesale markets, including a large number of independent generating companies, active participation by final consumers in the wholesale market, adequate transmission capacity, and a credible regulatory mechanism. Thus the introduction of unregulated bid-based spot markets could lead to significant problems in these countries. A less risky strategy might be to rely on marginal cost bidding systems.

Notes

1. This chapter draws heavily on Newbery (2001).

2. It is widely accepted that there must be a single network operator responsible for overseeing the operations of a control area—coordinating generator schedules, balancing loads in real time, acquiring ancillary support services to ensure network reliability, and coordinating with neighboring control areas (Joskow 2000a). Thus the system control function has attributes of a natural monopoly.

3. An important distinction between developing and transition economies is that the latter have achieved much higher service coverage in the electricity sector.

4. These are plants that use once-through boilers with operating pressures above 22.1 megapascals—the critical pressure point for water and steam.

5. When assets of a regulated utility are not used due to changes in economic conditions (such as the introduction of competition) or technology, they are considered stranded. Similarly, stranded costs are prudent costs incurred by a utility that may not be recoverable under competition or deregulation.

6. Simple-cycle combustion turbines are now being built with heat rates of 10,000 BTUs per kilowatt-hour, and this will fall to perhaps 9,500 BTUs in

the next cycle of technologies. This is as efficient as steam-turbine plants built in the 1970s, and far more efficient than combustion turbines built then.

7. Distributed generation is the integrated or stand-alone use of small, modular electric generation facilities close to the point of consumption. It encompasses many technologies that vary by size, application, and efficiency (see figure 3.3). Several important regulatory issues are associated with distributed generation. First, for distributed generation connected to the power grid (most customers will want to retain such a connection to guard against emergencies), interconnection terms and conditions will require regulatory oversight. Distribution utilities will demand a high price for providing such backup access. In addition, if distributive generators are permitted to sell all or some of their power into the grid, there will be a need for regulatory protocols to support these transactions. Second, if cross-subsidies are embedded in user prices, there is a question of whether customers who bypass these regulatory burdens by leaving the system should be required to contribute to these costs. Otherwise the remaining captive customers of local distribution companies will be saddled with an even larger share of these regulatory burdens. Third, significant regulatory issues also arise when distributed generation is not connected to the grid—for example, in terms of activities that require regulatory oversight and those that should be fully deregulated.

8. This is not true for all small-scale technologies. Combined heat and power technologies achieve much higher efficiencies than do microturbines and are rapidly becoming economical—even at the level of individual households. In addition, fuel cell technologies have a good chance of achieving efficiencies in the mid- to upper 40s by 2010.

9. Retail competition may not involve all customers. It may be limited to industrial customers, with residential consumers served by distribution companies that buy in a competitive wholesale market, or (as in the United Kingdom) a transition over time of competition from the largest to smallest customers.

10. It is not only the transmission company that can exercise the role of single buyer. It can also be assumed by load-serving entities. For example, distribution companies could create an entity to buy power on their behalf. Variants of this model existed for many years in the United States in the form of "joint action agencies" for municipal distribution systems.

11. This is the case when the entity responsible for real-time dispatch is bundled with the active single buyer.

12. If generators have apparent market power, there will be a strong temptation to choose the single buyer model to countervail against it.

13. This section is based on Joskow (1999).

14. These types of evaluations of institutional arrangements can be misleading. For example, France would score low based on these criteria, but its electricity system performs very well. For a more accurate evaluation these reform scores should be augmented by data on physical and economic performance.

15. For more accurate regional comparisons, it would be necessary to distinguish between investments in new capital facilities and sales revenue from the divestiture of existing capital facilities.

16. The improvements in labor productivity accelerated after the takeover of the formerly domestically controlled companies by foreign companies. Between 1999 and 2002 the number of employees in Chile's electricity system fell from 8,264 to 5,706.

CHAPTER FOUR

Managing Private Participation in Transportation

TRANSPORTATION IS ESSENTIAL TO A MODERN economy and a smoothly functioning society. Enormous changes in the world economy—including the dramatic increase in international flows of goods and services (globalization)—demand efficient transportation services. Indeed, recent findings suggest that productivity increases in transportation are the most important determinant of structural changes in the world economy (ECMT 2003). The competition generated by globalization has increasingly led users to demand faster, more reliable, more flexible transportation services. Thus increased demand, structural economic change, and new industrial logistics have placed enormous pressure on transportation systems.

National growth and international competitiveness are partly determined by how domestic transportation systems respond to these challenges.[1] For example, in the 1970s and 1980s national inventories of raw materials for manufacturing were two to three times larger (relative to GDP) in developing and transition economies than in the United States—in large part because of weak transportation services. These large inventories undermined these countries' competitiveness (Guasch and Kogan 2003).

Around the world, transportation has been among the most extensively regulated sectors. Vertical relationships, financial structure and accounting methods, and entry, operating, pricing, and exit rules have all been subject to government control. But in recent years limits on competition and ownership in this sector have been considered inimical to consumer and industry interests. After airlines, trucking, and freight railroads were deregulated in the United States in the late 1970s and early 1980s, many other industrial countries reviewed their transportation policies and liberalized their transportation systems (Gómez-Ibáñez and Meyer 1993; Oster and Strong 2000). Many developing and transition economies, facing huge fiscal pressures and poorly performing state enterprises, have also introduced wide-ranging policy reforms and realigned private and public roles in transportation (Estache and de Rus 2000; Estache 2001).

This chapter focuses on railroads and ports—two areas where the private sector has started to play a large role in many developing and transition economies. It identifies characteristics of these modes that have determined forms of private participation, and examines the implications that these characteristics and forms have for regulation.

Railroads: Restructuring Regulation for the Public Interest

SINCE THE EARLY 1950S THE RAILROAD INDUSTRY HAS EXPERIenced plummeting performance—financially and operationally—in both industrial and developing countries. In today's transition economies this decline was delayed by an emphasis on heavy industry and by policies that gave railroads favored status. But once central planning was abandoned, railroads experienced an even sharper drop in performance in these economies (figure 4.1; Thompson 2003).

Several factors have contributed to this worsening performance: growing competition from more advanced transport modes, monolithic industry structures and rigid management structures unresponsive to customer needs and market opportunities, excessive political interference, overstaffing, outdated technology, and regulation poorly suited to promoting the public interest. Most countries' rail networks were determined by the technologies and the industry and consumer locations of the 19th century. When these changed, large parts of many rail networks became almost obsolete. In passenger markets, advances in airplanes and automobiles made railroads much less competitive. In freight, the dominance of railroads was undermined by a shift away from bulk commodities toward high-value products, increasing the importance of quality and timely delivery—not characteristics common to traditional rail services.

Figure 4.1   Railroad Freight in Transition Countries, 1988–2001

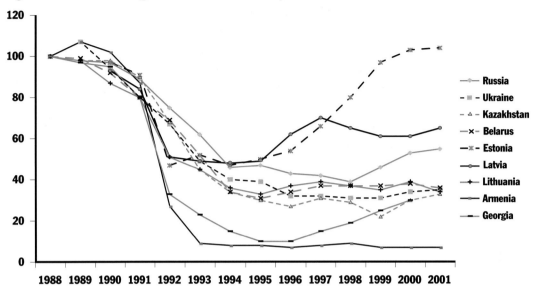

Source: von Hirschhausen and Meinhart (2001).

The railroad industry has had a hard time adjusting to these changes in its market environment. Misguided regulation has exacerbated the industry's problems, reducing its incentives and ability to respond to competition from other transport modes. For example, price restrictions and cross-subsidies from freight to passenger transport accelerated rail's loss of freight market share to trucking. In addition, the combination of public ownership and exclusive monopoly dulled incentives to control costs. Governments often imposed investment programs that did not reflect railroads' true priorities (World Bank 1994a), with more attention given to achieving physical targets than sound economic and financial planning.

In developing and transition economies most rail operations have also had extraordinarily high levels of excess employment. Labor costs have typically exceeded 50 percent of revenues, and have often been well above 100 percent. (China, at less than 20 percent, is a notable exception.) Chronic revenue shortfalls have impaired the industry's ability to maintain, replace, and modernize its equipment and operations. As a result railroad productivity has been extremely low relative to technological opportunities.

Thus government ownership and regulation have been largely responsible for the railroad industry's mediocre service, poor financial condition, deteriorating assets, and delays in introducing cost-saving innovations, as well as for misallocations of freight traffic between competing transport modes.

The industry's first signs of serious financial distress appeared in the United States, where tight regulation of the country's privately owned railroads largely ignored emerging competition between transport modes. In the early 1970s the bankruptcies of several major railroads threatened service in important parts of the country. These developments were followed by an enormous financial disaster in Japan. By the time the Japan National Railway was restructured and privatized in 1987, it had accumulated more than $300 billion in debt. Between the late 1950s and early 1990s British Railways also experienced a series of crises that made it financially unstable. In addition, rail systems in continental Europe lost substantial market shares in freight and passenger traffic.[2] These systems also suffered serious financial damage due to high labor costs—ranging from 80 percent of revenue to more than 200 percent (Kopicki and Thompson 1995; CEC 1996; Thompson 2003).

By the early 1990s railways in Latin America, Sub-Saharan Africa, and other developing regions were undergoing similar financial collapse, compounded by physical shortcomings. In many developing and transition economies railway traffic has been limited by poorly maintained track and shortages of trains. For example, in the early 1990s more than 40 percent of Brazil's track was in bad condition, and 35 percent of trains were immobilized at any given time, typically awaiting parts or funds for repairs (World Bank 1994a).

Railroad subsidies and losses have exacerbated fiscal crises in many developing and transition economies. Reductions in passenger traffic caused Poland's railroad to lose $300 million in 1998. Since 1999 the Bulgarian government's contribution to the rail system has hovered around 8 percent of GDP (World Bank 2001a). Uganda's Railways Corporation has consistently been among the three most heavily subsidized public enterprises (PPIAF 2001). And in the early 1990s Brazil's railroad received more than $250 million a year in public support (Estache, Gonzalez, and Trujillo 2002).

These problems led a wide range of countries to reassess policies toward railroads. Though reforms vary, common elements include:

- Rebalancing the supply roles of the private and public sectors.

- Adjusting the industry's vertical and horizontal structures.
- Modifying railroad regulation and giving railroads more pricing and structural flexibility.
- Increasing transparency in the provision and use of public subsidies.

U.S. reforms sought to free the railroad industry from regulatory constraints that crippled its performance and to replace regulation with market forces. In 1980 the Staggers Act substantially deregulated the industry, giving railroads pricing flexibility and allowing them to abandon unproductive and redundant track and other facilities. A program to restructure Japanese National Railways was launched in 1986, creating nine new enterprises: six vertically integrated passenger railways, a freight operator, an infrastructure holding company for part of the track, and a settlement corporation. This privatization lasted through the late 1990s.

In the early 1990s the United Kingdom restructured British Railways vertically and horizontally. The government subsequently privatized six freight businesses and all rail infrastructure and competitively awarded 25 franchises for passenger traffic. And during the 1990s most rail systems in Latin America and several in Africa moved from state ownership to private concessions (Thompson 2003).

Economic Characteristics of Railroads

The same economic characteristics that make the rail industry a natural target for government intervention also make it difficult to restructure and regulate in the public interest. Separating infrastructure ownership from train operations and marketing—a structural option that has attracted considerable attention in recent years—can generate significant benefits of competition. But it also makes it harder to coordinate essential services. Thus unbundling will likely be costly (Gómez-Ibáñez 1999). Moreover, old regulatory systems failed to solve the main regulatory problem facing railroads and some other network utilities (such as telecommunications and electricity): the mix of competition and monopoly in supply (Baumol and Willig 1987).

Structure of costs. The railroad industry's output is inherently multidimensional: at different times, different firms produce different services of different quality for different users at different origins and destinations. Thus the mix of output and shipment characteristics significantly influences a firm's costs. For example, railroads specialized in transporting coal incur much different costs than railroads specialized in moving passengers or manufactured commodities.

Moreover, rail activities involve significant economies of scale, scope, and density (Braeutigam 1999). Fixed costs are large because of the infrastructure—track, stations, and the like—that must be in place for trains to run.[3] Duplicating this infrastructure is inefficient, so the physical network has costs akin to a natural monopoly. And because rail infrastructure has little value for other purposes, its fixed costs are largely sunk—creating significant entry barriers.

The multiproduct nature of railroads implies that the same facilities, equipment, and labor are often used to produce different services. For example, passengers and freight are transported on the same track. In the movement of freight, low-value commodities and high-value manufactured goods often share the same services and facilities. These shared costs confer economies of scope on carriers offering a multiplicity of transportation services: a carrier that provides an array of services can do so at lower cost than a set of carriers producing each service separately. The multiproduct nature of railroads also implies that a large portion of rail costs cannot necessarily be attributed to a particular service at a particular point in time. Rather, a significant portion of costs are incurred on behalf of several activities and do not vary with the amount of the service provided.

The structure of railroad costs has significant implications for the competitive organization and behavior of rail markets. Indivisibilities in rail technology lead to increasing returns to scale and limit the number of competitors. As a result service prices are likely to exceed marginal costs. In addition, the multiproduct nature of rail operations makes it difficult to allocate costs and can complicate pricing policy and inhibit the achievement of financial viability.

When it comes to economies of scale in railroads, it is important to distinguish between economies of density (which result in less than proportionate increases in cost as more traffic is run over an existing set of track) and economies of system size (which result in less than proportionate increases in cost as more traffic is run over an enlarged track). Given the paucity of new track construction, economies of density are the more relevant measure (Pittman 2003).

Sources of competition.   High sunk costs and pervasive economies of scale and scope may suggest that the railroad industry is not structurally competitive or contestable. But while scale economies go hand in hand with natural monopoly, a railroad may or may not have the price-setting discretion of a textbook monopolist—and rail services are far more contestable than these impediments to entry suggest.

Although the provision of a rail network has natural monopoly characteristics, the operation of services on that network may be more consistent with active and potential competition. Providing services requires trains, crews, support facilities, and rights of way. Although hiring crews and buying or leasing rolling stock involve some sunk costs, they are small relative to those of establishing network infrastructure. And most of the costs of trains can easily be recovered by rolling them to other markets (Kessides and Willig 1995).

Competition in railroads can come from a variety of sources and forms (Baumol and Willig 1987). Rival products and sources of supply—including trucks, barges, buses, airplanes, pipelines, and even alternative rail routes—will likely impose competitive restraints on many rail activities. In freight, for example, coal shipped by rail competes with oil and natural gas shipped by pipeline. Thus competition from petroleum products can limit the prices that railroads can charge for transporting coal.

The relative costs of truck and rail in a given market depend on the distance covered and the types of commodities shipped. Rail has a cost advantage in long-distance shipments of bulk commodities because transit times are less of a concern. Trucking has an advantage in small, short-distance, time-sensitive shipments. Because of its flexibility, trucking is ideally suited for just-in-time movement of high-value-added manufactured goods. Despite recent technological improvements that have enhanced productivity and service, railroads still have a hard time serving just-in-time—and especially exactly-on-time—shipment needs.

Where navigable waterways exist, rail faces fierce competition from barges in moving bulk commodities. In the Unites States, for example, shipping wheat from Blackfoot, Idaho, to Portland, Oregon, costs about $0.73 a bushel ($26.83 a metric ton) for loads of fewer than 20 rail cars. Using a barge to ship wheat from Lewiston, Idaho, to Portland costs about $0.23 cents a bushel ($8.45 a metric ton; Capital Press 2003).

When transporting petroleum products, rail faces strong competition from pipelines—considered the most energy-efficient, cost-effective mode. Pipelines also minimize the environmental risks posed by the transportation of petroleum products: oil spills, gaseous emissions, and effluent leaks are negligible relative to other transport modes. In Brazil, for example, new pipelines have cut into railroad pricing power for petroleum transportation (Estache, Goldstein, and Pittman 2001).

Though it is generally not practical or economical to duplicate existing rail infrastructure, there are still opportunities for direct competition in rail, especially among large shippers. A large industrial plant can use:

- Direct services from two railroads with tracks that go directly into the industrial site.
- Competitive services from two railroads with a reciprocal switching agreement—that is, the railroads switch cars for each other at a given junction.
- Competitive services from two railroads through a terminal switching railroad that they own jointly and that switches cars for either in its junction.

These forms of intramodal competition are arguably the most intense. But there are also other, more subtle forms. A shipper directly served by just one rail carrier may benefit from the geographic proximity of a competing railroad: the shipper could ship its traffic to this other railroad by truck or by building a spur line. Similarly, a shipper with production facilities in different locations served by different railroads could generate competition between those carriers by adjusting production levels in its plants in response to the rail rates charged to each plant.

Moreover, a shipper deciding where to locate a plant could induce railroads to compete for its future business. Each railroad could offer favorable long-term contract rates to attract the shipper to locate on its own line. Finally, shippers could stimulate competition among rail carriers through product or geographic competition. An industrial plant (such as a power plant) captive to a railroad in a particular market (such as coal) may be able to obtain the same product, or use a substitute, shipped from a different location by a different carrier—at least up to a junction near the plant (Grimm and Winston 2000). But in reality, economic and other constraints often hold shippers captive to limited competition in the rail industry (box 4.1).

Box 4.1   Limited Rail Options Result in Captive Shippers

RESOURCE COMMODITIES—GRAINS AND OTHER agricultural products, minerals, fertilizers, coal, potash, sulfur, ores and concentrates, chemicals, forest products, petroleum products—are typically transported in large shipments over long distances, especially in large countries such as Brazil, China, India, Poland, and the Russian Federation, and in Africa. These commodities have low values relative to manufactured goods. The combination of large volumes, long distance, and low values often makes these commodities captive to the railroad industry, especially when roads are in bad shape.

About two-thirds of the traffic on Poland's state railway consists of hard coal, metals, ores, brown coal, and coke. Russia's railroads carry more than 90 percent of the country's shipments of coal, ore, ferrous metals, and cement, 80 percent of chemical and mineral fertilizers, and 70 percent of construction materials. Although competition from road transport is growing for containers, perishables, and high-value goods, it is largely limited to the Far East and to areas west of the Urals, where highways are well developed. Thus most Russian industrial customers continue to depend on railways for shipping. The situation is similar for several Brazilian mining companies, which lack meaningful competitive alternatives.

Commodity shippers are often captive not just to rail but also to a single carrier. Many chemical plants, for example, rely on one railroad for freight transportation. Similarly, coal mines (especially in remote areas) have few choices. Electric utilities also tend to be served by a single rail carrier. Such captive shippers must accept the rates and service levels offered by dominant rail carriers—and various analyses indicate that captive shippers pay much higher freight rates than noncaptive ones (by some estimates, more than 20 percent higher in the United States).

Source: Ordover and Pittman (1994); Campos (2002); Grimm and Winston (2000).

Regulatory Issues

The basic premises of railroad regulation, established many decades ago under entirely different market conditions, have become obsolete. This regulation was guided by the view that railroads held a monopoly (or near monopoly) on long-distance land transport—a condition that disappeared long ago, if it ever existed. Today competition for railroad traffic can be fierce. Where railroads do not dominate markets, they should be granted freedom in pricing. Where intramodal, intermodal, geographic, and product competition is weak or nonexistent, market forces may fail to prevent excessive prices. The resulting monopoly power is the basic justification for regulating rail rates and earnings and is the basic task for regulators.

Two main principles should guide regulatory reform in railroads (Baumol and Willig 1987). First, the competitive market should serve as the model for regulation. Market forces will contain prices for most rail services in most countries. Regulatory restraints should be imposed or maintained only if market forces are insufficient to enforce competitive behavior.

Second, regulatory impediments to adequate revenues should be eliminated. This should mean not a guarantee of profitability, but an opportunity to generate competitive earnings. Indeed, in a regime of deregulation without general subsidies, a key element in protecting the public interest is eliminating regulation that interferes with the rail networks financial viability. Thus regulatory reform should give railroads substantial flexibility in pricing and industry structure.

The regulatory issues identified below—cost allocation, demand-based differential pricing, regulatory protection for captive shippers, and access to rail infrastructure—cut across sectors, meaning they also arise in electricity, telecommunications, ports, and (to a lesser extent) water. Chapter 6 discusses these issues in more detail and suggests responses consistent with the features of developing and transition economies and their infrastructure sectors.

Cost allocation. The large fixed and common costs in the railroad industry create challenges for regulation. Perhaps the most troubling is that it is impossible to allocate these costs in a mechanical fashion based on economic logic (Baumol, Koehn, and Willig 1990). Historically, regulators have set rail tariffs using accounting cost allocation rules, the most common being the fully distributed cost methodology. Under this method regulators allocate a railroad's shared production costs to individual services in terms of some common basis of use, such as gross ton-kilometers (Braeutigam 1980).

Fully distributed cost pricing has several defects. The most serious one is that it does not necessarily measure marginal cost responsibility in a causal sense—taking into account how much costs would increase if more of a particular service were used (Kahn 1988). A further defect is this approach's neglect of demand data. Accounting and arbitrary cost allocation rules can undermine the efficient use of transport resources, cause misallocations of traffic among competing modes, and seriously damage the financial viability of railroads, as the U.S. experience indicates.

Demand-based differential pricing. Fully distributed cost pricing often overassigns or underassigns a rail carrier's unattributable fixed and common costs to certain services and almost invariably produces inconsistencies with patterns of shipper demands. If a carrier were forced to apply fully distributed cost pricing to all its traffic, some prices would be too high and the carrier would lose traffic to other modes (such as trucking) from which it is facing strong competition. The remaining captive shippers would then be saddled with a larger portion of the carrier's costs because they would no longer share those costs with the lost traffic. But other prices would be too low, leading the railroad to receive less than the optimal contribution from those services. Thus, in the multiproduct railroad industry, pricing individual services on the basis of accounting cost allocation rules that neglect demand characteristics is contrary to the interests of both carriers and shippers.

Demand-based differential (Ramsey) pricing overcomes this problem by apportioning all of a rail carrier's unattributable fixed and common costs among its services based on their demand characteristics. Each service is priced at a markup over marginal cost that is inversely related to the elasticity of demand for that service. Under Ramsey pricing it is the shortfall between total costs and the revenues that would accrue from pricing each service at its marginal cost that is apportioned on the basis of demand (Kessides and Willig 1995). Differential prices benefit all shippers, because lower prices for some shippers generate revenue that otherwise would have to be raised from those with the strongest demand for rail transportation.

Regulatory protection for captive shippers. Long-term contracts for rail service offer shippers protection from the exploitation of future captivity by a single railroad, particularly if such contracts can be negotiated when shippers are making their investment and location decisions. The costs of such decisions are often sunk, making it difficult for shippers to make competitive adjustments when facing higher rail rates. Thus regulations should focus on shippers caught in the transition to a privatized, less regulated rail system. This type of situation reveals the conflict between rate protection for shippers and rate flexibility for railroads, and highlights the need for regulatory intervention to strike the proper balance.

A critical issue for efficiency is the criterion used to set rate ceilings for captive shippers—that is, where the railroad has market domi-

> Railroads would lose customers if they had to charge everyone the same markup over variable costs

> To recover costs, railroads must price in line with the varying demands for rail service

nance. Although rate ceilings derived from fully distributed costs are inimical to the public interest, economically rational ceilings can be obtained from stand-alone costs. These are the costs of serving any captive shipper or group of shippers that benefit from sharing joint and common costs as if the shipper or group were isolated from the railroad's other customers (see endnote 4 of executive summary). The stand-alone cost method finds the theoretically maximum rate that a railroad could levy on shippers without losing its traffic to a hypothetical competing service offered by a hypothetical entrant facing no entry barriers or by a shipper providing the service itself.

The stand-alone cost test does not apply—and cannot be made to apply without disastrous consequences—if railroads are not allowed to abandon unremunerative facilities or services. If that freedom is denied, a railroad cannot earn adequate revenues from its potentially remunerative activities. For that reason it is unwise for public policy to limit the freedom of railroads to abandon uneconomic services unless public funds are provided to defray the costs of those services.

Access to rail infrastructure. Rail infrastructure remains a natural monopoly, regardless of the option adopted for the industry's structure. In most countries any operator seeking to run rail services between two points has the choice of only a single provider of infrastructure. Thus regulations are needed to govern the terms and conditions of access to bottleneck rail facilities (Nash and Toner 1998). The access problem is especially vexing if several railroad firms compete in the sale of final services and one is the monopoly owner of the track and other essential infrastructure facilities (competitive access option). In a variety of market settings the holder of bottleneck rail facilities has incentives to behave anticompetitively and create handicaps for its rivals.

Restructuring the Railroad Industry

For much of the 20th century most railroads in developing and transition economies were run by monolithic state-owned organization that controlled all facilities, operations, and administration and determined what services to provide to generally captive markets. But the conditions that generated this model no longer exist in most countries, forcing governments to consider fundamental restructuring of the railroad industry and its relationship with the state. Such restructuring has sought to introduce more innovative and efficient management, reduce railway deficits and public subsidies, increase competition with other transport modes, and make railroads more responsive to the needs of emerging private enterprises (Thompson 2003).

Options for vertical restructuring.   Three options are available for the vertical structuring of railways, addressing the relationships between a railway and other transportation entities (rail and other), markets served, and functions performed—including ownership, maintenance and improvement of fixed facilities, control of operations such as dispatching and freight classification, train movement, equipment provision and maintenance, marketing, and financial control and accountability. Determining which option is best is a complex policy decision.

The first option is often the status quo: a monolithic, integrated entity that owns and operates all railway facilities and vehicles. In theory this approach should maximize production efficiency by exploiting the economies of scale and scope of rail operations. But in practice the monolithic entity—lacking financial incentives and disaggregated information on profitability—is at best production oriented and unresponsive to demand, with a hierarchical (often bloated) organizational architecture.

Some Latin American and African countries are developing spatially separated but vertically integrated private railway companies (table 4.1). Competition comes primarily from road (or sometimes waterway) haulage. For example, most nonurban rail concessions in Latin America and Africa (including those in Cameroon, Côte d'Ivoire and Burkina Faso, and Gabon and the one being prepared in Senegal and Mali) are vertically integrated, predominantly freight carriers competing with deregulated road freight carriers.

Under the second option for vertical restructuring, competitive access, competing railway companies have exclusive control over some track and exchange access rights with other companies. Forms of competitive access include conferrals of track rights and joint terminal agreements, where a railway obtains the right to use the tracks or freight handling facilities of another railway at a particular location or along a particular route.

Table 4.1   Market Structure and Ownership Options in Railroads, Various Countries, 2001

	Private involvement		
	Public ownership	Partnerships: concessions or franchises awarded	Private ownership
Monolithic	China, Russia, and India (ministries), MAV, SRT, MZ, others (SOEs)	Argentina (13), Brazil (9), Mexico (5), Peru (3), Guatemala, Bolivia (2), Panama, Côte d'Ivoire/Burkina Faso, Cameroon, Congo (Brazzaville), Malawi, Madagascar, Jordan	New Zealand, Ferronor (Chile), CVRD (Brazil), A&B (Chile)
Competitive access	Amtrak, VI, Japan Freight, CN	Mexico City suburban, CONCOR (India)	U.S. Class I, CN, and CP East-West-Central, Japan Railways
Vertical separation	E.U. and Chile Passenger, Banverket	Swedish suburban, FEPASA (Chile), LHS line (Poland)	U.K. franchises and EWS, Polish and Romanian freight

(Left margin label: Structural change)

Note: MAV (Hungarian State Railways), SRT (State Railways of Thailand), MZ (Macedonian Railways), CN (Canadian National), E.U. (European Union), CP (Canadian Pacific), East-West-Central Japan Railways (East Japan Railways, West Japan Railways, and Central Japan Railways), EWS (England Wales and Scotland).

Source: Thompson (2001a).

Another arrangement may involve handing off traffic between railroad entities (interlining). U.S. railroads do a great deal of largely unregulated interlining, engage in regulated reciprocal switching, and exercise track rights as a result of both free negotiations and regulatory mandates (mostly achieved in settlements of disputes over rail mergers).

With the third option, vertical separation, the ownership of track and other fixed facilities is separated from other rail functions, with the track held by government, a consortium of operators, or a regulated private entity. A recent example is a joint terminal company in Mexico created to give the three main freight concessionaires nondiscriminatory access to Mexico City and ensure access to the track by future operators carrying suburban passengers (Campos and Jimenez 2003).

Vertical separation or competitive access?   Vertically separating the ownership of track and trains may permit active or potential competition among rail operators (Thompson 1997). Under this option operators need not be subject to detailed regulatory scrutiny, as competition creates strong incentives to be efficient and responsive to the needs of shippers and a growing entrepreneurial economy. But separation can create coordination problems, undermine economies of scope, and impose other unnecessary transaction costs.

A rail operator cannot offer reliable high-speed passenger service, for example, unless track is well maintained and made available by the infrastructure monopolist. In a vertically integrated railroad, track and rail operations are typically overseen by different departments. But because these departments are parts of the same corporate entity, they coordinate their actions to ensure consistency with corporate strategies and goals. Although their interests might not be perfectly harmonized, they are free of narrowly opportunistic behavior.

In a vertically unbundled system, on the other hand, coordination must be achieved through contracts between separate firms (Gómez-Ibáñez 1999). Though such firms might have a shared interest in the success of passenger or other services, they will likely have conflicting views on how to split the underlying investment costs and risks. Serious contractual and investment coordination issues arose, for example, in Britain's vertically unbundled rail system. The track owner (Railtrack) and operating companies often did not agree on the timing of needed track repairs. Coordination failures significantly increased broken rails, with obvious safety consequences (Yvrande 2000; Martin 2002). Such problems could be quite serious in many developing and transition economies, where significant new investments are required to rehabilitate track and other fixed rail facilities.

Powerful competition requires that entering operators believe they can avoid heavy sunk investments in rolling stock and specialized facilities. Trains may be an example of capital on wheels—as long as they can be transported to different points for productive use at reasonable costs. While this is feasible for services provided in the middle of a landmass with an extensive rail network, it may not be for specialized cars or an isolated market. In addition, the entering operator may not have yard, loading, maintenance, and other facilities. For these to be equally available to the entering and the incumbent operators, the infrastructure entity will have to have made the needed investments. But the more the infrastructure entity has to supply entrepreneurship and risk-taking investment, the less is gained from the separation.

Moreover, there is evidence that rail operations are characterized by significant economies of density (Ivaldi and McCullough 2001). This implies that firms offering rail services are likely to enjoy large market shares on specific routes. In that case vertical separation will generate limited competition.

The main alternative to vertical separation, competitive access, differs most clearly in allowing integrated operations by the rail entity. Competitive access may require that the integrated carrier make its facilities available to other entities on a fair and equal basis. But if the integrated carrier has strong incentives to keep out other entities, it is unclear how effective such equal access mandates will be (see chapter 1).

If regulation permits an integrated carrier to charge higher prices to captive shippers when it does more business, it would have incentives to exclude other participants. (This effect arises under rate of return regulation.) Similarly, if regulation limits the amount an integrated carrier can earn from the access it provides to another entity, it has incentives to undermine such cooperation (Ordover, Sykes, and Willig 1985). A carrier might also be motivated to exclude an efficient participant to weaken that participant's competitive impact in another market. Thus these approaches to rail regulation should be avoided in developing and transition economies.

Reform Experiences and Lessons

Railroad reforms are still at an early stage in most developing and transition economies. Still, emerging evidence seems to confirm what theory predicts: decentralized, market-oriented decisionmaking freed from excessive regulation and energized by market incentives is the surest way to develop efficient, innovative solutions to transportation challenges.

Progress on private participation.   In response to the declining financial and physical condition of railways over the past decade, many fiscally constrained developing and transition economies sought to restructure rail systems and increase private participation in their operations. Thus the 1990s marked the reemergence of private railways in some of these countries, after more than half a century of public ownership and management. More than 40 railways in 16 countries were concessioned or privatized in the 1990s. Another 7 railways in 7 coun-

Figure 4.2 Cumulative Investment in Rail Projects with Private Participation in Developing and Transition Countries, 1990–2001

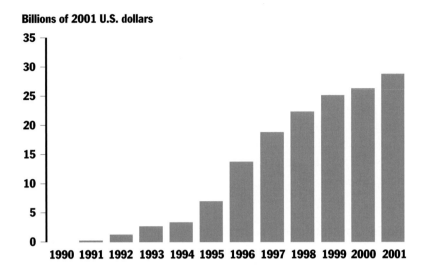

Billions of 2001 U.S. dollars

Source: World Bank, Private Participation in Infrastructure Project database.

tries are now being concessioned (Thompson 2003). During 1990–2001 more than 76 rail projects with private participation reached closure, with cumulative investment of $28.8 billion (figure 4.2; Harris and others 2003).

Only a few countries have fully privatized their railways. Several approaches to private participation have been used, combining varying degrees of private-public ownership and competitive restructuring (see table 4.1). These changes make clear that the monolithic, vertically integrated, state-owned railway is becoming obsolete and is no longer the preferred option. The dominant form of private participation in developing and transition economies is the concession (franchise) to operate and manage existing railways, with obligations for major capital spending to refurbish assets.

In some cases this is a complex arrangement. For example, in the Sitarail concession in Côte d'Ivoire and Burkina Faso, formal ownership of the infrastructure and operating assets remains with two national patrimony companies. The concessionaire must make payments into their investment and renewal funds and must service the debt on any investment they make on behalf of the concession.

Latin America has led the way in railway privatization. During 1990–97 seven countries in the region awarded private entities 26 rail contracts worth nearly $6.5 billion. The region's dominance in private railway projects can be attributed to its generally positive experience with private participation in other infrastructure sectors. Although countries in East Asia and the Pacific awarded fewer privatization contracts, their total investment—nearly $8.0 billion—exceeded that in Latin America due to the different nature of these projects (greenfield projects involving metropolitan rail systems and build-operate-transfer contracts). During this period only a few rail privatization projects reached financial closure in Sub-Saharan Africa and Europe and Central Asia, while Middle Eastern and North African countries have yet to transfer any railway operations to the private sector.

Effects of restructuring, deregulation, and privatization.   Since the Staggers Act went into effect in 1980, productivity gains in rail have exceeded those in nearly every other U.S. industry (Braeutigam 1993; Wilson 1997). Between 1981 and 2000 labor productivity increased 317 percent and locomotive productivity 121 percent. Lower rail rates—down 59 percent in real terms between 1981 and 2000 (figure 4.3)—and increased reliability have saved shippers and their customers

Figure 4.3   Performance of Class I U.S. Railroads, 1964–2000

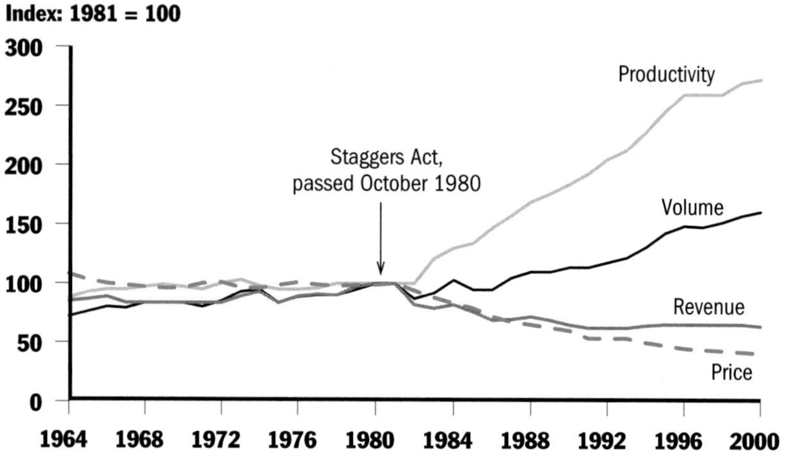

Source: AAR (2003).

more than $10 billion a year (1999 dollars; Grimm and Winston 2000). After decades of decline, rail's market share (measured in ton-miles) increased from 35 percent in 1978 to more than 40 percent today. These outcomes were achieved without vertical separation but with a great deal of consolidation: the number of class I railroads has fallen from more than 40 in 1980 to just 7 today, 2 of which are Canadian-based.

Restructuring, deregulation, and private participation have also generated significant benefits in developing and transition economies. Several policy options previously closed to state enterprises contributed to these gains. First, as part of their privatization agreements, new operators could cut excess employment—among the most vexing problems for state-owned railroads. Second, the freedom to change price structures (up to specified maximum rates) allowed concessionaires to attract traffic for which they had a comparative advantage. Third, in some cases freedom to withdraw from unremunerative activities (including passenger services) enabled concessionaires to focus on more profitable ones. Fourth, low spending on equipment and maintenance had hurt performance, so the physical refurbishment that preceded some concessions helped restore railways' ability to provide services.

Privatization significantly shrank labor forces in almost every case, ranging from an 8 percent reduction in Côte d'Ivoire and Burkina Faso to 44 percent in Estonia, 66 percent in Mexico, and 92 percent in Argentina. These reductions have usually not been due to service cuts but were achieved primarily through programs dealing with labor redundancy (Thompson, Budin, and Estache 2001; Thompson 2003).

Rationalization of the labor force, especially when combined with traffic growth, has dramatically increased labor productivity. In all but one case (Côte d'Ivoire and Burkina Faso) railway output per employee (measured as the sum of ton-kilometers and passenger-kilometers) has at least doubled—and has usually tripled or even quadrupled (figure 4.4; Thompson and Budin 2001).

Before concessioning, railroads experienced declines in traffic largely because of poor service, insufficient technological progress, and ineffective management. For example, in Argentina between 1965 and 1990 the railroad's share of freight traffic fell 50 percent. But concessions reversed this trend. In most concessions better service, combined with more flexible pricing and lower freight rates, has significantly increased the volume of freight carried.

Figure 4.4   Rail Labor Productivity in Argentina, 1974–2000

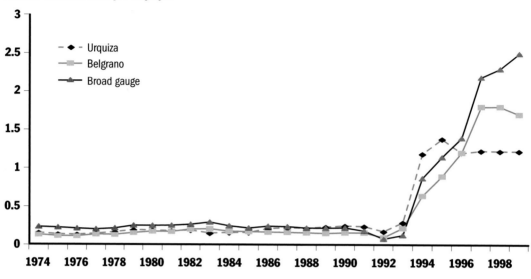

Millions of traffic units per employee

Source: Thompson (2001b).

Post-reform pricing in several developing and transition economies has provided considerable benefits to rail users. Among 16 privatized railroads (mostly in Latin America), 14 had lower freight tariffs in 1999 than when the concessions started (mostly in the mid-1990s; table 4.2). In Latin America rates dropped 8–54 percent, while in Côte d'Ivoire they fell 14 percent. These tariff reductions saved about $1 billion a year in transport costs for the six countries involved. Moreover, these estimates understate the total savings because they do not reflect the competitive pressures that lower rail tariffs exerted on trucking and other competing transport modes.

For most of its history Brazil's railroad system generated negative returns on its operations. In the early 1990s the country's freight railroads obtained higher unit revenues than most of those elsewhere on the continent. Still, the railroads were experiencing substantial losses. In 1995 Rede Ferroviaria Federal (RFFSA) lost $308 million and its debt reached $4 billion (Estache, Goldstein, and Pittman 2001).[4] Persistent losses reflected low productivity, pervasive organizational inefficiencies, government obligations that weakened railroads in the face of growing

Table 4.2 Rail Freight Tariffs in the Initial Years of Concessions and in 1999, Various Countries

Country, railway	Initial year	Tariff in initial year (PPP$ per ton-kilometer)	Tariff in 1999 (PPP$ per ton-kilometer)	Change in tariff (percent)	Savings (millions of U.S dollars)
Côte d' Ivoire	1995	0.123	0.106	–13.8	8.9
Argentina, broad gauge	1993	0.039	0.036	–7.7	20.7
Argentina, standard gauge	1994	0.032	0.043	34.4	–5.4
Bolivia, FCO	1996	0.147	0.123	–16.3	15.0
Bolivia, FCA	1996	0.061	0.098	60.7	–20.6
Brazil, FCA	1996	0.051	0.032	–37.3	138.1
Brazil, Novoeste	1996	0.043	0.027	–37.2	25.4
Brazil, Nordeste	1996	0.056	0.026	–53.6	21.3
Brazil, MRS	1996	0.027	0.022	–18.5	134.2
Brazil, ALL	1996	0.044	0.033	–25.0	113.1
Brazil, Tereza Cristina	1996	0.120	0.101	–15.8	4.9
Brazil, Bandeirantes	1998	0.038	0.023	–39.5	89.8
Chile, Fepasa	1994	0.089	0.053	–40.4	42.8
Chile, Ferronor	1996	0.072	0.046	–36.1	19.3
México, TFM	1997	0.054	0.043	–20.4	189.8
México, Ferromex	1997	0.041	0.036	–12.2	103.2
New Zealand	1992	0.104	0.081	–22.1	93.8
Total					994.2

Note: Tariffs and savings calculated using 1999 purchasing power parity (PPP) dollars.
Source: Thompson, Budin, and Estache (2001).

intermodal competition, and a failure to rationalize operations by shedding low-density lines, excess capacity, and redundant labor.

As part of restructuring, which started in 1995, Brazil split RFFSA into six freight concessions, cut its workforce from 110,000 in 1975 to 42,000 in 1995 (significantly increasing labor productivity),[5] eliminated subsidies for public service obligations, and gave the new operators considerable pricing flexibility. Operators were permitted to engage in demand-differentiated pricing and negotiate shipper contracts with confidential terms and conditions, and all operators significantly improved their performance. Losses fell quickly, with net operating profits turning positive in 1996 (Estache, Goldstein, and Pittman 2001). In addition, rail's declining share of freight traffic was stemmed: in 2000 Brazilian railroads carried 24 percent of the nation's freight traffic, up from 21 percent in 1996 (*International Railway Journal* 2000). One area where the expected benefits of privatization have not been fully realized, and could become a problem, is private investment. Most operators have not achieved the goals described in their investment plans (Campos and Jimenez 2003).

Concessions have also led to increased use of suburban passenger rail. After Buenos Aires, Argentina, unbundled its metropolitan rail services into seven concessions in the mid-1990s, suburban rail traffic more than doubled in just a few years—suggesting significant benefits for consumers (Thompson 2001b). The main reasons for the jump appear to have been more reliable services and increased passenger safety, though more attention to collecting fares may have overstated the increase in passengers. Still, lower fares were not among the initial reasons for increased use.

Lessons.   Over the past decade the railroad industry has undergone some of the most sweeping structural changes ever observed in the transport sector. But in most developing and transition economies railroad restructuring and privatization is at too early a stage to permit a clear assessment of long-term impacts. Still, the experience to date offers general insights into the reform process:

- Restructuring raises several difficult policy questions with no clear-cut or universal answers: Is the organizational separation of track ownership and train operations conducive to economic efficiency? How much pricing freedom should an infrastructure entity have to recover its replacement costs? What regulatory restrictions should be imposed on pricing by a dominant service provider facing weak intramodal and intermodal competition?
- Injecting competition into the railroad industry is not easy. It requires introducing new and complex regulations. Although many developing and transition economies might lack the expertise to implement such schemes, maintaining the status quo—a monolithic, state-owned railroad—is likely the most costly option.
- A variety of approaches can be used to increase competition in the railroad industry and its vertical relationships. But few reforms have significantly enhanced intramodal competition. Most of the benefits of structural reorganization seem to come from unsettling embedded business cultures and providing managers with

the flexibility, independence, and incentives needed to become efficient and fiscally responsible and to respond to growing intermodal competition. Thus it may be appropriate for public policy in developing and transition economies to focus on freeing rail entities from unnecessary regulatory restraints and creating a level playing field between rail and other transport modes, rather than trying to create rail competition through aggressive structural remedies. This is especially important in Central and Eastern Europe and the Commonwealth of Independent States, where rail still accounts for a large share of freight traffic. Although this situation is partly explained by physical impediments—such as underdeveloped and poorly maintained highways—to the use of alternative transport modes and a continued emphasis on extractive and heavy industries, policies favoring the rail industry have also played a major role.

- Ownership and market structure options form a continuum in the rail industry. Choosing one of these options is a complex policy decision: many country- and industry-specific characteristics must be considered. Countries differ significantly in size, level of development, institutional capacity, density of the rail network, condition of fixed rail facilities, strength of intermodal competition, and efficacy of public finances. Thus an uncritical choice among extreme options (entirely private or public, complete vertical integration or separation) could reflect ideology rather than carefully designed policy for the public interest.

Ports: Alternatives for Organizing a Multiproduct Activity

IN MOST COUNTRIES PORTS HAVE PLAYED A VITAL ROLE AS GATEways for trade and commerce.[6] Shipping remains by far the main mode for international transport of goods, and more than 80 percent of trade involving developing countries is waterborne (measured in tons; al Khouri 1999). As an important determinant of maritime transport costs, port efficiency is critical to the success of any strategy to integrate a country with the global trade system (Clark, Dollar, and Micco 2002). Excessive port costs make a nation's products less competitive in world markets and can impede economic development.

Recent technological innovations and changes in the content of trade have led to far more integrated operations in international transport. Ports have become nodes in a seamless global logistics supply chain. Globalization of economic activity and strong competition in the shipping industry have increased the demand for optimal capacity use and effective delivery of integrated logistics services. Moreover, port container throughput is expected to reach 270 million TEUs (20-foot equivalent units) by 2005—55 percent higher than in 1998 (al Khouri 1999).

Even with increased productivity, considerable investment is needed in new port facilities: 200–300 additional full-fledged container terminals. Thus port operators and authorities are under enormous pressure to adapt their roles and functions and, in particular, increase their efficiency and labor productivity (Juhel 1998). Doing so will require a fundamental reorganization of ports, a rebalancing of the roles of the private and public sectors, and regulatory reform aimed at eliminating administrative constraints that stifle port productivity and investment.

Many countries have taken steps to reorganize port operations and management (Haarmeyer and Yorke 1993; World Bank 2001d). These reforms have dramatically increased private activity in ports—especially in developing countries where the public sector could no longer finance investments in modernization and expansion. There is evidence of increasing competition between ports, and there are pressures to increase it within ports (van der Veer 2001). There is also a widespread belief that private management improves port strategies and operations, reduces excessive government control, and deals more effectively with restrictive labor practices. The efficiency gains from increased private activity largely depend on the efficacy of port regulation. Inadequate economic regulation could result in inefficient, costly port services.

Economic Characteristics of Ports

From a technical perspective, ports have a large, indivisible initial capacity requirement that is immobile (sunk) and long-lasting. From an economic perspective, port operations involve large fixed costs (especially for container terminals, where up to 80 percent of costs are fixed), strong economies of density (unit costs fall as more ships and cargo are handled through existing port facilities; Walters 1979), and increasing returns to scale (costs per unit of traffic handled decline as a port expands; Button 1993). Thus ports have traditionally been viewed as exhibiting natural monopoly characteristics, justifying direct public involvement in provision (to ensure sufficient investment) and operations (to limit monopoly power).

Multiproduct character. This simple characterization breaks down on elaboration, however, because ports are multiproduct entities, encompassing diverse activities with entirely different economic characteristics. These activities involve both infrastructure and services, and the range of both creates scope for unbundling and competition (Trujillo and Nombela 2000b).

In terms of infrastructure, a port typically requires several types of capital assets. It needs infrastructure for maritime access (channels, protective works, sea locks, lights, buoys) and land access (roads, railways, inland navigation channels). In addition, port activities require basic infrastructure (berths, docks, storage areas, internal links) and so-called superstructure (terminals, sheds, office buildings, fuel tanks, cranes, pipes).

Maritime and land access infrastructure entail long-lived, largely sunk assets with costs that cannot be easily assigned to specific users. Thus these assets are not an attractive proposition for private investors and are typically owned by governments. They could also be held by a consortium of port operators. Although a lot of basic port infrastructure and superstructure are also long-lived assets, their costs can be assigned to users without much difficulty. Accordingly, there is much greater scope for private participation and investment in such infrastructure.

Ports use this infrastructure to provide a range of services (box 4.2). For example, movement of freight traffic through a port generally involves the following distinct activities. On arrival, a vessel is allocated a berth and typically requires piloting and towing to navigate through the appropriate channels into and within the port. On berthing, the vessel requires cargo handling, both onboard (stevedoring) and on land. Cargo usually also requires stacking or storing (not least for customs purposes) before being released for land transport out of the port area. Other value-adding activities often also occur in ports. Vessels require a range of services while in ports, including bunkering, tank cleaning, and repairs and maintenance. The appropriate form of private participation, and hence regulation, may differ by function.

Box 4.2   Examples of Port Services

Services to vessels
- Piloting
- Towing
- Mooring
- Dredging
- Utilities
- Ship repair
- Environmental services

Services to cargo
- Stevedoring
- Wharf handling
- Transfers to land transport
- Storage
- Processing (consolidation, bagging, mixing)
- Cargo tracking
- Security
- Rental of specialized equipment

Source: Trujillo and Nombela (2000a).

As with other network utilities, most port infrastructure is likely to have natural monopoly characteristics. But unlike other utilities, ports provide a wide variety of services rather than a few specific products. Most of these services may be conducive to competition. Although provision of these services involves economies of scale and some sunk costs, they are smaller than those associated with port infrastructure. For example, most of the capital costs for towing and related services involve the purchase of tugs. There is an active international market for tugs, including second-hand ones. The costs of acquiring tugs are not a material barrier to entry, because only a small portion of such costs is sunk. Thus towing is a contestable activity.

Unbundling—that is, separating activities that are naturally competitive or entail no structural impediments to contestability (arguably most of the services and parts of port superstructure) from those with extensive scale economies or heavy sunk costs (such as access and basic infrastructure)—offers considerable opportunities to introduce competition and reduce the need for regulatory oversight in ports. In naturally competitive segments, interference with market mechanisms and truncation of property rights should be minimized, and scope for introducing competition should be fully exploited. By contrast, the public sector should regulate or even run segments with an unavoidable natural monopoly or substantial sunk capital.

Ports have also gotten more involved in providing, within their surrounding premises, logistical services (such as storing, packing, and distributing) that add value to a product. The private sector would likely be able to profitably develop such activities.

Models of port organization. Numerous activities occur simultaneously in a port because ships are constantly entering, unloading and loading, getting serviced, and exiting. Thus all ports need a coordinating agent to ensure the proper use of common facilities, ensure safety, and perform systemwide planning. These functions are usually performed by a public institution called the port authority.

The four main port models (in order of decreasing public involvement) are public service ports, tool ports, landlord ports, and private service ports (box 4.3). The services they provide depend on the role of the port authority and the degree of private participation. More than 90 of the world's 100 largest container ports are landlord ports (Cass 1996). The trend in developing and transition economies has been to move from the public service and tool models to the landlord model. For example, many Latin American countries have been adopting the landlord model (Hoffmann 2001; Micco and Perez 2001). However, some major ports—such as those in India and Sri Lanka—remain the public service type.

Box 4.3 Organizational Structures of Ports

There are four main port models:

- *Public service ports*—public sector owns land, infrastructure, and equipment and provides services.
- *Tool ports*—public sector owns land, infrastructure, and equipment but leases equipment and space to private providers on a short-term basis.
- *Landlord ports*—public sector owns land and infrastructure; private sector provides services on a long-term basis through concessions or build-operate-transfer (BOT) contracts.
- *Private service ports*—private sector owns all land, infrastructure, and equipment and provides services.

Source: van der Veer (2001).

Introducing competition in ports. Most of the benefits of private participation in port activities result from competition. Competition also reduces the scope of needed regulatory oversight. Thus the critical question is, how can governments foster competition in line with port characteristics and market opportunities for innovation? Several types of competition are possible:

- *Interport competition* can be fierce, as between the major container ports of East Asia. Major shipping enterprises are extremely demanding and expert at playing one port against another. A port's success in these contests may depend on its ability to process traffic quickly and reliably and integrate its activities with inland or feeder networks. Such external competition may be the most important determinant of the internal regulation a port requires.

- *Intraport competition between terminals* allows technically efficient integration of port functions without sacrificing competitive pressure within the port. Terminal operators have complete jurisdiction over their terminal areas, from berth to gate. This approach was adopted to great effect in the liberalization of the port of Buenos Aires.

- *Intraterminal competition between service suppliers* is encouraged by many ports. Competition in stevedoring, warehousing, forwarding, and other services is highly desirable whenever it can be physically accommodated. From a port authority's viewpoint, such competition may be influenced by licensing requirements, which limit the number of competitors but make the concessions attractive for competitive tendering.

- *Competition for the exclusive right to provide services* is an extension of the competitive tendering of licenses and may be the only way to attract private investment in small ports. When local monopoly rights are granted, the question usually arises: to prevent monopoly exploitation, should contracts be used or a regulatory authority established?

Governments and port authorities can take a number of steps to enhance competition, including introducing new berths and terminals, dividing ports into competing terminals (terminalization), dividing port operations within terminals, and introducing short-term operating leases or management contracts. The form of competition and regulatory requirements are closely related and largely depend on the size of the port, the extent of external competition, and the degree of captive traffic that needs protection.

Effects of Restructuring, Deregulation, and Privatization

Private participation in ports has had impressive results. In developing and transition economies more than $18 billion was invested in 177 port projects during 1990–2001 (figure 4.5; Harris and others 2003). Latin America and East Asia led such activities, with five countries accounting for two-thirds of the investment. Ports have recently been privatized in Brazil, China, Colombia, Estonia, Latvia, Lithuania, Malaysia, Mexico, Mozambique, Panama, Poland, the Russian Federation, and Tanzania.

One of the key arguments for privatization is that, relative to private owners and operators, public owners and operators are less able (and have fewer incentives) to control costs, are slower to adopt new technologies and management practices, and are less responsive to the needs of users. An early test of this claim came with the 1986 divestiture of the container operations of the Kelang Port Authority. (Port Kelang is

Figure 4.5 Cumulative Investment in Port Projects with Private Participation in Developing and Transition Countries, 1990–2001

Billions of 2001 U.S. dollars

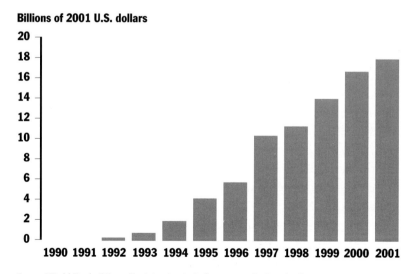

Source: World Bank, Private Participation in Infrastructure Project database.

Table 4.3 **Operating Performance of Ports in Colombia before and after Reforms, 1993 and 1996**

Indicator	Before 1993	1996
Average vessel waiting time (days)	10	No wait or hours, depending on the port
Working days per year	280	365
Working hours per day	16	24
Tones per vessel per day		
Bulk cargo	500	2,500 minimum
General cargo	750	1,700
Containers per vessel per hour (gross)	16	25

Source: Gaviria (1998).

Malaysia's largest port.) Privatization generated significant efficiency gains (Peters 1995). Crane handling improved from 19.4 containers an hour in 1985 to 27.3 in 1987, bringing Kelang's performance very close to Singapore's (Tull and Reveley 2001). The return on fixed assets grew at an average annual compound rate of just 1.9 percent in 1981–86, but jumped to 11.6 percent in 1986–90. The higher return was due to improvements in productivity and throughput, not higher prices. Workers also benefited from the gains in productivity: by 1990 they were paid 60 percent more an hour in real terms, put in 6 percent more hours, and produced 76 percent more than before privatization (Galal and others 1994).

Privatization and deregulation have produced similar improvements in port performance in other countries. In 1993 Colombia concessioned its four main ports to separate regional port authorities. These authorities do not provide services directly but contract with operators that use the facilities. In addition, new laws allow stevedoring services to compete freely at each port. Although the initial concessions involved little investment, the main reason for their success seems to have been the development of effective competition—not only within but also between ports. These reforms have significantly improved port performance (table 4.3).

Port reforms in Argentina also show the powerful effects of deregulation and interport and intraport competition. Before reforms, port operations were costly and inefficient because of restrictive labor practices, overregulation by multiple agencies with poorly defined responsibilities, and weak organization. As a result Argentine ports were losing market share to roads and to more efficient Chilean ports (Estache and Carbajo 1996).

In the early 1990s the Argentine government deregulated and decentralized port operations and increased private participation and competition. It deregulated piloting and towing services, eliminated controls on contracts with stevedoring companies, permitted Argentine ship owners to temporarily register their ships under foreign flags, allowed foreign ships to practice cabotage (pick up and deliver freight within Argentina), and allowed operators to set tariffs. One of the most important reforms was authorizing private entities to build and operate ports for public use—undermining the market power of existing ports. The government also reorganized the largest port, in Buenos Aires, into three areas with separate functions and administrations. One of these was further split into six terminals that were concessioned to compete with each other (Estache, Carbajo, and de Rus 1999).

Deregulation and privatization had dramatic effects on port investment and performance. In the port of Buenos Aires between 1991 and 1997, annual container traffic jumped from 300,000 TEUs to more than 1 million, the number of cranes increased from 3 to 13, labor productivity almost quadrupled, and the average stay for full containers dropped from 2.5 to 1.3 days. As a result the port of Buenos Aires was able to successfully compete with Santos, Brazil—South America's largest port. In fact, from 1997 onward the port of Buenos Aires surpassed that of Santos in terms of cargo handling (Hoffman 1999).

Some port services in Argentina were supplied by the private sector before reforms were initiated in 1990. For example, the private sector managed stevedoring at the Buenos Aires port. But because of excessive regulation, inadequate competition, strong labor unions, and low investment by the port authority, no significant improvements in performance were achieved in the early years of private participation (Micco and Perez 2001). This points to the importance of substituting competition for regulation whenever feasible. Yet in many developing and transition economies competition within and between ports has not been an important part of reforms (Estache, Gonzalez, and Trujillo 2001).

Port reforms can also provide significant fiscal benefits. In the mid-1990s Mexico introduced an aggressive decentralization program that led to the concessioning of the country's major ports to private operators. In addition to resulting in much lower tariffs and vast improvements in efficiency and productivity, privatization has enabled the port system to cover its costs. Indeed, the system now generates substantial tax revenue for the government, whereas before it depended on public support. This improvement in the system's financial condition has allowed the port authorities and concessionaires to undertake substantial investment in system expansion and modernization.

The Need for Post-privatization Regulation

The primary objective of port policy is to support national development. Although some emphasis has recently been placed on port services that add value to products, the development objective is usually best served by securing cheap and fast movement of traffic through ports. To that end, the landlord port model introduces competition either in the market for the provision of port services (between or within terminals) or for the exclusive right to provide services where the market is too small to support multiple providers. This approach may require structural controls to secure or maintain an appropriately competitive framework or, where structural measures are insufficient, controls to prevent monopolistic exploitation or distortion.

Structural approaches. The most complete form of privatization involves transferring ownership of entire ports or terminals to a single private operator. When there are many competing ports, complete privatization may generate the most intense competition. But where external competition is absent—as is often the case in developing countries—severe problems arise. In such circumstances the private owner's ability to exploit its monopoly position may provide a compelling reason to stop short of complete privatization. It is likely to be easier to regulate a port concession, albeit for a monopoly location, than to protect assets critical for national development once a country has transferred their ownership.

In recent years global carriers have sought to entrench their competitive position through long-term contracts for dedicated terminals in strategically located ports. Such vertical integration of terminal operations with shipping activities can ensure competition in large ports. But in smaller ports this approach can damage competition by enabling the integrated company, as the terminal operator, to use its monopoly power to favor its associated shipping activities—as with American President Lines' operation at the Karachi International Container Terminal in Pakistan. To avoid that outcome, a recent round of concessions in Chile stipulated that no more than 40 percent of a concessionaire could be owned by any shipping company, exporter, or importer operating more than 25 percent of the transfers at the concessioned terminal or more than 15 percent of the transfers in ports in the region in the previous year (Foxley and Mardones 2000).

Horizontal integration can be equally threatening. A limited number of global stevedoring companies emerged in the 1990s, including Hutchison Port Holdings (Hong Kong, China), International Container Services (Philippines), and PSA Corporation (Singapore). The threat here is that a company controlling a large portion of the terminals in a region could manipulate port use to its advantage, against national interests. For example, P&O Ports (Australia) has concessions for two of the five main container ports in India and may obtain two more. If successful, the company would control three-quarters of India's container terminal capacity. In 1999 the European Commission refused to allow Hutchison International to buy a controlling interest in Europe Combined Terminals, Rotterdam because it already owned Felixstowe, Thamesport, and Harwich, and the additional expansion would have given Hutchison a dominant market position in northwestern Europe.

Regulation of behavior. Ports require many technical, environmental, social, and safety regulations. For example, technical oversight is needed to ensure safe movement, avoid environmental pollution, and so on, and social oversight is needed to ensure fair treatment of workers and healthy working conditions. In most countries these functions are regulated by sector agencies or specialized agencies that are usually attached to or part of line ministries. Agencies independent of port management should oversee technical regulation, whatever the degree of private participation.

Tariff regulation is required only when there is insufficient competition, internally or externally. Competition has increased substantially not just between ports, but also between companies that may or may not be located in the same port (Meersman, Van de Voorde, and Vanelslander 2002). Hence overall tariff regulation should be very light handed.

But ports encompass multiple activities with significantly different economic characteristics, and so require different regulatory treatment. Moreover, ports differ substantially in terms of size and hence opportunities for introducing intraport competition and degrees of desirable regulation. Thus there is no single solution to the problem of port pricing (Pettersen-Strandenes and Marlow 2000).

As a rule of thumb, ports handling less than 30,000 TEUs a year are too small to have several terminals and operators. The best approach in those ports is to have a single operator and regulate its charges. Ports handling more than 30,000 TEUs can facilitate intraterminal competition, and those with over 100,000 TEUs can support interterminal competition. Finally, regions where container traffic exceeds 300,000 TEUs a year can have several ports competing with each other. The need to exercise regulatory control over private operators' prices is clearly lessened as one moves from single operator ports to interport competition (Trujillo and Nombela 2000a).

Countries have adopted different institutional approaches toward port competition and regulation. In Mexico the Ports Law states that the Federal Competition Commission shall determine when to establish tariff regulation. If the commission deems competition inadequate, it may stipulate rate of return regulation or price controls to prevent monopolistic exploitation. In such cases rates may be set based on benchmarks from comparable ports in more competitive situations or a synthesis of rates from cost data. Both methods are difficult, and the problem is that the regulated bodies are almost inevitably better informed than regulators. One way to do so, adopted in port regulations for Sri Lanka, is to involve the regulator only in cases of disputed rates. Adjudicating disputes between port operators or between port users and operators may be the most important function of a regulator in a liberalized port sector.

Notes

1. For example, the international competitiveness of agriculture is highly sensitive to changes in transportation services and costs. Consider soybean production, which is rapidly increasing in Bolivia, Brazil, and Paraguay—where production costs are lower than in Iowa, the most important soybean-producing U.S. state. As transportation systems improve in Latin America, the

region's soybeans and other agricultural products will become more competitive worldwide (Bertels 1998).

2. Between 1970 and 1994 rail passenger traffic rail grew 25 percent—while overall passenger traffic doubled. During the same period rail freight traffic fell from 283 to 220 billion ton-kilometers, while overall freight traffic grew nearly 70 percent—meaning that rail lost half its market share in freight traffic (CEC 1996).

3. As much as 30 percent of the long-term costs of providing rail services are fixed and largely sunk (Pittman 2001).

4. In 1957 several railroads that the government had to bail out in previous decades were consolidated into RFFSA, a holding company controlled by the Ministry of Transport.

5. Before privatization the government implemented a staff reduction program that included early retirement and voluntary separation incentives, training assistance for outplacement, and severance packages for dismissed workers (Estache, de Azevedo and Sydenstricker 2000).

6. The discussion on ports draws heavily on Gwilliam (2001).

CHAPTER FIVE

Reforming the Water Sector

TWO FEATURES DISTINGUISH THE WATER SECTOR from other infrastructure. First, the supply is finite and location-specific. Second, because safe water is crucial for life and health, its availability and affordability for the entire population are of enormous welfare (and political) importance (ADB 2000). These features, combined with the sector's economic and technological characteristics, limit institutional options for supply, create regulatory challenges, and highlight water's significance in achieving social and economic development goals—especially poverty reduction and environmental sustainability.

Since the early 1990s there has been growing recognition that water should be managed as an economic good and that its scarcity requires policies and institutions that can achieve economically and financially sustainable provision (WMO 1992). At the same time, the inclusion of a water access target among the Millennium Development Goals—seeking to halve between 1990 and 2015 the portion of people without sustainable access to safe drinking water—underscores the sector's close link to social equity. The challenge for regulation is to meet both efficiency and social welfare objectives in the water sector, balancing the needs of operators, consumers, governments, and the environment.

The state of the water sector is far from where it needs to be in developing and many transition economies in terms of both services and efficiency. Globally, 1.1 billion people lack access to safe water supplies (31 percent of the rural population and 8 percent of urban) and 2.4 billion lack adequate sanitation (65 percent of the rural population and 23 percent of urban; WHO/UNICEF/WSSCC Joint Monitoring Program 2000).[1] But these averages are misleading because they do not reflect the quality, regularity, affordability, or convenience of services. For example, an urban slum dweller is considered to have access if a public tap or latrine is within 100 meters of the home, even though it may be shared with hundreds of other residents (IIED 2003). Indeed, in the rapidly growing small cities of low-income countries, less than half the residents (many of whom live in informal, periurban settlements) have water connections (Hewett and Montgomery 2002).

One major cause of inadequate coverage is that water utilities, which mainly serve medium-size and large urban settlements, are often extremely inefficient in developing and transition economies. In many systems more than one-third of production is lost, overstaffing is pervasive, revenues do not cover operating costs, piped water flow and pressure are inconsistent, and water is often unsafe to drink.

Faced with poor service, high unmet demand, often deteriorating water resources, and an inability to finance needed rehabilitation and expansion, many countries and cities have embarked on reforms. But structural and policy changes in the water sector have been slower, less sweeping, and harder to sustain politically than those in other infrastructure sectors. Despite the significant scope for better performance, the sector's economic and technological characteristics disallow the possibility of an institutional "magic bullet" that would significantly increase efficiency. Ultimately, designing and sustaining effective water reforms depend on managing the political agenda.

Economics of Water Supply

THE ECONOMICS OF PROVIDING WATER SERVICES ARE DEtermined by supply and demand, the high fixed costs of delivery systems, the sector's natural monopoly characteristics, externalities involving public health and the environment, the need for and features of sanitation, and technological changes in supply systems. The complexity and importance of these features, in turn, provide a rationale for sector regulation.

Supply and Demand

Water supplies are determined by basic water resources and by the location, quantity, and quality of freshwater available in a given area for agriculture (which typically accounts for 80–90 percent of consumption), industrial and municipal uses, hydropower (which requires a steady flow), and often ignored ecological needs (such as wetland protection). The geographic radius of natural supply is determined by the cost of transporting surface water or pumping from aquifers.

The sustainability of a water resource depends on whether net extraction rates (including water returned to the source) are less than inflows. The quality of the water source determines the spending needed for treatment before use. A growing number of countries are experiencing economic water scarcity—meaning that the costs of capture, treatment, and transport make supply and distribution unaffordable. For most developing countries the supply problem is not an issue of absolute scarcity but of deteriorating resource quality, insufficient connections for a growing population—especially poor households—and unreliable services (ADB 2000).

Competition for water among users and economic sectors is often intense and rises with population growth, urbanization, and industrialization. Many countries do not recognize private ownership rights over water but do recognize use rights, which are the focus of legal and institutional protections. Urban demand for water has both quantity and quality implications: most population growth is urban, and urban users demand higher quality, but urban industrial and household discharges can harm the quality of water sources unless properly disposed of or treated (Saleth and Dinar 1999).

Sharpening competition for water has led many policy and institutional reforms to focus (though not nearly enough) on allocation issues, such as tradable water rights; on strategies for decentralized water management and control (while recognizing the need for integration and coordination across jurisdictions and user groups); and on ensuring the economic viability and physical sustainability of water provision.

Because water is essential for life, at a certain minimum level of consumption demand is price inelastic. But the minimum supply required to sustain life and health is very small: the World Health Organization guideline is 25 liters per capita per day. This is far below the level of consumption subsidized in many countries, where lifeline tariffs may extend up to 30 cubic meters a month per connection—or about 200 liters per capita per day for a five-person household (Boland and Whittington 2000).

Table 5.1 Ratios of Prices Charged by Water Vendors and Public Utilities

Country	City	Ratio
Bangladesh	Dacca	12–25
Colombia	Cali	10
Côte d'Ivoire	Abidjan	5
Ecuador	Guayaquil	20
Haiti	Port-au-Prince	17–100
Honduras	Tegucigalpa	16–34
Indonesia	Jakarta	4–60
	Surabaya	20–60
Kenya	Nairobi	7–11
Mauritania	Nouakchott	100
Nigeria	Lagos	4–10
	Onitsha	6–38
Pakistan	Karachi	23–83
Peru	Lima	17
Togo	Lomé	7–10
Turkey	Istanbul	10
Uganda	Kampala	4–9

Source: Bhatia and Falkenmark (1993).

Even in the poorest urban areas many water uses are not for subsistence, so consumption is somewhat price elastic. Thus demand management, especially to reduce waste under users' control, is a relevant policy objective (Noll, Shirley, and Cowan 2000).

Because they are typically underserved by formal providers, poor people often pay extremely high rates and large shares of their income for water—far above the levels spent by the better-off despite much lower consumption (table 5.1). Where utility water is of poor quality, even middle- and upper-income households buy from vendors (Komives, Whittington, and Wu 2001). Willingness to pay for water varies for poor people (reflecting desired quality and convenience) and must be assessed to achieve a financially sustainable system. Although there is ample evidence linking adequate water supply and quality—combined with sanitation—to health outcomes (Esrey 1996), private consumers' valuation of safe water and especially of sanitation's health benefits may be less than the social value of public health. Thus incentives (such as subsidies), coupled with public education, may be needed to ensure socially desirable minimum consumption.

High Fixed Costs

Water delivery systems involve four components: capture of the natural resource (for example, through reservoirs and wells), treatment to ensure adequate quality for use, transportation (for example, through aqueducts and mains—the primary network), and delivery to users (through pipelines and taps—the secondary network; Noll, Shirley, and Cowan 2000).[2] All these components require fixed capital investment in long-lived assets, many of them underground.

The fixed costs of water supply are typically high relative to variable costs, more so than for other utilities such as electricity. For example, fixed costs account for more than 80 percent of water supply costs in the United Kingdom (Armstrong, Cowan, and Vickers 1994). Such cost structures mean that most revenues in self-financing water utilities are returns to capital. It also implies that a water provider may be able to operate for many years without recovering fixed costs, and in such cases will likely face political difficulties when prices need to be raised. Accordingly, water providers have an economic incentive to extract monopoly rents—but at the same time are vulnerable to political pressures to keep prices low, preventing adequate returns that would permit capital replacement and attract new investment.

Natural Monopoly

Much of a water supply system involves engineering scale economies that contribute to conditions of natural monopoly, especially for water capture and transportation. But these economies do not necessarily dictate that an organizational monopoly is the most efficient structure throughout a system, even at the supply end. In a system with multiple reservoirs, for example, each reservoir could function analogously to an electricity generation facility in a large electrical grid (see chapter 3), enabling a decentralized wholesale water market in which competing reservoirs bid to furnish water to bulk water transportation networks or directly to user groups (Noll, Shirley, and Cowan 2000).

But unlike electricity, water is not a homogeneous product. Thus each supplier into the distribution network has to undergo quality monitoring. And because water has a low unit value relative to its transport costs, centralized transmission through a large national or regional network—as with an electricity grid—is impractical. So, water systems tend to be highly decentralized geographically and often operate under local (municipal) or provincial jurisdiction (Foster 1996).

Although there is increasing experimentation with third party access, especially to service poor neighborhoods, the capture, treatment, transportation, and delivery of water from each natural source are generally a natural monopoly.[3] A single vertically integrated utility is the usual industry structure,[4] especially in small and medium-size markets. In metropolitan areas with larger markets and reliance on multiple water sources, several vertically integrated entities can coexist, with each operating a separate distribution network in a separate zone of the city. This arrangement can be seen in metropolitan Manila (the Philippines), which is served by two contiguous water systems.

The network features of water systems imply, as in other infrastructure sectors, a need for system coordination—especially to control the quantity and quality of water intake. The large amount of capital stock underground also means that information on system conditions and operations is not easily observed or compared, creating a challenge for regulation.

Health and Environmental Externalities

Water provision and use involve extensive externalities in terms of public health and environmental impact. Excessive water offtake from private wells leads to costly building subsidence. Poor disposal of untreated wastewater contaminates groundwater and degrades natural resources in the region, such as watersheds and coastal habitats. Water spillage and pooling from bad drainage contribute to disease risks.

Many of these negative effects can be diffuse and long term, making them difficult to identify and prevent. Water and sanitation reform has historically received political impetus when the health dangers from inadequate provision have spilled beyond individual (usually poor) neighborhoods to affect middle-class and business interests—as with the cholera epidemic in Lima, Peru, in 1991 and the spread of typhoid in Santiago, Chile, in the late 1980s (Shirley and Menard 2002).

Policies governing water use rights, command and control regulations, and tax- or fee-based restrictions ("polluter pays") may be appropriate to limit harmful externalities and achieve socially desirable outcomes. But specifying and enforcing such rules and charges correctly—without under- or over-restricting behavior—are difficult. Command and control approaches are often less effective than financial incentives at curbing pollution, or than institutional pressures such as monitoring and public exposure of polluters' performance by citizen groups or the media (World Bank 2001b).

The Case of Sanitation

Much of what has been said about the cost structure and natural monopoly characteristics of water supply also pertains to piped systems of sanitation, namely sewerage, and to stormwater drainage. There are economies of scale in sewerage and economies of scope in combining water and sewerage transportation and delivery (Armstrong, Cowan, and Vickers 1994). But cost recovery is harder for sanitation than for water, partly because piped sewerage is costly and because more of the benefits are external to individual users.[5] Few lower-middle-income countries have been able to meet the necessary conditions—adequate piped water flow, consumer willingness to pay, and fiscal ability to sustain financial subsidies for revenue shortfalls—to provide access to sustainable sewerage to more than a small minority of the urban population. Demand for piped sewerage is stronger at higher income levels, where users place more value on convenience, amenities, and environmental impacts.

Satisfactory health benefits can be obtained from less sophisticated sanitation methods—such as ventilated pit latrines, shallow (condominial)[6] sewers, and septic tanks—that are only partly or not at all networked but require correct construction and maintenance.[7] The benefits and costs of these less expensive technologies are still not fully internal to households, so provision and use of such systems often require organization at the neighborhood level and may justify public subsidies for construction costs. Regulation or oversight is usually best provided by communities, nongovernmental organizations (NGOs), or local governments (PPIAF/WSP 2001). The rest of this chapter focuses on water supply and sanitation activities that are integral to a water utility.

Technological Changes in Delivery

A significant difference between water supply and most other infrastructure is that water has seen much less technological change over the past few decades, and the change that has occurred has had less effect on the underlying economics of supply. Unlike in telecommunications, there has been no revolution in the product and in underlying costs. Unlike in electricity generation, there have been no new production methods. And unlike in some segments of transportation, there have been no fundamental improvements in operations, management, or availability of critical information.

The most significant technological innovation in conventional water systems has been the widespread introduction of metering at the point of consumption, which enables utilities to set tariffs that reflect the marginal cost of water used and to bill for actual consumption. For metering to be worthwhile, the efficiency gains from encouraging customers to conserve water must be as great as the transaction costs of meter installation and meter-based billing. Thus metering is most attractive in situations of water scarcity. In addition, if a water system faces high costs from externalities (for example, if there are serious problems with drainage or wastewater pollution), metering can permit usage-based prices to internalize these externalities (Noll, Shirley, and Cowan 2000).

Overall, for reasons of efficiency, conservation, and externalities, metering of consumption is recommended in most developing and transition economies. But metering can also bring political advantages, by making information about consumption and pricing more widely available. In Santiago metering is seen as giving consumers more control, by informing them of their consumption and making billing more transparent (Clarke 2001). In Guinea the extension of metering to all administrative connections after 1996 helped reduce government water bills and consumption—but also underscored the seriousness of official nonpayment (Menard and Clarke 2000).

In response to the demands of poor consumers for better access to water, cheaper technologies have become more common in urban water systems.[8] For the most part these innovations were not the result of organized research and development by formal utilities or government agencies, but rather a recognition and legitimization of existing alternative arrangements for self-provisioning and small-scale private distribution. Low-cost pipe technologies, some based on small pipes laid above ground, have reduced the economies of scale of secondary distribution. When they purchase bulk water from the utility, these small-scale providers benefit from the network economies of scale and the utility's water treatment (Tynan 2000).

But even if the chemical quality of the water is the same as that from the main system, it is not identical for consumers because of lower pressure. Alternative providers meet a segment of user demand typically not served by the network and provide contestability to the utility within this market. In the El Alto area of La Paz, Bolivia, when consumers were required to connect to the utility (which had exclusivity rights), they resisted because they preferred to maintain alternative arrangements, which provided satisfactory service (Komives 1999).

Rationale for Regulation

The existence of natural monopoly and the importance of fixed costs, externalities, and social welfare concerns create a strong rationale for government regulation in the water sector, to protect both producers and consumers. Water provision is not highly contestable, and consumers cannot assess whether water is safe to drink. Regulation in the public interest aims to guard against extraction of monopoly rents and ensure adequate water quality while guaranteeing that investors earn a necessary return on long-lived assets. Government ownership of water systems is no substitute for regulation because public monopolies also have incentives to overcharge consumers with no alternative supply, and to run down the capital stock and underinvest.

It is a major challenge to establish effective regulation that avoids the many problems of government control (see chapter 1 and 2). Ensuring that water supply can keep up with demand in a sustainable manner requires institutional arrangements that introduce competition wherever possible and improve access to information for the regulator and consumers, to instill incentives for efficiency. The next two sections discuss how options for market structure and regulatory rules may meet these objectives. The final section describes recent experiences with structural and regulatory reform.

Options for Competition and Market Structure

ALTHOUGH THERE IS LESS SCOPE FOR COMPETITION IN water than in other infrastructure sectors, encouraging competition is still a good principle when setting the structure of

Table 5.2   Institutional Options for Water Supply

Option	Ownership	Financing	Operations
Service contract	Public	Public	Public then some private
Management contract	Public	Public	Private
Lease contract	Public	Public	Private
Concession	Public	Private	Private
BOT (build-operate-transfer) contract	Private then public	Private	Private
BOOT (build-own-operate-transfer) contract	Private then public	Private	Private
Reverse BOOT	Public then private	Public	Private
Joint ownership	Private and public	Private and public	Private and public
Sale	Private	Private	Private

Source: Ringskog (1998).

the market. Local conditions will determine which structural options are relevant, with the most important being the size of the water market, the fixed costs of accessing water resources, and the minimum efficient size of the treatment facility. The system's attractiveness to private investors and the possible benefits from privatization will also depend on regulatory arrangements, which are discussed in the next section.

The natural monopoly character of water supply is so strong that structural unbundling is rare, making vertical integration of utilities dominant even in industrial countries. Horizontal integration is also common, in the sense of a single utility being responsible for an entire urban market (multiple utility providers within a city are relatively rare, though more likely in large cities). Three options for direct competition are discussed below: direct competition for specific services, competition within the product market, and competition for the market. Competition for the market is the main area of involvement by the international private sector. Indirect competition, known as yardstick competition, is discussed later as a mechanism of regulation. The main institutional options for water supply are summarized in table 5.2.

Laying the Groundwork for Competition: Decentralization and Corporatization

When it comes to managing water supply, there is widespread consensus on the need for subsidiarity—that is, assigning responsibility to the lowest level possible relative to the area affected (WMO 1992). Decentralization poses a tradeoff between locating allocative decisions close to sources of demand and relevant information, thereby increasing accountability and efficiency, and losing control over coordination and spillover effects. Some urban water companies remain owned by the national government (as in Honduras) or provincial government (as in São Paulo, Brazil). But in many countries ownership and control have been transferred to local governments as part of comprehensive political and fiscal decentralization, as in Hungary (Lobina and Hall 1999).

A common structure, especially in Sub-Saharan Africa and Central America, is a single water company responsible for several or all of a country's water services, rural and urban (box 5.1). The intent is usually to cross-subsidize systems in small towns with revenues from larger cities. But in Africa this setup has not been effective in extending service relative to a more decentralized structure. Service coverage is lower in capital cities and other urban areas in African countries with a single water provider than in countries where provision is organized locally. Coverage outside capitals is also no higher in countries with a single provider. These results suggest that cross-subsidies have been ineffective and that monopoly supply, at least at the national scale, has not expanded service (Clarke and Wallsten 2002).

Box 5.1   Water Systems in Small African Towns and Rural Areas

CÔTE D'IVOIRE AND SENEGAL EACH RELY ON A single operator to run their water systems. This setup is designed to generate cross-subsidies between regions, with capital cities providing most of the revenues to cover the costs of serving smaller urban areas. In Côte d'Ivoire this system has done a decent job of incorporating towns into the service area of the national water company, SODECI. But villages are starting to outgrow their community management systems, and the national operator has been unable to expand to all small communities—making apparent the limitations of this system.

Côte d'Ivoire and Senegal both plan to decentralize water services and strengthen incentives for competitive private providers to improve services in smaller markets. In Senegal the national entity's failure to expand services to rural communities has stimulated the development of community water systems headed by village water committees. Reforms are raising the legal standing of the village committees and creating a system that could promote local small-scale private providers. Some small towns on the perimeter of the formal network have opted to continue controlling water services locally, even preferring to pay higher tariffs if the revenues are used to support community activities.

Source: Tremolet, Browning, and Howard (2002); Tremolet (2002).

In many countries reform of urban water management involves sep-arating the water business from government departments and creating autonomous, self-financing, utility-type entities (World Bank 1994b), as in the European Union (Hall 1998a), Brazil, Chile, China, Mexico, and Morocco (Saleth and Dinar 1999). Though publicly owned, these corporatized and commercialized structures offer the minimum condi-tions for competition—direct or indirect—by making the business of water supply more transparent.

Encouraging Competitive Procurement by State Enterprises

Water utilities can introduce a focused form of competition by con-tracting specific functions. When potential contractors bid for such work to standards specified by the utility, it can increase efficiency and bring the utility new skills and practices. Service contracts typically have short durations (several months or one to two years) and can be subject to frequent rebidding. But without open bidding, service con-tracts do not encourage increased efficiency.

Competitive contracting is the simplest form of private participation because the utility remains responsible for operations and fixed assets (box 5.2). The practice can help "break the ice" for public-private collaboration and elicit valuable information about operational costs

---

Box 5.2 Problems with Service Contracts in Mexico City

IN 1993–94 MEXICO CITY ISSUED SERVICE CONTRACTS TO FOUR PRI-vate companies for meter installation, reading, and billing. The main objective was to make water and sewerage operations more efficient by reducing waste and increasing revenues. Another goal was to ac-quire better information on the condition of physical assets, as a pre-requisite to a full management concession (which has since been de-layed indefinitely). The contracts covered different zones of the city, but their specifications and bids were not sufficiently comparable to benchmark costs and performance across the zones.

Source: Haggerty, Brook, and Zuluaga (1999).

(Idelovitch and Ringskog 1995). Before its partial divestiture Empresa Metropolitana de Obras Sanitarias (EMOS), the public water utility in Santiago (Chile), contracted billing, meter reading, planning studies, construction and rehabilitation, general repair and maintenance, computer and payroll services, public relations, and industrial relations (Alfaro 1996). In Chennai, India, the Metropolitan Water Supply and Sewerage Board has achieved cost savings of 45–65 percent by contracting private operators for its sewage pumping stations (World Bank 1999b).

Privatized and concessioned utilities often procure goods and services at preferential rates from their subsidiaries. This need not be a concern if the concession was awarded competitively and the contract promotes the right overall incentives. But if a private operator exhibits excess reliance on its subsidiaries, it can undermine public trust in the utility.

Competition in the Market

There have been few instances of competing utility companies operating in the same water market. In Paris (France) and Manila (Philippines), two large metropolitan areas, the water market is split into service areas covered by companies that do not compete directly but that can be compared by a regulator (yardstick competition). In addition, competition for customers can occur at the boundaries of such service areas.

Most product competition in water markets occurs between piped and unpiped sources (such as vendors and wells), although piped water can be provided much more cheaply. But customers may seek unpiped alternatives if utility water is overpriced or of poor quality. Utility networks may also be bypassed by large customers able to provide their own supply systems.

Australia and the United Kingdom have tried to foster product competition in their water markets by allowing third party access to network infrastructure. But because transporting water is extremely expensive, common carriage and cross-border competition are not very economical—and so are uncommon (ADB 2000; Cowan 1997).

Competition in a water market can become significant only if a utility does not have an exclusive right to service customers in a particular area (Klein 1996b). Exclusivity is often awarded to enable cross-subsidies and to make concessions or equity shares more attractive to private investors. Governments may also use exclusivity to discourage consumers from using unsafe water sources and to avoid negative externalities from private well drilling. But exclusivity can work against the public interest if water coverage is low and utility performance is poor—as in most cities in low-income countries.

In Paraguay independent small-scale operators use low-cost small pipes to distribute water in periurban neighborhoods not connected to the main network (Solo 1998). Alternative providers are also at least tolerated in many African cities (Collignon and Vezina 2000). Formal utilities typically have little experience providing standard connections to poor people's unplanned, quasi-legal settlements, which are often characterized by extreme density, difficult topography, erratic layouts, and unclear land tenure. In cities where many residents live in such conditions, encouraging alternative operators (as well as utilities) to extend service using innovative methods is vital to providing poor people with water in a reasonable time at a reasonable cost (PPIAF and WSP 2001).

Competition for the Market

In addition to the long-lasting concessions that are the main form of private participation in and competition for the market of network utilities, the water sector also involves two less common types of private involvement: management contracts and leases. Management contracts last about five years and are limited to operations and maintenance. They are fee-based and do not entail any financial risk for the contractor or responsibility for investment. The potential for management contracts to increase operational efficiency largely depends on how performance targets are defined, what incentives are provided for the operator, and how the contract is monitored.

As with other forms of private participation, management contracts require a supportive institutional and political environment. Mexico City, for example, does not have an institutional structure conducive to successful management contracts. There is no single regulator for water supply; instead, responsibilities are fragmented across numerous agencies and 16 municipal governments. Moreover, there is no legal basis for cutting service to nonpaying customers. Although service contracts were awarded in the mid-1990s, delays in preparing for the next stage reduced the government's credibility with the private sector and undercut support for issuance of a broader management contract.

In the late 1990s in Johannesburg, South Africa, the municipal water service was corporatized and bid out for a management contract at the same time, because public opposition precluded attempting a long-term concession. The contract includes several incentive provisions that are paid only if a reputable international firm gives an independent, positive assessment of the utility's performance (PPIAF and WSP 2001). A management contract is also being used for water services in the West Bank and Gaza, and seems to be working well.

An operations concession is generally longer than a management contract—usually lasting 15–20 years—and covers operations and maintenance as well as some asset replacements. The operator receives all revenue and is the residual claimant, meaning that it keeps whatever cash it receives after paying operations and maintenance costs and a preset fee to the public utility related to investments (which are the utility's responsibility).

This fee can be structured in various ways. In the classic *affermage* contract, as developed in France, the fee is proportional to the volume of water sold. (The operator collects this part of the tariff on behalf of the public utility.) In a typical lease contract the fee is a fixed periodic payment. Variations are possible. For example, bonuses can be offered for good performance. Moreover, there is no sharp distinction between an operations concession and a full concession, because under an operations concession the operator can be made responsible for a limited range of investments.

Among developing and transition economies, water leasing has operated longest in Abidjan, Côte d'Ivoire (since 1957), and is being practiced (among other places) in Guinea, Mozambique, Niger, Poland, Senegal, and Turkey.

In concessions the contractor acquires a long-term right (typically 20–30 years) to use all utility assets, as well as a responsibility to finance new investments with specified performance targets. The assets are returned to the public utility at the end of the contract, and the contractor is compensated for own investments not fully amortized. In developing and transition economies water concessions (including sewerage in some cases) are functioning in Bucharest (Romania), Buenos Aires (Argentina), Lima (Peru), Manila (Philippines), and Sofia (Bulgaria), as well as for water and electricity services in Gabon (making it the first true concession in Sub-Saharan Africa). Given their long duration, concessions require government credibility and should allow adjustments in major contract parameters (see below).

Water supply, wastewater, and water treatment utilities have also been established under build-operate-transfer (BOT) and build-own-operate-transfer (BOOT) concessions in Chengdu (China), Ho Chi Minh City (Vietnam), Pusan (Republic of Korea), and west Bangkok (Thailand; Haarmeyer and Coy 2002). These contracts, which typically involve greenfield facilities rather than investments in existing water systems, have take or pay provisions (revenue guarantees) that can subject governments to contingent liabilities. Moreover, investing in bulk water supply without curbing waste in distribution may worsen utility performance and environmental damage. Although projects for new supply are often easier to negotiate than system reform and restructuring, they underscore the urgency of adjusting retail tariffs and demand management (ADB 2000).

Privatization of Ownership

Sales of equity shares in water companies, with or without restructuring or regulatory changes, are also occurring—though less often than in electricity and telecommunications. In 1999 Chile initiated equity sales in several water companies, including Santiago's EMOS (subsequently renamed Aguas Andinas), which had one of the best performance records of any public water enterprise in a developing country. The sales were intended as a prelude to concessions, but political resistance halted further reforms.

The water sector does not exhibit wide variation or innovation in market structure, and private participation has been modest (box 5.3). Although competition is inherently limited, opportunities are often not fully tapped. For example, major private concessions in the Czech Republic, Hungary, Poland, Timisoara (Romania), and Jakarta (Indonesia) have been awarded without competitive tendering (Bayliss, Hall, and Lobina 2001; Lobina 2001). Few long-term concessions have been terminated by governments or lost by the original winners during rebidding and renewal. Internationally bid contracts are dominated by two large French multinational corporations (Vivendi and Suez-Lyonnaise, which together hold two-thirds of the world's privatized water market) and several smaller European companies (Société d'Amenage-

Box 5.3   Private Sector Transactions in Water and Sanitation

PRIVATE INVESTMENT IN WATER AND SANITATION IS FAR BELOW that in other infrastructure sectors, accounting for just 5 percent of global private investment in infrastructure in developing and transition economies during 1990–2001. Private flows for water supply and sanitation averaged $4.6 billion a year in 1999–2001, down from a decade high of $9.3 billion in 1997 (all measured in 2001 dollars). Latin America has the most private water and sanitation projects, while East Asia has the most investment. All other developing regions trail well behind. Concessions are by far the most common type of project in the sector, accounting for more than 80 percent of investments in the 1990s. Over half of private water and sanitation projects, and three-quarters of investment, has gone to just six countries, including Argentina and Brazil.

Source: World Bank, Private Participation in Infrastructure Database; Izaguirre (2002).

ment Urbaine et Rurale, Thames, Anglian, and International Water Limited; Hall and Lobina 2002). But these companies collaborate as often as they compete, since they frequently form partnerships to win contracts (Bayliss, Hall, and Lobina 2001). Thus regulatory design and enforcement are crucial determinants of water sector performance.

Choosing Regulation

WATER REGULATION NEEDS TO ACHIEVE THREE ECOnomic and social welfare goals, the weight of which will depend on local water conditions, economic development, and politics:

- Efficiency—producing and delivering water at the lowest possible cost, maintaining assets, and conserving supply.
- Equity—ensuring that all residents have access to affordable, quality service.
- Environmental sustainability—minimizing pollution and damage to natural resources.

The main challenges for regulators involve dealing with insufficient information and balancing the interests of investors, consumers, and taxpayers. Asymmetric information on costs is a bigger constraint in water than in other infrastructure sectors because of limits on competition as a discovery mechanism and because a lot of water infrastructure is underground and not readily observable. Similarly, consumers can only partly assess the quality of water (in terms of clarity, taste, and smell); complete assessment requires regular expert testing.

To satisfy investors, regulators must provide credible assurances of adequate returns on long-lived capital assets, which implies curbing public sector performance risk. To protect consumers, regulators must ensure that water will remain safe and affordable. And for taxpayers, regulator assurances must extend to future generations without creating undue fiscal or debt burdens or irretrievably damaging natural resources. This section focuses on pricing regulation but also discusses other regulatory efforts (particularly quality and other performance targets, especially as they relate to service expansion) to establish incentives and behaviors consistent with these concerns.

Pricing Policy

As in all infrastructure sectors, successful water reforms require efficient pricing policies. But water pricing policy is especially controversial because of the conflicting objectives of such policy (box 5.4) and because of the severe problems in measuring elasticities of demand—that is, how price changes affect the amount of water consumed by different groups of customers and their decisions to connect or remain connected to the water system.

There are two basic structures for water tariffs: a single-part tariff and a two-part tariff. Under a single-part tariff a consumer's water bill is based on a fixed charge or a water consumption charge. With a two-part tariff the bill is based on both a fixed charge and a consumption charge.

Single-part tariffs. The simplest single-part tariff is the fixed charge, where the water bill does not reflect the volume of water consumed. In the absence of metering, fixed charges are the default tariff structure. They are still used in many countries with abundant water resources.

> ### Box 5.4   Objectives of Water Tariff Design
>
> WATER TARIFFS ARE DESIGNED TO ACHIEVE THE FOLLOWING GOALS:
>
> - *Cost recovery.* Tariffs must be consistent with revenue adequacy—that is, they should generate revenue that covers the financial cost of water supply.
> - *Economic efficiency.* Prices should provide signals for efficient actions by consumers, suppliers, and investors. In particular, prices should indicate to consumers the financial and environmental costs that their consumption decisions impose on the economy.
> - *Equity.* Consumers with similar characteristics should be treated similarly.
> - *Affordability.* Given its importance for well-being, water should be provided at minimal cost to poor people, through well-targeted subsidies if needed.
>
> *Source:* Whittington, Boland, and Foster (2002).

Fixed charges can vary across households or groups of customers. For example, more valuable residences and businesses might be assigned higher fixed charges because of their likely greater consumption of water, greater ability to pay, or both. Fixed charges might also be differentiated based on the diameter of the pipe connecting users to the water system.

The main disadvantage of fixed charges is that they provide no incentive for consumers to economize on their water consumption. Moreover, if some households lack a connection, connected users could resell water—frustrating the utility's cost recovery efforts.

A single-part tariff can also be based on the amount of water consumed. There are three types of consumption charges:

- Uniform volumetric charge—the household bill is the product of the quantity of water consumed multiplied by a uniform price per unit.
- Block tariff—the unit price is fixed for a specified quantity (block) of water but shifts up (increasing block tariff) or down (decreasing block tariff) for water consumed beyond that quantity and up to the limit of the second block, and so on.

- Increasing linear tariff—the unit price increases linearly with the quantity of water consumed.

An important advantage of the uniform volumetric charge is its simplicity. In addition, it can send a clear signal about the marginal cost of consuming water.

In theory the increasing block tariff could achieve the goals of affordability (by setting a low rate for the first "subsistence" block), economic efficiency (by aligning rates for higher blocks with marginal costs), and cost recovery. But increasing block tariffs often fail to achieve these goals, partly because of design problems. Many poor urban households share water connections, and their combined consumption can place them in the highest price block—causing them to pay higher unit prices than rich households. Increasing block tariffs may also fail to achieve economic efficiency and cost recovery goals because the prices of the higher blocks are not set high enough or the subsistence block is so large that most households do not go beyond it (Whittington 1992).

Under an increasing linear tariff water prices increase continuously with the quantity consumed. Not only is each additional unit of water more expensive, but all preceding units are sold at the last (high) price. Thus this type of single-part tariff sends a powerful signal that increased water consumption is costly. As such, it represents an effective tariff structure for dealing with water shortages. But increasing linear tariffs bear no direct relationship to marginal costs and so generally conflict with the goal of economic efficiency.[9] Especially for large-volume industrial and commercial users, they could drive prices well above marginal costs.

Two-part tariffs. In most cases the economically efficient pricing structure for water is a two-part tariff, with the first part being a fixed capacity charge and the second reflecting marginal costs. This second part, a volumetric consumption charge, is more important when water is scarce (Noll, Shirley, and Cowan 2000). Ideally the consumption charge should vary to reflect periods of peak demand relative to supply.

If properly designed, two-part tariffs can achieve the goals of economic efficiency and cost recovery. If marginal costs are low because of recent capacity expansion, the fixed component can be set to recover the costs of expansion and the variable component can be aligned with marginal costs. Thus the fixed component allows prices to reflect marginal costs (as allocative efficiency requires) while ensuring recovery of the firm's fixed costs. This is a distinct advantage over single-part tariffs. In similar circumstances a single-part tariff could not recover costs without distorting the price signal contained in the volumetric charge.

Imposing a uniform fixed charge to recover "nonmarginal" costs—that is, the shortfall between total costs and the revenues from pricing water at marginal costs—might cause poor consumers to drop out of the system. That outcome is inefficient because such consumers might be willing to pay marginal costs for some units of water. It is also undesirable on distributional grounds.

On the other hand, it is desirable to keep prices close to marginal costs for reasons of allocative efficiency. Striking a balance between economic efficiency and social equity would call for a marginal price somewhat above marginal cost and a correspondingly lower fixed charge. Alternatively, different two-part tariffs could be used. For example, a tariff with a low fixed charge and higher consumption charges (especially after a given level) could be aimed at the low-demand end of the market, while a tariff with a high fixed charge and lower consumption charges could be applied to customers who consume more water (Armstrong, Cowan, and Vickers 1994).

The short-run marginal costs of consuming a unit of water include variable operations and maintenance costs as well as a resource or opportunity cost (from withdrawal of water from alternative uses, such as agriculture) and a discharge cost (of untreated wastewater to the environment). Including the discharge cost in the tariff would make it possible to internalize the externalities of water use. Payments for the opportunity cost and externalities of water consumption can be collected with the tariff but should not be kept by the utility. Instead they should be kept by the owner of the water resource, such as a water management authority. But few water systems (especially in developing and transition economies) charge for all these elements of true marginal costs—even when environmental impacts and cross-sectoral allocations are burning issues (PPIAF and WSP 2001).[10]

Indeed, tariff revenues often fail to cover even basic operations and maintenance costs. As an extreme illustration, in Lima (Peru) in 1989, operating costs were 50 percent higher than operating revenues (Alcazar, Xu, and Zuluaga 2000). Because of the high ratio of fixed to variable costs noted earlier, in a self-financing utility a large share of revenue is quasi-rents. Whether a utility is publicly owned or private and regulated, political pressures will be strong to expropriate these quasi-rents by imposing low prices. Even if expropriation does not occur through prices, it may occur through government nonpayment of its water bills—as has been a major problem for water companies in Abidjan (Côte d'Ivoire) and Conakry (Guinea), where chronic payment arrears by public customers undercut tariff schemes (Shirley and Menard 2002).

Information Handicap

Even when supported by the strongest political will, a regulator will have a hard time committing to efficient water prices because it will have less information than the operator. In the face of information asymmetries, regulation can be a blunt instrument insensitive to the basic economic parameters underlying the industry. As a result regulation will likely veer from efficiency.

Simple cost-plus pricing regulation is common because it relies on what the operator reports—but it does not provide incentives to increase efficiency. In Guinea the regulator of the water supply lease has limited authority to demand information from the leaseholder, SEEG. External audits showed that because of this weakness and political interference, the cost-plus formulas used to adjust tariffs had been misapplied, resulting in excessive price increases (Menard and Clarke 2000). Two approaches are used to combat information asymmetry and reveal cost information: auctioning and yardstick competition.

Auctioning. Auctioning is especially appealing in the water sector because it can be applied to all the contract arrangements described earlier. Successful auctioning requires careful design and a minimum number of bidders. In 1993 Buenos Aires, Argentina, auctioned its water and sewerage concession to the bidder offering the lowest water price for a defined set of performance parameters. The winning bidder agreed to deliver water for 27 percent less than the prevailing price and committed to annual investments in the first five years well beyond those under state ownership (Klein 1996b). In 1988 Côte d'Ivoire renewed its lease contract with SODECI without rebidding, but used the threat of an auction to win a 20 percent cut in the real tariff—an outcome that suggests the company was enjoying high rents (Kerf 2000).

Because lack of information can also deter private operators, making system information available to potential bidders is critical to a competitive tender and a major responsibility of due diligence prior to inviting private participation. And even when the water price has been set by auctioning a long-term contract, it may need to be renegotiated in response to changed circumstances beyond the operator's control. Investors need assurance that they will be covered in case of adverse external circumstances, while the regulator needs to keep pressure on the operator to sustain high efficiency and pass on to consumers or taxpayers part of the gains from external or unforeseen cost reductions.[11] This tension has turned some water concessions into a battle of wills even where economic and institutional conditions should ensure success (box 5.5).

Rebidding a major franchise is too costly and disruptive to be a practical approach to price adjustment, so between auctions the regulator needs a more calculated method of adjustment. The shortcomings of rate of return regulation are discussed in chapter 2, and for the water sector this approach is far too information-intensive. An alternative increasingly considered more appropriate for the water sector, first adopted in 1990

Box 5.5   An Aborted Attempt at Water Concessioning in Atlanta, Georgia

IN THE UNITED STATES 94 PERCENT OF MUNICIPAL water systems—some 5,000 separate utilities—are publicly controlled, and most require extensive repair and rehabilitation. In an effort to improve operating efficiencies and access to private capital, more than 1,000 of these systems have turned to private long-term concessions (up from 400 in 1997). Atlanta, Georgia, undertook the largest such concession in 1999, signing a 20-year contract with United Water, a subsidiary of Suez. United Water was to make $800 million in repairs over five years. But by January 2003 both sides conceded failure and agreed to cancel the contract.

What happened? In the three years under the concession, city residents and officials complained that service was poor and unresponsive, fraught with water main breaks and safety failures leading to occasional "boil before drinking" alerts. But United Water argued that the system's infrastructure was in a much worse shape than it had been led to believe when the concession was signed, and that it lost $10 million annually under a $22 million a year contract that the city refused to renegotiate.

Source: Douglas Jehl, "As Cities Move to Privatize Water, Atlanta Steps Back," *New York Times,* 10 February (2003).

by OFWAT (the Office of Water Regulation in England and Wales), is a price cap method of adjustment (known as RPI–X) that can encourage increased productivity. During its first periodic (five-year) review of prices under the formula, OFWAT determined (in the face of consumer dissatisfaction) that the approved prices had been too high and tightened the parameters in the formula. The transparency of this method reduces the risk that the regulator could abuse such a review (ADB 2000).

Yardstick competition.   Even under a price cap, information on efficiency and other parameters is still needed for the regulator to monitor a utility's performance. In the face of information asymmetries and incomplete observability of actions, yardstick competition—where regulated monopolies in different markets or regions enter into virtual competition through the regulatory mechanism—is an attractive regulatory option (Shleifer 1985).

Yardstick regulation is based on relative efficiency and entails indirect or proxy comparison among actual or stylized providers. Agents (regulated firms) are effectively forced to compete with a (nonexistent) "shadow" firm whose performance is determined by the industry average or best practice. Incentives make the rewards of agents contingent on their own performance as well as that of other agents. By making rewards dependent on a firm's performance relative to other firms, yardstick competition strongly encourages efficiency: because a firm's price depends on the cost performance of other firms, it retains part of the surplus generated by its cost-reducing activities. The incentives for cost efficiency mitigate the problem of information asymmetry. Although regulated firms do not transfer information directly to the regulator, informational rents are extracted.

Two requirements must be met to apply yardstick competition. First, firms must operate in similar environments and face similar technological opportunities, so that cost conditions are correlated across regions. Second, firms should not be able to collude. The comparability requirement is likely to prove too demanding in many cases because of substantial firm heterogeneity. Even though a regulator can capture certain factors of firms' heterogeneity, the application of yardstick competition remains inherently subjective. There is no objective basis for attributing unexplained cost differences to inefficiency (Williamson and Toft 2001).

Moreover, obtaining relevant comparators is not easy because the required information may be specific to a firm or a water system. Using partial indicators of productivity can lead to inconsistent rankings of performance across utilities; where possible, regulators should use estimates of the industry's overall efficiency frontier (Estache and Rossi 2001). OFWAT has relied on benchmarking most intensively for price regulation, while Chile's regulator relies on long-run marginal cost calculations for a model company (Klein 1996b).

Balancing Interests and Allocating Risks

A general principle of risk allocation is that each party should bear the risks it is best able to mitigate. Contracts and regulations should require the operator to bear commercial risks (of demand and payment) but be able to cut off delinquent customers, construction risks (for concessions), and risks that can be hedged, such as normal foreign exchange and interest rate risk.

Households should be required to pay for services, but within a social contract where costs of connection and minimum consumption are shared for those unable to pay. The government (taxpayers) should bear these social commitments. Individuals should also be responsible for their own behavior related to water and sanitation use and disposal—but again, where basic hygiene education and access to minimum services are inadequate, the public sector must correct these failures. Risks associated with political change, water resource quality, and major macroeconomic setbacks are best borne by government (ADB 2000). In practice, however, the magnitude and cost implications of external shocks are not always immediately evident and may require some burden sharing among the government, the utility, and its customers.

Interests of investors. A clear mechanism for adjusting prices can curb risks for an investor, but only if the public utility and regulator make credible commitments—so that the investor can be assured that political pressures will not undermine the best-laid plans through expropriation. Credibility can be established through rules that separate regulation from the government's ownership role, protect the independence of the regulator, and strengthen the legal security of investors (see chapter 2). Further commitment devices include public sector performance bonds, dispute resolution mechanisms (such as international arbitration in major cases), and roles for consumer representation. Multilateral institutions have helped back government commitments—as in Guinea, where the World Bank provided partial financing for a revenue subsidy during a period of phased tariff hikes.

Because international experience with concession design is still evolving and each situation is different, flexibility on the part of the regulator is important. Side-by-side water concessions instituted in west and east Manila in 1997 were generally considered well prepared and designed (ADB 2000). But one feature allocated the debt portfolio of the parent utility to the west Manila concession, obligating the east to seek new financing for its larger investment requirements. This setup had the unanticipated effect of saddling west Manila with massive foreign exchange losses stemming from the 1997 East Asian financial crisis, which struck shortly after the contracts were signed. The consortium for this concession has demanded a doubling of the prices agreed at initial bidding (Public Services International 2000). Resolving this financial problem, which could not have been fully foreseen, may be critical to continuing the west Manila concession.

Interests of government (taxpayers).   A contrary risk to expropriation, and one greater from the perspective of taxpayers (and consumers), is the risk of regulatory capture.[12] Capture is evident in some long-term concessions where the public authority has been reluctant to challenge the incumbent. But capture has not prevailed in the face of extreme political opposition to a concession's performance.

For example, in Tucuman, Argentina, a 30-year water concession granted to a subsidiary of Générale des Eaux (now Vivendi) in 1995 was terminated in 1998 because consumers rebelled against the doubling of tariffs and the company failed to meet investment and quality targets. Water service in the province has since been returned to public operation (Hall and Lobina 2002). However, in Cochabamba (Bolivia) and Szeged (Hungary), as well as in Tucuman, multinational concessionaires have pursued legal claims for compensation after disputes, which could make it costly and difficult for governments to end such contracts (Bayliss, Hall, and Lobina 2001).

A regulator can be captured by powerful interests other than the utility, such as user groups or suppliers. To guard against excessive influence by any well-organized party, it is essential for regulation to allow open access to information on its decisions and procedures, provide opportunities for all stakeholders to voice their concerns, and submit to judicial reviews (Noll, Shirley, and Cowan 2000).

Interests of consumers.   In addition to tending to the basic structure and level of water tariffs, the regulator is also concerned with their application to different groups of customers. Like electricity and some transportation services, many water systems subsidize households with revenues from industrial and commercial users. The general drawbacks of internal subsidies are discussed in chapter 1. Subsidies are especially problematic for the water sector when large shares of the population are very poor or lack connections. In such cases subsidies impose an enormous burden on certain groups of customers—such as large firms—and could entice them to leave the network (as in Lima and Mexico City).

Pricing and regulatory policies for households in developing and transition economies should encourage sustainable, affordable water consumption for all, with incentives for residents to avoid waste and for the utility to extend coverage to unserved areas. To that end, regulation should be carefully examined to see how its benefits and costs affect different consumers. For example, in Parana, Argentina, several proposed water concessions were subjected to stakeholder analysis to determine how they would affect the government and consumers. The analysis found that the initial regulatory terms featured a tariff structure favorable to existing users but weak provisions for funding new connections. Moreover, the strongest gains were anticipated to accrue to the government through fees paid by concession operators (figure 5.1). The concession was redesigned to convert net losses to customer groups to net gains—except for the poorest customers, for whom further tariff reform was needed (van den Berg 2000).

Ensuring Access and Affordability for Poor Households

The urgency of meeting the needs of poor households through urban water sector reform has been getting increasing international recogni-

Figure 5.1 Winners and Losers before and after Adjustments to a Water Concession in Parana, Argentina

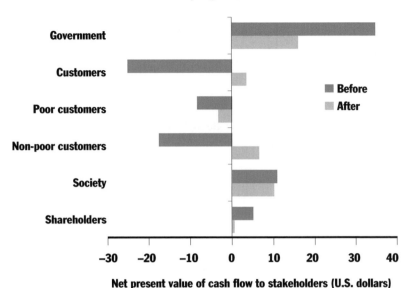

Source: van den Berg (2000).

tion (PPIAF and WSP 2001). In many cities of the developing world more than half the population lives below local poverty lines (World Bank 2003). And while official data on access to water often suggest that most urban residents are already serviced, these averages mask major gaps and inadequacies.

Residents of quasi-legal and periurban settlements—representing millions of people in many large cities—are often not considered part of urban jurisdictions and so are not included in official data. Moreover, many residents with nominal connections have extremely poor water access and quality. For example, coverage data in Conakry, Guinea, include people using standpipes, which in Africa serve an average of 15 people. And when Lima, Peru, began reforming its state-owned water company in the early 1990s, 48 percent of the connected population received water for less than 12 hours a day—and 28 percent for less than 6 hours (Shirley and Menard 2002).

Subsidies and other support. Policies aimed at promoting access and affordability for poor customers have included guarantees of free

---

Box 5.6 Creative Management of South Africa's Commitment to Free Water

SOUTH AFRICA RECENTLY PASSED A LAW THAT PRO-
vides every household with 200 liters of free water a
day. Thus Durban Metro Water does not bill households for the first 6 cubic meters of water consumed
each month. But instead of allowing this subsidy to
impose a financial burden on customers who consume more or rationing water through poor service
or insufficient connections, the utility has applied innovative low-cost schemes to meet the needs of its
poor customers. In partnerships with two private
firms (Lyonnaise des Eaux and Vivendi) responsible
for designing and managing projects to test these

schemes, the utility is developing a range of service
levels geared to customers' actual demand. Options
include semi-pressure systems with water tanks on
household roofs, which permits smaller mains than
usual, and metered delivery. Low-cost sanitation,
complementary to the semi-pressure water systems,
includes improved latrines and condominial sewers
maintained by communities. Arrangements restrict
water flow to minimize waste and theft, include provisions for credit to pay for connections, and incorporate user education and community mobilization.
In addition, sanctions for nonpayment are enforced.

Source: Brocklehurst (2001).

---

minimum service, increasing block tariffs, direct (nontariff) subsidies,
community service obligations, and performance incentives and fiscal
transfers for utilities (Clarke and Wallsten 2002; Chisari, Estache, and
Laffont 1999). Durban, South Africa, has used the country's free water
policy to encourage innovation (box 5.6). In Côte d'Ivoire and Senegal
social tariffs cover consumption up to 18 and 20 cubic meters per
household per month, respectively, and each country's government ab-
sorbs connection costs for eligible households (Tremolet 2002). Otherwise, increasing block tariffs are used—that is, tariffs that rise progressively with consumption.

Increasing block tariffs are widely used in developing countries because they are perceived as being fair and discouraging excessive consumption. In reality, though, they can have perverse effects (Boland
and Whittington 2000). As noted, if many poor households share a
connection, such tariffs can shift these users into higher rate categories.
They can also discourage private operators from extending service to
low-volume consumers (PPIAF and WSP 2001) and can be maintained
only under exclusivity. A uniform volumetric charge is more equitable
but may be less popular politically.

In most countries water subsidies provided through social tariffs are
regressive, ineffective at reaching poor people, and (when inadequately
funded by government) contribute to utility deficits and water ration-

ing. In Belem, Brazil, in the mid-1990s the poorest fifth of the population received no subsidy spending, the second fifth received 12 percent, and the richest fifth absorbed almost 40 percent (Alfaro and others 1997; World Bank 1994b).

Chile is one of the few developing countries to provide a direct water subsidy that is means tested and administered by municipal governments. The nationally funded subsidy is transferred to the utility and subtracted from the water bills of eligible customers, who must remain in good standing. Despite being one of the best examples of subsidy design, this model has not been widely replicated—possibly because it requires strong administrative capacity (Foster, Gomez-Lobo, and Halpern 2000).

If subsidies are required to ensure affordable water for poor people, ideally they should focus on access rather than consumption, to avoid distorting incentives for efficient use. Connection costs typically pose a greater barrier to affordability than do normal tariffs (Tynan 2000). In recent years lease and concession contracts have encouraged new connections using various approaches, with mixed success. Whatever the approach, incentives for consumers (affordability) and investors (profitability) need to be right, and contracts should encourage flexible, innovative approaches to meeting service targets.

After a rocky start, Buenos Aires, Argentina, has found a satisfactory way to finance new connections, though expansion has been slower than expected (box 5.7). In the parallel water concessions in east and

---

Box 5.7 Making New Connections Affordable in Buenos Aires

THE 1993 WATER CONCESSION IN BUENOS AIRES, Argentina, set targets for new connections, with priority given to poor areas. A fee was introduced to cover the new connections, payable by the new customers over two years. But poor households could not afford the fee, and new customers considered it unfair because before the concession the costs of connections were shared by all customers. Although the fee was adjusted several times, affordability concerns and resentment led to renegotiation of the concession in 1997. As a result a bimonthly charge was introduced for all customers, and connection charges were reduced and made repayable in interest-free installments spread over five years.

Although these changes cut the average water bill by three-quarters for households in poor neighborhoods, affordability remains a problem. There are also concerns that the contract renegotiation lowered expansion targets, which will mainly affect poor neighborhoods.

Source: PPIAF and WSP 2001; Alcazar, Abdala, and Shirley (2000).

west Manila, the concessionaires are allowed and even encouraged (under certain circumstances) to relax their exclusivity by awarding service licenses to third parties, such as a bulk provider. Retail sales by these licensees are counted toward the concessionaires' coverage targets (PPIAF and WSP 2001).

Implications of quality and other performance regulations.   Water regulation typically includes standards that utilities must meet for water safety, pressure, service levels, equipment, technologies, and procedures (such as for billing). Though well intentioned, such standards often make it impossible for a utility to incorporate cheaper approaches or provide a menu of services in line with poor households' willingness to pay, as shown by the experience in El Alto, Bolivia (box 5.8).

Especially where large shares of the population do not have connection, regulators need to take a flexible approach to standards to en-

---

Box 5.8   Adapting Quality Standards to Permit Extensions of Low-cost Service in El Alto

IN LA PAZ, BOLIVIA, THE SUEZ-LED WATER CONCESSION AWARDED in 1997 to Aguas del Illimani contained explicit targets for connecting poor households but did not provide adequate financial incentives for the company to do so. Moreover, the government did not provide targeted transfers to ease affordability. The concession contract stated that metered, in-house water and sewer connections were the only acceptable technology, which put service out of reach of poor households and essentially guaranteed that the company would fail to meet its ambitious target of universal water coverage within four years. Recognizing this dilemma, the regulator and the company agreed to experiment with a cheaper condominial technology for water and sewerage. The technology was found to be acceptable to the unserved population, and has allowed affordable service to be extended in the poor neighborhood of El Alto. In 2001 the condominial technology was legitimized by the Bolivian Institute for Technical Norms and Standards.

Source: Hall and Lobina (2002); PPIAF and WSP (2001); Komives (1999).

249

Box 5.9   Providing Incentives to Extend Service in Côte d'Ivoire

THE WATER LEASE CONTRACT BETWEEN THE GOV-
ernment of Côte d'Ivoire and SODECI, a private
company, contains provisions to expand service
among low-income households. To aid such efforts,
the government promotes the installation of "social
connections" in households that meet eligibility criteria. These connections are financed by a charge,
separate from the water tariff, that SODECI collects from all customers. The proceeds are deposited
in a separate account, and the company retains the
same profit as on regular connections. Since the
lease was renewed in 1988, more than 300,000 new
connections have been established—90 percent of
them social connections.

Although SODECI has no financial disincentive
to serve new customers, a major drawback of the lease
contract is that the company is allowed to install connections only in legal settlements. Yet an estimated
70 percent of the unserved population are guest
workers and immigrants living in illegal settlements.

Source: PPIAF and WSP (2001).

courage innovation. To provide the strongest incentive for a utility to
seek creative and efficient approaches to meeting targets, quality and
performance regulations should be output-based rather than input-
based (PPIAF and WSP 2001). Minimum health standards for water
quality and pressure should not be compromised—but these are often
below the levels imposed by regulation. Legal restrictions on a utility,
such as exclusivity provisions or proscriptions against connections to
households without formal land title, can be formidable barriers (box
5.9). Rigid business practices, such as monthly billing, can also exclude
customers with low purchasing power (Baker and Tremolet 2000).

Organizing Water Regulation and Ensuring Enforcement Capacity

As with other infrastructure sectors, water can be regulated at the national, regional, or local level.[13] Because water is usually provided as a
local service that (especially after decentralization) is the responsibility
of local governments, these authorities must be well represented in the
regulatory agency. Few municipal governments have the capacity to design competitive contracting or carry out regulation, so obtaining expert advice may be essential to ensure balanced negotiations with more
knowledgeable private partners.

Municipalities have agreed to guarantee concessionaries against revenue losses in the Czech Republic and Hungary, creating a major risk
for taxpayers (Hall 1997). Municipal involvement in the regulatory

board of Buenos Aires and interference by several municipalities in Mexico City undermined regulatory autonomy and contributed to problems of politicization (Shirley and Menard 2002). Because municipalities are often water providers, conflicts of interest need to be avoided. In the water lease for Gdansk, Poland, the city is both the regulator and a contractual party, owning 49 percent of the consortium that holds the contract (Ringskog 1998).

Unclear relationships between levels of government can create problems for water regulation. In the water concession for Cordoba, Argentina, poorly defined responsibilities for the provincial government, which owned the infrastructure, and the municipality, which retained responsibility for making residential connections (the concessionaire was responsible only for extending the primary network), undermined the public sector's regulatory role (Nickson 2001). Such circumstances can strengthen the private operator's bargaining power. Sometimes the regulator has been bypassed entirely in critical decisionmaking—as in Buenos Aires, where the Ministry of the Economy and Department of Natural Resources renegotiated the water concession in 1997 without any involvement by the regulator. The outcome was appealed by consumer associations and the national ombudsman, partly because the process undercut the regulator's credibility (Conte Grand 1998).

Consumer involvement in water regulation can be an invaluable way to provide information to the regulator (especially on the needs of poor consumers) and create oversight of regulatory and operator behavior. Consumer representation in regulatory reviews is more common in industrial countries than in most developing and transition economies (even those that have implemented water reforms). Indeed, limited public disclosure of key information and contract provisions is common, and advocated by multinational corporations to protect commercial secrets.

For example, documents about the Budapest Sewerage Company, in which a consortium made up of Vivendi and a German company holds an equity share, are not available even to the city council, and matters concerning the company are debated in closed council sessions (Public Services International 2000). Transparency and two-way flows of information with the public on system performance, coupled with sound policies and institutions supporting regulation (including the rule of law, checks and balances, and protection of property rights and contracts), may be the best way to ensure that regulation fairly balances the interests of multiple stakeholders.

Reform Experiences and Lessons

STRUCTURAL AND REGULATORY REFORMS AND PRIVATE PARTIC-
ipation are more recent and less common in water than in other
infrastructure sectors, making it harder to obtain a clear picture
of outcomes. Most large public-private partnerships are only about five
years old (with a few much longer-lived exceptions such as the water
lease in Abidjan, Côte d'Ivoire, and the water concession in Macau,
China—which was launched in 1982 as the first of its type in Asia, but
built on decades of experience with private provision). Assessing reforms is also complicated because changes in institutional arrangements, especially those that convert public operations into formal
contracts with private providers, make explicit conditions that may
have been hidden—such as nonpayment of water bills by government
agencies, other implicit taxes and subsidies, and backlogs in system
maintenance.

Any assessment of reforms and institutional arrangements should
take full account of sector and economic conditions and of regulation
as applied. Such thorough analysis is not available for many cases over
time, especially not in a form that allows comparisons among regulatory and contractual regimes. This section summarizes findings from
the comparative analyses (across cities, countries, and institutions) that
have been done to date. Definitive conclusions about success or failure
are not yet possible, but many of the factors contributing to positive
and negative outcomes are becoming better understood.

Comparing Water System Reforms

Shirley and Menard (2002) compare the content and outcomes
(through 1996) of six water system reforms initiated between 1988–93:
the concession in Buenos Aires, service contracts in Mexico City, state
ownership and operation in Lima (where a concession was planned but
not implemented) and Santiago (including contracting), and leases in
Abidjan and Conakry. Initial conditions in the six cities are summarized
in table 5.3. Connection rates were lowest for the two African cities,
which were also the poorest and fastest growing. Water stress (unsus-
tainability of resources) was most severe in Lima and Mexico City.

Table 5.3 Initial Conditions and Reforms in Six Water Systems

Indicator	Buenos Aires	Mexico City	Lima	Santiago	Abidjan	Conakry
Year reform started	1993	1993	1992	1989	1988	1989
Type of reform						
Planned	Concession	Management contract	Concession	Sale	Lease[a]	Lease
Implemented	Concession	Service contract	State owned	State owned	Lease	Lease
Population in service area at start of reform (millions)	8.7	8.4	6.4	4.6	2.0	1.0
National GDP per capita at start of reform (U.S. dollars)	8,861	7,647	3,462	7,101	1,582	1,398
Population connected at start of reform (percent)						
Water[b]	70	97[c]	75	99	60	38[d]
Sewerage	58	86[c]	70	88	35	10
Annual population growth, 1980–95 (percent)	1.5[e]	3.1	2.4	1.8	5.1	5.6
Annual water production at start of reform (millions of cubic meters)	1,402	1,113	527	478	67	163

a. Before reform, the lease in Abidjan had characteristics similar to a management contract.

b. Includes private taps in yards of dwellings. These were predominant in Abidjan and Conakry, important in Mexico (20 percent of connections) and probably Lima, and minimal in Santiago and Buenos Aires.

c. 1990.

d. Includes people with access to standpipes or neighbors' taps.

e. 1980–91.

Source: Shirley and Menard (2002).

Regulation. Competition occurred only in Buenos Aires, Abidjan, and Conakry, through competitive bidding. With the only concession, regulation in Buenos Aires imposed a fuller range of financial risks on the operator (investor) than did the other systems. But the two leases also provided for efficiency pricing and full metering, with tariffs covering marginal costs as in Buenos Aires. Every city but Santiago provided cross-subsidies from high-volume to low-volume customers. Only Santiago both set expansion targets for the operator and made it affordable for poor people to connect (although this improved in Buenos Aires after contract renegotiation). None of the regulatory regimes had a very strong or formal institutional structure (commitment devices, regulatory neutrality, enforcement mechanisms, consumer representation), but Santiago had the best—which, perhaps ironically, represented state ownership and operation.

Results. Changes in economic welfare after the reforms—combining the effects to government, consumers, workers, and domestic investors—can be estimated and compared to a counterfactual (no reform) scenario. For the cases where data permit, the per capita welfare gains are estimated to be largest in Buenos Aires ($150 in 1996 prices), followed by Santiago ($64) and Conakry ($12). If Lima's concession had been implemented as designed, welfare gains are estimated at $85, compared with $8 in the actual case (see Shirley and Menard 2002).

The results of a few years of reform can be seen by comparing before and after indicators of efficiency and other performance measures. After reforms, labor productivity (measured in employees per connection) increased and operating costs dropped in every city (with operating costs falling below revenues everywhere except Mexico City). In addition, water and sewerage coverage expanded everywhere except Lima, though expansion would have occurred there if the concession had not been abandoned (table 5.4). New connections grew at a faster pace in every city except Lima, where the growth rate stayed the same. And unaccounted-for water—a measure combining physical losses (due to poor maintenance) and commercial losses (due to poor financial management or illegal use)—fell significantly in Buenos Aires, Lima, and Santiago but the improvement was less evident in the other three cities.

Quantitative Studies

Few studies have subjected performance data from different water systems to econometric analysis to determine factors driving better or worse outcomes. One such study by Estache and Kouassi (2002) derives

Table 5.4 Effects of Reforms on Access and Waste in Six Water Systems
(percent)

Indicator	Buenos Aires	Mexico City	Lima without concession	Lima with concession[a]	Santiago	Abidjan	Conakry
Water coverage[b]							
Pre-reform	70	95[c]	75	75	99	72[d]	38[e]
1996	81	97[f]	75	85	100	82[d]	47
Sewerage coverage							
Pre-reform	58	86[c]	70	70	88	35[d]	g
1996	62	91[f]	70	83	97	g	9[f]
Annual growth in new connections							
Pre-reform	2.1	n.a.	4.0		2.9	4.0	−0.1
Post-reform	2.8	5.1	4.0		3.8	6.7	8.5
Unaccounted-for water							
Pre-reform	44	37–47	42	42	34	13	35–60
1996	34	37	36	30	20	16	50

Note: Pre-reform refers to the year before reform started; see table 5.3. Post-reform refers to a span of dates.
a. Estimates based on draft concession contract.
b. Does not include public standpipes.
c. Data are for 1990.
d. Data are for all urban areas served by private operators.
e. Data are for 1989.
f. Data are for 1995.
g. Though data are not available, sewerage coverage in Abidjan and Conakry is not believed to have changed much.
Source: Shirley and Menard (2002).

a combined productivity indicator for 21 African water utilities and determines how each compares with an estimated "production frontier" for the group. The analysis finds considerable heterogeneity in performance and large scope for improvements. The authors conclude that a country's institutional capacity and quality of governance are key factors determining efficiency, and are more important than private participation in itself.[14] In a study of alternative efficiency measures for 50 Asian water utilities, Estache and Rossi (2001) find statistically significant evidence that private operation is correlated with greater efficiency.

Clarke and Wallsten (2002) compare the performance of African water systems in terms of their piped water coverage of urban households headed by individuals with different education levels (used as a measure of household welfare). This analysis finds that in countries with public operators, coverage of households where the head has no education is lower (25 percent) than in countries with established private operators (31 percent). Similar conclusions emerge when comparing the share of connected households with uneducated heads to the share of connected households whose heads have secondary education (thus controlling for the country's level of development). This study also concluded from cross-country analysis that there was no evidence that water and other infrastructure reforms harm low-income consumers, and that poor people seem to benefit in terms of having better chances of becoming connected to network services.

Lessons

In many countries the political economy of water has not been highly favorable to reform, which partly explains why the water sector is behind electricity, telecommunications, and transportation in restructuring and privatization. Major water reforms have tended to be provoked by public health crises and by fiscal and macroeconomic pressures that reduce water revenues. Inflation, mounting budget deficits, and rising government debt contributed to the reforms in Buenos Aires, Conakry, Lima, Mexico City, and Santiago in the late 1980s and early 1990s (Shirley and Menard 2002).

The condition that mattered most to the course of reform in the cities analyzed above was the relative power of potential winners and losers. Water reform typically has high social benefits but low political benefits, especially relative to other utility reform (Menard and Shirley 2001). The political benefits may come from expanded coverage, typically to poor urban households, and better service for middle-income groups. But these political gains may be smaller than the risks from necessary price increases and employment cutbacks in public utilities. Water reforms have been politically most difficult to sustain in cities where the marginal supply price of water is increasing quickly and wastewater creates large externalities—as in Lima and Mexico City. In Buenos Aires, by contrast, a cheaper, renewable water resource made it possible to cut water prices and still attract private investment (Noll, Shirley, and Cowan 2000).

Although it is too early to draw firm conclusions about what kinds of water reforms and institutional arrangements are most effective in different circumstances, the following observations can be made:

- Identifying winners and losers in advance, and adjusting the balance where possible, may increase the sustainability of reform. A perception of fairness is important—as evidenced by protests in Buenos Aires when newly connected households were charged fees that existing customers had not incurred.
- Price increases can be acceptable when customers see that quality and service are improving, when they are well informed, and when they can control their consumption. Where supply is limited, higher prices can help expand coverage and so benefit poor people.
- Where expanded coverage to poor households is a policy objective, it must be a deliberate focus of regulatory and contract design. Where necessary, subsidies should be provided to support connections—not consumption—and regulation should favor innovation and competition by providers.
- Lack of information is a major constraint to the private sector (especially potential entrants), to the public sector as regulator, and to consumers. Improving access to information may ease distrust and defuse political volatility.

Notes

1. "Safe" water includes water obtained through a household connection, public standpipe, borehole, protected dug well, or spring water and rainwater collection. "Adequate" sanitation includes connection to a public sewer or septic system, or possession of a pour flush, simple pit, or ventilated improved pit latrine.

2. Wastewater capture and treatment may be considered the fifth and sixth components of supply, or a separate system of their own (possibly also including sludge disposal).

3. Water treatment and transportation are most likely to be the bottleneck elements of natural monopoly in urban water systems (Noll, Shirley, and Cowan 2000).

4. Vertical integration can also be justified as well as a way of internalizing the environmental externalities of sewage discharge and of permitting cross-

subsidization of sewerage costs by water payments, since sewerage services cannot be disconnected for nonpayment (Foster 1996).

5. In Durban, South Africa, for example, a conventional household water connection costs about $180, while a sewerage connection costs $800 (McLeod 2002).

6. Condominial sewers involve small bore pipes at a shallow depth running through yards linking household connections to a neighborhood receptor. The system requires neighbors to maintain the network and so substitutes an institutional input (collective action) for capital (the physical assets).

7. These methods are not suitable for very dense settlements or some geological conditions because they can contaminate underground water.

8. Although in rural areas non-networked water provision has long been the norm, the low-cost technologies becoming more formally recognized in urban areas may be linked to the network.

9. Increasing linear tariffs do not necessarily assign marginal cost responsibility in a causal sense because a utility's marginal cost of providing water does not change appreciably as a household's water use changes.

10. Because some users are not able to participate effectively in water markets and because of collective action problems, poorly defined property rights, and transactional and information costs, water pricing can take into account only some opportunity costs and externalities (Noll, Shirley, and Cowan 2000).

11. In the United Kingdom periodic cost adjustments for unforeseen circumstances can include price reductions if external factors generate significant savings for the utility (Klein 1996b).

12. Most of the research literature on the politics of regulation focuses on risks of capture, not expropriation (Noll, Shirley, and Cowan 2000).

13. Issues related to water resource management, however, often need to be addressed at a high level, which may be cross-regional and even cross-border.

14. The sample of 21 utilities included only 2 that involved the private sector (through leases). According to the analysis of efficiency, these were not the best-performing companies during the period under study.

CHAPTER SIX

An Agenda for Action

I NFRASTRUCTURE POLICY IS UNDERGOING MULTIFACETED revision. More than a decade has passed since the first widespread efforts to restructure and privatize network utilities. During that time the high-tech (especially Internet) bubble inflated, then burst—leading to the collapse of stock markets around the globe. In addition, developing and transition economies experienced a series of financial crises and a sharp drop in private investment in infrastructure (from a peak of US$130 billion in 1997 to about US$60 billion in 2001). More recently, California's electricity crisis has confounded regulators, analysts, and other experts.

As a result policymakers in developing and transition economies are seeking clear answers on what to do about infrastructure, and reassurances on (or qualifications of) confident messages from the past. The world's media, which just a few years ago was praising privatization in near harmony, is now focusing on the growing skepticism and social costs of shifting infrastructure activities from public to private control (box 6.1).

There is compelling evidence that restructuring and privatization, when designed and implemented well, can significantly improve infrastructure performance. Still, critics of reform are right to point out the many cases where privatization has been undertaken without institutional safeguards and conducted in ways widely viewed as illegitimate. Under those circumstances transferring state assets to private control may have been a dubious achievement (Stiglitz 1999). Moreover, concerns are growing about the distributional effects of privatization and market liberalization—especially their effects on basic services for poor households and other disadvantaged groups (Chisari, Estache, and Waddams Price 2003).

> ## Box 6.1   The World Bank Wonders about Utility Privatizations
>
> THE WORLD BANK, THE APOSTLE OF PRIVATIZATION, IS HAVING A crisis of faith. What seemed like a no-brainer idea in the 1990s—that developing nations should sell off money-losing state infrastructure to efficient private investors—no longer seems so obvious, especially when it comes to power and water utilities. Investors who once seemed eager to risk their money on Brazilian power plants or African sewers are pulling back. Commercial banks' power-project financing in the developing world and former Eastern bloc nations, which peaked at $25.9 billion in 1998, totaled just $5.7 billion last year, according to Dealogic, a British data firm. Consumers, feeling deceived, increasingly associate privatization with higher rates for them and higher profits for foreign companies and corrupt officials. The unexpected turn of events has left privatization enthusiasts at the World Bank wondering what went wrong.
>
> *Source:* Michael M. Phillips, *The Wall Street Journal,* 21 July 2003.

Thus there is an urgent need to analyze the successes and failures associated with past reforms and to identify the instruments and policies that should guide ongoing and future efforts. The agenda proposed in this chapter focuses on the efficiency and distributional effects of restructuring and privatization programs and on several second generation regulatory reforms—of pricing, access to bottleneck facilities, and subsidies—that will be needed if such programs are to achieve their public interest goals (Jacobs 1999).

Assessing Reform's Effects on Performance and Distribution

A LOT OF WORK HAS BEEN DONE ON THE ECONOMIC AND social impacts of infrastructure reform in developing and transition economies. But except in Latin America, brief reform histories impede empirical analysis of the performance of restructured and privatized industries. Expanding pre- and post-reform analysis will require systematically collecting cross-country data (box 6.2), defining

---

Box 6.2   The Need for Data on Infrastructure Reform

EXTENSIVE INFORMATION IS REQUIRED TO EMPIRICALLY ANALYZE the links between specific policy reforms and infrastructure performance. Cross-country and time-series data are needed on measures of market structure (industry concentration, vertical and horizontal integration, ownership structure), conduct and performance (profits, prices, productivity, investment, quality of service, coverage ratios), and numerous governance and institutional variables (regulatory independence, discretion, and budget, structure of regulatory agencies, market structure regulation, method of controlling prices).

Because comprehensive data on these basic economic variables are not currently available, it is imperative that a systematic cross-country data collection effort be undertaken. International financial institutions have collected a lot of useful data in the context of their infrastructure activities. At times these institutions have imposed conditions on their loans to promote better infrastructure performance, and have periodically tried to review experiences and outcomes. Thus they have some of the needed data. A systematic collation of these data, coupled with collection of additional variables noted above, could help overcome critical knowledge deficiencies.

---

and constructing basic economic measures for various aspects of reform and industry performance, and determining appropriate techniques for econometric estimation.

Structural Options and Post-Reform Performance

Many options are available to countries with strong political commitment to reforming publicly owned network utilities. Much of the debate on how to restructure and privatize such utilities focuses on industrial structure. Accordingly, policymakers and government advisers pay a lot of attention to questions such as:

- Should all assets—such as generation, transmission, and distribution networks in electricity, or rolling stock, track, and stations in railroads—be privatized? Or should private ownership be limited to segments where competitive markets are feasible?

- Should competition be pursued in small markets?
- What is the optimal degree of vertical integration between various stages of production (for example, between generation, transmission, and distribution in electricity)—bearing in mind that investments or operational decisions in one area can influence operational efficiency in others?
- Similarly, to the extent that investment and operational coordination is needed between and within regions (as with electricity), what is the optimal degree of horizontal fragmentation?

Despite this analysis and debate, there is not sufficient evidence that in a given utility a certain structural configuration is more likely to attract long-term private investment and improve performance. Thus, far more before and after analysis is needed to clarify the relationship between structural reform and industry performance. Such analysis should take into account numerous country and sector characteristics—particularly the industry's regulatory framework. Preliminary findings indicate that successful restructuring is associated with the extent to which regulation enables asset owners to resolve disputes independently and earn a fair return on their investments.

Indeed, because no organizational structure is obviously superior, some analysts believe that what Levy and Spiller (1996) call "regulatory governance" is more important than industrial structure when it comes to attracting long-term private investment and improving performance. According to this view, successful reform requires first establishing credible regulation, and only then refining the industry's structure.

Sequencing strategies. Among the first considerations for any reform program is whether there is a logical sequence for reforms—and if there is, whether it is costly to undertake them out of order. Early reforms should address the most important problems and, if possible, build momentum for future reforms and minimize risks of failure and policy reversal. Reversible and less risky reforms can be undertaken more readily than irreversible (or costly to reverse) and more risky reforms. Some irreversible reforms can have the advantage of establishing commitment to future changes, and privatization is often seen as one such reform. But irreversible reforms require more careful design and assessment.

Evidence is emerging on what constitute robust, self-sustaining, and desirable reform strategies and what strategies are risky and may lead to undesirable outcomes. Privatization is reversible only at high external cost (diminished reputation among foreign investors), and poorly designed privatization can complicate subsequent reforms. Structural choices, such as the degree of vertical or horizontal integration, can also be costly or difficult to reverse.

Next steps. Several factors may explain the varying performance of restructured and privatized network utilities: the industrial structure adopted, the extent of market liberalization, the speed and sequencing of reforms, the quality of regulatory governance, and the interaction between market rules and structure. To get a better sense of how these factors contribute to cross-country variations in utility performance, there is a need for more empirical assessments of different structural configurations and unbundling schemes, changes in ownership and regulatory governance, market designs and rules, and regimes governing access to bottleneck facilities. By pooling cross-country and time-series data and examining different approaches to liberalization, regulation, and privatization, future empirical studies should seek to identify and disentangle the effects of initial conditions, policy design variables, and other country characteristics. Thus future studies should shed light on both basic questions and contentious issues such as:

- The proper scope, pace, and sequencing for reforms—for example, whether restructuring should occur before privatization, whether restructuring coupled with corporatization and the creation of regulatory institutions but without privatization is viable, what political condition require slow progress through the various stages, and what conditions permit a compressed schedule—and how costly it is to undertake reforms in the wrong order.
- How to improve incentives for efficiency in operations while maintaining incentives for (and the ability to finance) efficient expansion, and whether the presence of coordination economies implies that vertical separation will undermine the ability to undertake investments based on long-term systemwide planning in each utility.
- How to ensure that the gains from improved efficiency are shared with consumers.

- Whether there are significant gains from restructuring moderately well-run utilities.
- How market rules, and regulatory, ownership, and restructuring choices affect pricing (level, structure, and volatility) and operating efficiency.
- What is the minimal set of regulations needed under ideal circumstances and how this set should be expanded in response to equity concerns, consumer protection, and other social goals.

By assessing how regulation, market design, and industry structure affect performance, future studies could provide valuable guidance to policymakers in developing and transition economies seeking to strengthen incentives for efficient operation of network utilities. In particular, for each feasible option these studies could discuss a relevant role model and examples close to the recipient country's initial conditions, questions to ask, problems that may arise (including unintended consequences of reforms) and how hard they are to fix, regulatory and institutional requirements, sequencing options, and the costs and benefits of competitive restructuring, deregulation, and privatization.

Distributive Impacts of Infrastructure Reforms

Most evaluations of infrastructure restructuring and privatization have focused on operating and financial performance—labor productivity, service quality, investment and network expansion, profitability, and market valuation. But increased efficiency and profitability might come at the expense of workers, customers, and other groups as a result of higher prices, reduced levels and worsened terms of employment, and lower-quality services. Thus a comprehensive welfare assessment of infrastructure reforms must consider their effects on these groups. In particular, it is important to analyze how reform-induced changes in service prices, quality, and access affect the welfare of households in different expenditure categories, and how reform-induced changes affect employment, wages, and earnings inequality. Such an assessment requires systematic household income, expenditure, and employment surveys (McKenzie and Mookherjee 2003).

One of the most serious defects of infrastructure policy during the pre-reform era was its failure to expand services to poor areas, both rural and urban. As a result most of the world's poor people had no access to basic infrastructure services, or very limited access and very poor quality. Thus any welfare assessment should also analyze how restructuring and privatization affect service expansion and improvements for poor households.

Promoting access to poor households.   In recent years there have been growing concerns about how privatization and market liberalization have affected low-income households in developing and transition economies (Estache, Foster, and Wodon 2002). Some observers are concerned that competition will make the traditional method of financing access for low-income households—cross-subsidies from higher-income customers—difficult if not impossible. The fear is that new service providers entering the market will target only the most profitable customers, eroding the profits that incumbent enterprises used to subsidize service for low-income groups and high-cost areas. So, even if privatization and competition result in service expansion and lower average tariffs, poor households might end up paying higher prices and governments might need to find new sources of financing for universal access—a difficult task in developing and transition economies due to inefficient and distorted tax systems.

Low service coverage among low-income households in urban or periurban areas of informal settlement, slums, and rural areas in most developing economies indicates that public monopolies have failed to achieve universal access (figure 6.1). But it is not clear that privatization and liberalization will automatically benefit these households. Although public monopolies are often overstaffed, inefficient, and lack the resources needed to expand services, governments often heavily subsidize tariffs. Moreover, many utilities subsidize certain customers and services—though these funds do not always reach poor people (see chapters 1 and 5). Thus the impact that reform has on coverage will depend on how it influences incentives for investment and prices for poor customers.

The limited data on how reform affects poor people—drawn from case studies and household surveys—suggest important trends. First, there is little evidence that reform consistently reduces access for poor urban or rural households (Clarke and Wallsten 2002; Foster and Irusta 2003). Even when service prices have increased for these households, the share of poor urban and rural residents with connections has often not fallen, and in many cases has even increased. Further, allowing

Figure 6.1   Telephone and Water Access in Urban and Rural Areas of Developing Regions, 1990s

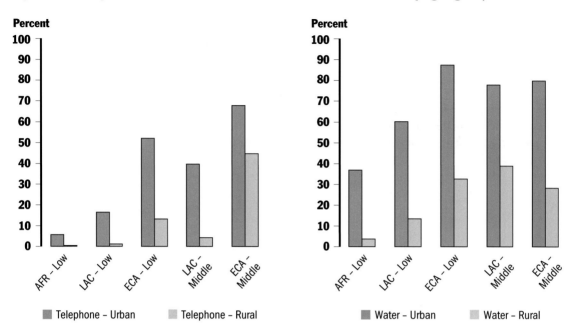

Note: AFR is Sub-Saharan Africa; LAC is Latin America and the Caribbean; ECA is Europe and Central Asia; Low are low-income countries; Middle are middle-income countries. Income classifications for countries are based upon classifications in World Bank (2002b). Regional averages are computed as simple averages (i.e., no weighting).
Source: Clarke and Wallsten (2002).

competition can dramatically improve infrastructure services for poor people. Competition can allow a range of price and quality options, making service possible to regions and customers that a monopoly provider would never have found profitable.

Still, the impacts of reform vary by country and city. Where coverage is already high among poor households or many poor customers have informal or illegal connections, large price hikes and formalization of customer accounts can reduce coverage among poor households even if overall coverage increases. By contrast, if service was heavily rationed before reform, privatization and liberalization can increase coverage for poor households even if prices rise.

Designing more effective subsidies.   Many of the infrastructure subsidies in developing countries are very poorly targeted. As a result poor people and other vulnerable groups capture only a small share of these

266

Box 6.3   Criteria for Designing Subsidies

SUBSIDY SCHEMES AND REFORMS SHOULD BE DESIGNED TO achieve:

- *Effective targeting*—benefits should accrue to the intended beneficiaries, such as poor people or rural populations.
- *Positive net benefits*—subsidies should pass a cost-benefit test.
- *Administrative simplicity*—schemes should have reasonable administrative costs.
- *Transparency*—financial costs and payment channels should be clearly defined and open to public scrutiny.

---

subsidies (Foster, Pattanayak, and Prokopy 2003). A key reason for this shortcoming is that most poor households in developing countries lack access to basic infrastructure services. In transition economies, where service coverage is much higher, subsidies have done a better job of reaching poor people (Lovei and others 2000).

There is no universally appropriate model for designing subsidies. Every support program must be tailored to national and local characteristics, including the country's stage of development, institutional capacity, and economic conditions and state of public finances. Still, several basic principles should be applied when designing and implementing subsidy reforms (box 6.3).

Effective targeting is arguably the most important consideration—and greatest challenge—in designing and reforming subsidies. A variety of targeted subsidy mechanisms have been devised that rely on observable indicators of poverty: the amount of services consumed, the characteristics of the neighborhood or region (geographic targeting), and the characteristics of the individual household or dwelling (individual targeting). Preliminary analyses suggest that explicit targeting—geographic or individual—performs better than implicit schemes that rely on modifications of the tariff structure (for example, changing the size of the lifeline first block under an increasing block tariff structure). Explicit targeting reduces errors of inclusion (the extent of subsidy leakage to unintended beneficiaries). But it also tends to substantially increase errors of exclusion (the share of intended recipients who do not benefit).

These tradeoffs can be resolved only with reference to the policy goals underlying each subsidy program, and require considerable empirical analysis. Moreover, targeted connection subsidies perform much better than targeted consumption subsidies by reducing both inclusion and exclusion errors. Recovering connection fees through moderate monthly access charges or providing credit to finance connections (or both) might be especially appropriate in countries with underdeveloped capital markets for personal loans (Kebede 2002). Otherwise, high connection fees can preclude low-income households from obtaining infrastructure services, even if such households could afford equivalent monthly payments (World Bank 1992).

Every price subsidy scheme, no matter how well designed, suffers from limitations—such as distortion of relative prices, leakage to untargeted groups, or wasteful consumption—that reduce economic efficiency. The redistribution goals embodied in such schemes can be achieved with less distortion of economic efficiency through targeted income transfers under a broader social safety net. Governments can allow prices to signal their true economic scarcity costs while providing direct subsidies to consumers who cannot afford those prices (Foster, Gomez-Lobo, and Halpern 2000a). But the administrative requirements of direct subsidies may be beyond the capacity of many developing and transition economies. Moreover, there are practical difficulties in designing eligibility criteria. Thus, despite their imperfections, targeted price subsidies might still be preferable.

Next steps.   To design pro-poor regulation and more effective subsidies, more consistent and comprehensive household data on consumption, willingness to pay, and various socioeconomic characteristics should be collected and rigorously evaluated (Foster, Gomez-Lobo, and Halpern 2000b). In particular, poor people's demand for services needs to be analyzed more thoroughly—including factors that affect their decision to connect, the role of alternative and informal service providers, and how the presence of alternatives affects household connections.

Understanding poor people's willingness to pay and their demand for services is critical to assessing the effects of reform and expanding access. For example, data constraints prevent policy analysis from determining whether households remain unconnected because they are unwilling to pay for service in the presence of (perhaps informal) alternatives, or whether those alternatives exist because households cannot afford to connect or the utility does not provide service in the area. Knowing the reasons for nonconnection is crucial for developing policies that enhance access and for designing subsidies that extend services to poor and rural customers.

The performance of alternate subsidy mechanisms in terms of targeting, extent of pricing and other economic distortions, extent of service expansion to poor households, administrative costs, and other criteria (see box 6.3) requires rigorous empirical assessment. In particular, the relative merits of consumption, connection, and direct subsidies need to be empirically analyzed to evaluate their appropriateness in different country and industry environments.

Pricing Reform—Balancing Efficiency and Equity

SUCCESSFUL RESTRUCTURING AND PRIVATIZATION REQUIRE pricing policies that provide signals and incentives for efficiency by customers, suppliers, and investors. Yet in many developing and transition economies pricing continues to undermine economic efficiency (World Bank 1994b). Prices are often still set by ministries with mandates to establish price controls that support macroeconomic goals (Bruce, Kessides, and Kneifel 1999). So, in addition to adopting privatization timetables and establishing regulatory institutions, developing and transition economies must rebalance and regulate prices as part of second generation reforms (see chapter 1).

Some deviations from optimal pricing are due to political and social constraints: noneconomic and equity considerations inevitably influence efforts to implement economically efficient pricing (Kahn 1988; Dinar 2000). Indeed, inefficient pricing is often the outcome—and instrument—of a complex system of cross-subsidies under the broad domain of social policy. But deviations are also due to lack of appreciation for alternative pricing schemes that could better balance economic efficiency and social equity. In particular, price differentiation and competitive pricing flexibility—potentially valuable tools for achieving adequate revenue and expanding service to poor people—have not been sufficiently exploited in developing and transition economies.

Policy solutions consistent with both economic efficiency and social equity are not always available or politically feasible. Accordingly, price

269

reform is among the most challenging tasks for policymakers in developing and transition economies (Kessides 1997; Newbery 2000b, 2000c, 2000d, 2000e; Noll 2000d). It is also a policy area where replicating approaches in industrial countries will likely prove extremely problematic, and where technical assistance from multilateral organizations and other external advisers has been highly unsatisfactory.

As a first step developing and transition economies should examine differentiated, nonlinear, and other pricing schemes that could ease the transition to cost-reflective, competitive prices. The emphasis should not be on setting "optimal" tariffs but on reforming tariffs—to find feasible changes in tariff structures that both improve welfare and generate adequate revenue (Armstrong and Rees 2000). Even optimal prices, if instituted extremely quickly and without enough notice, can lead to a damaging and costly transition (Baumol 1995). Moreover, customers without viable alternatives will suffer the most. Thus policymakers should plan early for a smooth transition to cost-reflective prices (Monson and Rohlfs 1993). This point has been ignored in some restructuring and privatization programs, creating public disenchantment with reform and a danger of policy reversal.

Pricing Issues in Developing and Transition Economies

The main pricing issues for policymakers in developing and transition economies are inadequate revenue and unsustainable social pricing.

Inadequate revenue. Inefficient pricing was one of the main reasons for the deteriorating performance of infrastructure sectors in developing and transition economies prior to the reform era. Although inefficient pricing was also a problem in industrial countries, their less developed counterparts were less able to afford the costs of misallocated resources and inefficient production. The failure of many governments to prescribe cost-reflective tariffs hindered service expansion and decapitalized network utilities. Service quality suffered, and the inability to provide better and more varied services constrained domestic growth and hampered international competitiveness. This problem was particularly pronounced in telecommunications but also serious in electricity and transportation.

Unsustainable social pricing. Because the demand for many infrastructure services is highly price and income inelastic, their pricing has important distributional implications. Subsidizing basic services such as electricity and water appears politically attractive because it can approximate a lump-sum grant based on the number of household members. Conversely, raising the price of basic services appears like a lump-sum tax that bears heavily on the poor, the elderly, and those with large families (Newbery 2000a). Not surprisingly, moves toward cost-reflective tariffs often encounter strong political obstacles.

Thus past infrastructure policies have resulted in prices with systematic cross-subsidies (Kahn 1984; World Bank 1994b). The publicly articulated rationale is that such policies foster social goals (helping customers who would otherwise be disadvantaged) and economic externalities associated with universal service. But economic theory and regulatory experience suggest that it is impossible to maintain significant cross-subsidies in the structure of prices for long, with open entry and no remedial policies, regardless of whether that seems desirable (box 6.4).

Box 6.4   Picking Apart Cross-Subsidies

TO USE THIS TERM RIGOROUSLY, A CUSTOMER SERVICE that is priced above its stand-alone cost provides a cross-subsidy to another customer service that is priced below its incremental cost. Economic logic teaches that prices with cross-subsidies are unsustainable in an environment of open entry, and that such competition predictably leads to inefficiencies. The reason is simple—entrants will be impelled by the profit motive to divert the overpriced business, regardless of these entrants' efficiency, while entrants are unlikely to relieve the incumbent service provider from the financial burden of serving customers whose prices do not compensate the costs required to serve them. Thus, even suppliers with inefficiently high costs may find entry profitable in reaction to pricing that has the mandate of providing a flow of cross subsidies. Entry of this kind not only raises industry costs, but it also erodes the very ability to finance the subsidies that motivate the policy.

The other side of the cross-subsidization coin is the set of prices that lie below their services' incremental costs. While these prices convey the subsidies that motivate the policy, they also discourage the competitive entry of alternative suppliers who would contribute to industry efficiency. An entrant might have incremental costs of providing services that are lower than the incremental costs of the incumbent service provider, but are greater than the level of the cross-subsidized prices. Such a supplier might enter and enhance consumer welfare in an undistorted competitive environment, and yet find it financially unrewarding to enter in the face of cross-subsidies.

Source: Willig (1994a).

So, policymakers in developing and transition economies suffer from a seemingly irreconcilable dilemma. Social development goals and political pressures have led them to set infrastructure prices with significant cross-subsidies. Yet in recent years these policymakers have sought to restructure, liberalize, and privatize their infrastructure sectors. These two goals are incompatible (Baumol 1999), because competitive entry will destroy the cross-subsidies.

Possible solution—competitive pricing flexibility.   How can countries achieve adequate revenue while protecting disadvantaged groups? Economics offers well-established principles and insights from both theory and regulatory experience around the world.

Uniform pricing and regulatory prohibition of price differentiation can seriously undermine revenue adequacy by limiting the ability of infrastructure operators to exploit demand characteristics and extract more revenue from high-value customers. As an alternative, demand-differentiated pricing can alleviate the need for radical tariff rebalancing. If an economy is to benefit from market liberalization, infrastructure entities must be allowed to compete with flexible prices and terms. Prices will best serve the public interest if they are allowed to vary among classes of users in accordance with the value of service and in response to the marginal costs of service. The need to set some prices low to retain business means that other prices should be allowed to be higher to secure adequate revenue.

In telecommunications, for example, policymakers should permit the rapid installation of new telephone lines—wired or wireless—based on prices that reflect differences in the value of service and clear service backlogs. In addition, customers who place more value on a service should contribute more revenue to cover unattributable, fixed, and common costs. By offering discounts with nonlinear prices to noncaptive customers, the utility will be able to recover the costs of the local loop with marginal access prices much closer to incremental costs and keep all customers in the network, benefiting all.

Next steps.   The priority for action, involving both applied research and detailed policy analysis, is to develop practical, flexible, differentiated pricing rules for infrastructure services that balance economic efficiency and social equity. This agenda will also entail creating a cross-country database on infrastructure prices and regulations that permits emerging regulators to draw on international benchmarks.

Reform programs in several countries have been criticized as excessively increasing prices and hurting poor people, yet reform is essential to achieving development goals—including poverty reduction. Pricing is an area of policy where practical research is needed to aid the real-time design and application of better—second best, but workable—reforms. This applied research should draw on the theoretical literature on competitive pricing flexibility and nonlinear pricing to design transitional approaches that allow cost-reflective prices in restructured and privatized network utilities, taking into account regulatory and information constraints and perceptions of social fairness.

A Practical Pricing Regime

Data shortcomings are a key obstacle to economically efficient pricing regulation. And because of weak auditing and inadequately trained regulators, information problems are likely to be especially severe in developing and transition economies (Beato and Laffont 2002). In particular, information is generally unobtainable on demand elasticities and other attributes of demand.

Constrained market pricing. Constrained market pricing offers a promising solution to this dilemma (ICC 1985). This approach divides the setting of product prices into two stages. In the first stage the regulator imposes floors and ceilings on the prices of the regulated firm. These limits can be determined solely with the aid of information on costs. The second stage of price setting is left to the firm, which will be driven by self-interest to take into account demand conditions. The firm is prohibited from setting prices that violate the limits imposed by the regulator but is free to select prices that best promote its interests.

Regulated ceiling and floor prices are derived from the competitive market model. Thus the firm cannot adopt a price higher than what an efficient entrant (rival) could afford to charge for the product in a competitive market where inputs are available on competitive terms. This price ceiling is the stand-alone cost of the product or service (see executive summary, endnote 4). A price constrained not to exceed the stand-alone cost ensures that customers pay no more than they would have if the item had been sold in an effectively competitive (contestable) market. The floor price reflects the product's marginal or average incremental cost. This approach, in essence, seeks to enforce competitive behavior where such behavior is not the automatic result of market conditions (Baumol and Willig 1988).

The main purpose of the stand-alone cost ceiling, aside from its role in eliciting economic efficiency, is to protect consumers from monopolistic exploitation by the regulated firm. Similarly, the main purpose of the floor price, economic efficiency aside, is to protect actual or prospective rivals of the regulated firm from predatory pricing and related practices that can handicap these competitors or drive them from the field.

The application of differentiated pricing in developing and transition economies, when it has even been considered, has often been dismissed as being too difficult and contrary to social equity. But it is possible, and indeed imperative, for such a pricing approach to be made practical in infrastructure sectors facing chronic revenue inadequacy, underinvestment, and low coverage. Differentiated pricing rules should be considered a source of qualitative guidance rather than a generator of precise, definitive pricing prescriptions. Price differentiation can do much more to alleviate revenue inadequacy than can standard uniform price rebalancing schemes (such as across the board price hikes), and can provide greater potential for social equity than unsustainable internal cross-subsidies under uniform prices.

Next steps. Stand-alone and incremental costs will have to be calculated if constrained market pricing is to be used to help determine the reasonableness of utility rates. Given the likely difficulties of estimating these costs in developing and transition economies, international benchmarking should be carefully considered. At the least, the potential applicability of software developed to estimate stand-alone costs, especially in the United States, should be examined. Moreover, there is a need to assess whether the ceilings on pricing imposed by constrained market pricing sufficiently address concerns about higher prices for poor consumers. Further empirical evidence is required to address these concerns.

Facilitating Access to Bottleneck Facilities

U TILITY RESTRUCTURING REQUIRES POLICYMAKERS IN DE-
veloping and transition economies to address a difficult new
issue. As a part of restructuring, potential competitors often
require access to essential (bottleneck) network facilities. Thus the removal of legal barriers to competitive entry is not sufficient to ensure
effective competition in infrastructure. Competitors must also have access to bottleneck facilities on nondiscriminatory terms if they are to
have a reasonable opportunity to compete. Explicit regulatory intervention may be required to ensure such access, particularly if these facilities are controlled by the incumbent infrastructure operators, who
will often have business incentives to deny rivals fair access.

Emerging experience from several countries indicates that the allocation of bottleneck facilities and the broad issues of access and interconnection are extremely important in infrastructure deregulation and competitive restructuring. Regulators must identify appropriate terms and
scope for sharing these facilities. The benefits of liberalizing the potentially
competitive segments of infrastructure industries will not obtain without
a proper framework for access and interconnection (Armstrong and Doyle
1995; Valetti and Estache 1998; Kessides, Ordover, and Willig 1999).

Regulators in developing and transition economies must ensure that
competitors have access to bottleneck facilities on terms consistent with
efficient competition—setting a level and structure of access prices that
promote dynamic efficiency through entry and investment decisions
while enabling the owner of the network to remain financially solvent.
Prices should be high enough to be compensatory (at least covering the
long-run incremental cost of the entrant's use of the network), yet not
so high as to preclude efficient operations by the entrant.

The access problem is especially vexing when competitors require a
bottleneck input controlled by one of their rivals. Monopoly control of
bottleneck facilities can create powerful incentives to behave anticompetitively and cross-subsidize unregulated competitive activities from
regulated monopoly ones. Without regulatory constraint, the holder of
the bottleneck monopoly can repress competition by creating artificial
handicaps for its rivals for the final products sold to consumers. The
monopolist can impose costs on its competitors by impeding their access to the bottleneck, thereby raising the prices that they must charge
to cover their elevated costs and so weakening their ability to compete.

**Access and
interconnection rules
are one of the central
regulatory tasks for
network utilities**

275

Two Approaches

The economic literature offers two ways to price bottleneck facilities efficiently: the Baumol-Willig efficient component pricing rule, or parity pricing, and the Laffont-Tirole global price cap rule (Baumol, Ordover, and Willig 1997; Laffont and Tirole 1994, 1996). Under efficient component pricing the holder of the bottleneck facility should charge as much for its services as it would earn from providing them itself. This approach is consistent with efficient competition—it ensures that responsibility for supplying contested services is distributed among actual and potential rivals in a way that minimizes total costs. But it does not permit competition to fulfill other important functions of eliminating allocative inefficiency and eroding monopoly profits. Thus regulation must determine how large a markup of the retail price above marginal cost is economically efficient and what level of contribution should then be included in access charges. This requirement is likely to be violated in developing and transition economies with deficient regulation, where regulated price structures are often inefficient.

The Laffont-Tirole rule recognizes that the profit of the integrated incumbent is an increasing function of both the access charge and the final retail price. Under a breakeven constraint a higher access charge would permit the regulated firm to lower its final price. A regulator concerned with consumer welfare would take this tradeoff explicitly into account. The socially optimal access charge will depend on the benefits of reducing the retail price (which will depend on the elasticity of demand) and the effects on productive inefficiency of raising the access charge (which will depend on entrants' elasticity of supply).

Despite their internal consistency and powerful theoretical results, translating either approach into workable rules and actual access prices has been proven extraordinarily difficult and contentious. The first approach suffers from restrictive assumptions that limit its applied policy content. Indeed, the case for adopting the efficient component pricing rule is not so unequivocal if allocative and dynamic efficiency are important issues, as is likely in many developing and transition economies—that is, when even inefficient competition could make a substantial contribution to allocative efficiency and to increased efficiency and service innovation (Kahn and Taylor 1994). The Laffont-Tirole rule has substantial information requirements (demand and supply elasticities are hard to estimate). Thus it is challenging to translate it into operational rules than can be applied in real world settings.

Next Steps

An important policy priority in the restructured utilities of developing and transition economies is developing regulation for network access that has realistic prospects of being implemented effectively. There is an urgent need to translate the principles and results of theoretical and analytic work on access into workable rules and procedures, especially in the face of severe problems measuring relevant economic variables. One promising direction for applied policy analysis is to build on the powerful insights of the efficient component pricing rule and the Laffont-Tirole price cap rule, and develop a hybrid model that combines the two approaches with the objective of promoting productive and allocative efficiency. Moreover, in developing and transition economies it is imperative to identify the conditions, if any, under which it is appropriate to use access pricing as an instrument to promote supplementary goals (such as expanding service to poor people) that go beyond attainment of economic efficiency.

References

AAR (Association of American Railroads). 2003. "Why the Rail Reregulation Debate Is Important." Policy and Economics Department, Washington, D.C.

ADB (Asian Development Bank). 2000. *Developing Best Practices for Promoting Private Sector Investment in Infrastructure: Water Supply.* Manila, Philippines.

ANRT (Agence National de Reglementation des Telecommunications). 2000. "Interconnection Conflicts: The Moroccan Case." Paper presented at an International Telecommunication Union workshop on Fixed-Mobile Interconnection, 20–22 September, Geneva.

Ahortor, C. 2003. "Regulatory Impact in Ghana." Paper prepared for a University of Manchester conference on Regulatory Impact Assessment: Strengthening Regulation Policy and Practice, 26–27 November, Manchester, U.K.

Alcazar, L., M. Abdala, and M. Shirley. 2000. "The Buenos Aires Water Concession." Policy Research Working Paper 2311. World Bank, Washington, D.C.

Alcazar, L., L. Xu, and A. Zuluaga. 2000. "Institutions, Politics and Contracts: The Attempt to Privatize the Water and Sanitation Utility of Lima, Peru." Policy Research Working Paper 2478. World Bank, Washington, D.C.

Alexander, I., C. Mayer, and H. Weeds. 1996. "Regulatory Structure and Risk and Infrastructure Firms—An International Comparison." Policy Research Working Paper 1698. World Bank, Washington, D.C.

Alfaro, R. 1996. "Introduccion de la Competencia en un Monopolio Natural y del Elemento Social en un Empresarial." Privatizacion y Responsabilidad Social, Programa de Gestion Urbana PGU Oficina Regional para America Latina y el Caribe. Serie Gestion Urbana, Volumen 5.

Alfaro, R., V. Blanlot, R. Bradburg, and J. Briscoe. 1997. "Reforming Former Public Monopolies: The Case of Water Supply." World Bank, Washington, D.C.

al Khouri, R. 1999. "Maritime and Air Transport: The Potential Gains from Liberalization." Paper presented at the Third Mediterranean

Development Forum, 5–8 March, Cairo, Egypt.

Apoyo Consultoria. 2002. "Feedback to Regulators from Consumers." Paper presented at the International Telecommunication Union Global Symposium for Regulators, Hong Kong, China.

Arellano, M. 2003. "Diagnosing and Mitigating Market Power in Chile's Electricity Industry." Cambridge Working Paper in Economics CWPE 0327, University of Cambridge.

Arizu, B. 2003. "Market Surveillance—Lessons Learned in Latin America." Paper presented at the World Bank Energy Forum, February, Washington, D.C.

Armstrong, M., and C. Doyle. 1995. "The Economics of Access Pricing." Organisation for Economic Co-operation and Development, Paris.

Armstrong, M., and R. Rees. 2000. "Pricing Policies in the Infrastructure Sectors." Background paper prepared for the World Bank's *World Development Report 2002*, Washington, D.C.

Armstrong, M., and D. Sappington. 2003. "Recent Developments in the Theory of Regulation." In M. Armstrong and R. Porter, eds., *Handbook of Industrial Organization, vol. III*. New York: North-Holland.

Armstrong, M., S. Cowan, and J. Vickers. 1994. *Regulatory Reform: Economic Analysis and British Experience*. Cambridge, Mass.: MIT Press.

Arnback, J. 1997. "Technology Trends and Their Implications for Telecom Regulation." In W. Melody, ed., *Telecom Reform: Principles, Policies and Regulatory Practices.* Lyngby: Technical University of Denmark.

Arocena, P., and C. Price. 2002. "Generating Efficiency: Economic and Environmental Regulation of Public and Private Electricity Generators in Spain." *International Journal of Industrial Organization* 20 (1): 41–69.

Aubert, C., and J-J. Laffont. 2000. "Multiregulation in Developing Countries." University of Toulouse, Institut d'Economie Industrielle, Toulouse, France.

Bacon, R. 1994. "Restructuring the Power Sector: The Case of Small Systems." Public Policy for the Private Sector Note 10. World Bank, Washington, D.C.

Bacon, R., and J. Besant-Jones. 2001. "Global Electric Power Reform: Privatization and Liberalization of the Electric Power Industry in Developing Countries." *Annual Reviews of Energy and the Environment* 26: 331–59.

Baker, B., and S. Tremolet. 2000. "Regulation of Quality of Infrastructure Services in Developing Countries." Paper presented at a conference on Infrastructure for Development: Private Solutions and the Poor. 31 May–2 June, London.

Balzhiser, R. 1996. "Technology—It's Only Begun to Make a Difference." *The Electricity Journal* 9 (4): 32–45.

Barker, J., L. Mauer, and T. Storm van Leeuwen. 2003. "The Evolution of the Single Buyer Model and Introduction of Competition." World Bank, Washington, D.C.

Baron, D. 1989. "Design of Regulatory Mechanisms and Institutions." In R. Schmalensee and R. Willig, eds., *Handbook of Industrial Organization, vol. 2.* New York: North Holland.

Baumol, W. 1993. "On the Perils of Privatization." *Eastern Economic Journal* 19 (4): 419–40.

———. 1995. "Modified Regulation of Telecommunications and the Public-Interest Standard." In M. Bishop, J. Kay, and C. Mayer, eds., *The Regulatory Challenge.* Oxford: Oxford University Press.

———. 1999. "Having Your Cake: How to Preserve Universal-Service Cross Subsidies While Facilitating Competitive Entry." *Yale Journal on Regulation* 16 (1): 1–17.

Baumol, W., and J. Sidak. 1994. *Toward Competition in Local Telephony.* Cambridge, Mass.: MIT Press.

Baumol, W., and R. Willig. 1987. "Using Competition as a Guide." *Regulation* 11 (1): 28–35.

———. 1988. "Competitive Rail Regulation Rules." *Journal of Transport Economics and Policy* 33 (1): 43–54.

Baumol, W., M. Koehn, and R. Willig. 1990. "How Arbitrary Is 'Arbitrary'? Or, Toward the Deserved Demise of Full Cost Allocation." *Public Utilities Fortnightly* 120 (5): 16–21.

Baumol, W., J. Ordover, and R. Willig. 1997. "Parity Pricing and Its Critics: A Necessary Condition for Efficiency in the Provision of Bottleneck Services to Competitors." *Yale Journal on Regulation* 14 (1): 146–63.

Baumol, W., J. Panzar, and R. Willig. 1988. *Contestable Markets and the Theory of Industry Structure.* Cambridge, Mass.: International Thomson Publishing.

Bayless, C. 1994. "Less Is More: Why Gas Turbines Will Transform Electric Utilities." *Public Utilities Fortnightly* 132 (22): 21–25.

Bayliss, K. 2001. "Privatisation of Electricity Distribution: Some Economic, Social and Political Perspectives." Report 2001-040E. University of Greenwich, Public Services International Research Institute Unit, London.

Bayliss, K., D. Hall, and E. Lobina. 2001. "Has Liberalisation Gone Too Far? A Review of the Issues in Water and Energy." University of Greenwich, Public Services International Research Unit, London.

Beato, P., and J-J. Laffont. 2002. "Competition in Public Utilities in Developing Countries." Report IFM-127. Inter-American Development Bank, Washington, D.C.

Benitez, D., O. Chisari, and A. Estache. 2003. "Can the Gains from Argentina's Utilities Reform Offset Credit Shocks?" In C. Ugaz and C. Waddams Price, eds., *Utility Privatization and Regulation: A Fair Deal for Consumers?* Northampton, Mass.: Edward Elgar.

Bergara, M., W. Henisz, and P. Spiller. 1998. "Political Institutions and Electricity Utility Investment: A Cross-Nation Analysis." *California Management Review* 40 (2): 18–35.

Bertels, P. 1998. "Infrastructure Improvements by International Competitors." U.S. Department of Agriculture, Agricultural Marketing Service, Washington, D.C.

Besant-Jones, J. 1993. "Reforming the Policies for Electric Power in Developing Countries." World Bank, Washington, D.C.

Besant-Jones, J., and B. Tenenbaum. 2001. "The California Power Crisis: Lessons for Developing Countries." World Bank, Energy Sector Management Assistance Program, Washington, D.C.

Bhatia, R., and M. Falkenmark. 1993. "Water Resources Policies and the Urban Poor: Innovative Approaches and Policy Imperatives." United Nations Development Programme–World Bank Water and Sanitation Program, Water and Sanitation Currents, New York.

Bialek, J. 2004. "Recent Blackouts in US and Continental Europe: Is Liberalization to Blame?" University of Edinburgh, School of Engineering and Electronics.

Bitran, E., and P. Serra. 1998. "Regulation of Privatized Utilities: The Chilean Experience." *World Development* 26 (6): 945–62.

Boland, J., and D. Whittington. 2000. "The Political Economy of Water Tariff Design: Increasing Block Tariffs versus Uniform Price with Rebate." In A. Dinar, ed., *Political Economy of Water Pricing Reforms.* Oxford: Oxford University Press.

Bond, J. 1997. "The Drivers of the Information Revolution—Cost, Computing Power, and Convergence." Public Policy for the Private Sector Note 118. World Bank, Washington, D.C.

Borenstein, S., 2000. "Understanding Competitive Pricing and Market Power in Wholesale Electricity Markets." *The Electricity Journal* 13 (6): 49–57.

Borenstein, S., and J. Bushnell. 2001. "Electricity Restructuring: Deregulation or Reregulation?" *Regulation* 23 (2): 46–52.

Borenstein, S., J. Bushnell, and C. Knittel. 1999. "Market Power in Electricity Markets: Beyond Concentration Measures." *The Energy Journal* 20 (4).

Borenstein, S., J. Bushnell, and F. Wolak. 2000. "Diagnosing Market Power in California's Restructured Wholesale Electricity Market." NBER Working Paper 7868. National Bureau of Economic Research, Cambridge, Mass.

Bortolotti, B., D. Siniscalco, and M. Fantini. 2000. "Privatization and Institutions: A Cross-country Analysis." Working Paper 375. CE-Sifo, Munich.

Bortolotti, B., J. D'Souza, M. Fantini, and W. Megginson. 2001. "Sources of Performance Improvements in Privatized Firms: A Clinical Study of the Global Telecommunications Industry." Working Paper 26-2001. University of Oklahoma, Department of Finance.

Boubakri, N., and J-C. Cosset. 1998. "The Financial and Operating Performance of Newly Privatized Firms: Evidence from Developing Countries." *Journal of Finance* 53 (3): 1081–1110.

Bouin, O., and C. Michalet. 1991. *Rebalancing the Public and Private Sectors: Developing Coun-*

try Experience. Paris: Organisation for Economic Co-operation and Development.

Boylaud, O., and G. Nicoletti. 2002. "Regulation, Market Structure and Performance in Telecommunications." ECO/WKP(2000) 10. Organization for Economic Co-operation and Development, Paris.

Braeutigam, R. 1980. "An Analysis of Fully Distributed Cost Pricing in Regulated Industries." *Bell Journal of Economics* 11 (1): 182–96.

———. 1993. "Consequences of Regulatory Reform in the American Railroad Industry." *Southern Economic Journal* 59 (3): 468–80.

———. 1999. "Learning about Transport Costs." In J. Gomez-Ibanez, W. Tye, and C. Winston, eds., *Essays in Transportation Economics and Policy: A Handbook in Honor of John Meyer.* Washington, D.C.: Brookings Institution.

Braeutigam, R., and J. Panzar. 1993. "Effects of Change from Rate-of-Return to Price-Cap Regulation." *The American Economic Review* 83 (2): 191–98.

Brennan, T. 1995. "Is the Theory Behind U.S. v. AT&T Applicable Today?" *The Antitrust Bulletin* 40 (3): 455–82.

Broadman, H., J. Anderson, S. Claessens, R. Ryterman, S. Slavova, M. Vagliasindi, and G. Vincelette. 2003. *Institutional Reform for Investment and Growth in South Eastern Europe.* Washington, D.C.: World Bank.

Brocklehurst, C. 2001. "Durban Metro Water: Private Sector Partnerships and the Poor."

Water and Sanitation Program—Africa, Nairobi, Kenya.

Brook, P., and T. Irwin, eds. 2003. *Infrastructure for Poor People: Public Policy for Private Provision.* Washington, D.C.: World Bank.

Bruce, R., and R. Macmillan. 2002. "Telecommunications in Crisis: Perspectives of the Financial Sector on Regulatory Impediments to Sustainable Investment." Debevoise & Plimpton, London.

Bruce, R., and A. Marriott. 2002. "Use of Alternative Dispute Resolution Techniques in the Telecom Sector." Debevoise & Plimpton, London.

Bruce, R., I. Kessides, and L. Kneifel. 1999. *Overcoming Obstacles to Liberalization of the Telecom Sector in Estonia, Poland, the Czech Republic, Slovenia, and Hungary: An Overview of Key Policy Concerns and Potential Initiatives to Facilitate the Transition Process.* Washington, D.C.: World Bank.

Bushnell, J., and S. Soft. 1997. "Improving Private Incentives for Electric Grid Investment." *Resource and Energy Economics* 19: 85–108.

Button, K. 1993. *Transport Economics.* 2nd ed. Cheltenham, U.K.: Edward Elgar.

CAISE (Camara Argentina de Inversores en el Sector Electrico). 2002. *Electricity in Argentina: A Great Achievement Facing Serious Problems.* Buenos Aires, Argentina.

Calderon, C., W. Easterly, and L. Serven. 2003. "Infrastructure Compression and Public Sector Solvency in Latin America." In W. Easterly and L. Serven, eds., *The Limits of Stabilization—Infrastructure, Public Deficits, and Growth in Latin America*. Palo Alto, Calif.: Stanford University Press.

Campos, J. 2002. "Competition Issues in Network Industries: The Latin American Railways Experience." *Brazilian Electronic Journal of Economics* 5(1).

Campos, J., and J. Jimenez. 2003. "Evaluating Rail Reform in Latin America: Competition and Investment Effects." Paper presented at the First Conference on Railroad Industry Structure, Competition and Investment, 7–8 November, Toulouse, France.

Casanueva, C., and R. del Villar. 2003. "Infrastructure Regulation Difficulties: The Basic Telecommunications Industry in Mexico, 1990–2000." In W. Thissen and P. Herder, eds., *Critical Infrastructures—State of the Art in Research and Application*. Boston, Mass.: Kluwer Academic Publishers.

Cass, S. 1996. *Port Privatisation: Process, Players and Progress*. London: Cargo Systems.

Casten, T. 1995. "Electricity Generation: Smaller Is Better." *The Electricity Journal* 8 (10): 69–73.

Cave, M., and R. Crandall. 2001. *Telecommunications Liberalization on Two Sides of the Atlantic*. Washington, D.C.: American Enterprise Institute-Brookings Joint Center for Regulatory Studies.

CEC (Commission of the European Communities). 1996. "A Strategy for Revitalizing the Community's Railways." White Paper, COM (96) 421 Final. Commission of the European Communities, Brussels, Belgium.

Chisari, O., Estache, A., and J-J. Laffont. 1999. "The Needs of the Poor in Infrastructure Obligation: The Role of Universal Service Obligations." World Bank, Washington, D.C.

Chisari, O., A. Estache, and C. Romero. 1999. "Winners and Losers from the Privatization and Regulation of Utilities: Lessons from a General Equilibrium Model of Argentina." *The World Bank Economic Review* 13 (2): 357–78.

Chisari, O., A. Estache, and C. Waddams Price. 2003. "Access by the Poor in Latin America's Utility Reform: Subsidies and Service Obligations." In C. Ugaz and C. Waddams Price, eds., *Utility Privatization and Regulation: A Fair Deal for Consumers?* Northampton, Mass.: Edward Elgar.

Clark, X., D. Dollar, and A. Micco. 2002. "Maritime Transport Costs and Port Efficiency." Policy Research Working Paper 2781. World Bank, Washington, D.C.

Clarke, G. 2001. "Thirsting for Efficiency: a) The Politics of Water Reform, b) Effect of Reform on Performance of Urban Water Utilities." Paper presented at a Regional Conference on Reform of the Water Supply and Sanitation Sector in Africa, 26–28 February, Kampala, Uganda.

Clarke, G., and S. Wallsten. 2002. "Universal(ly Bad) Service: Providing Infrastructure Services to Rural and Poor Urban Consumers." Policy Research Working Paper 2868. World Bank, Washington, D.C.

Collignon, B., and M. Vezina. 2000. "Independent Water and Sanitation Providers in African Cities." World Bank, Water and Sanitation Program, Washington, D.C.

Conte Grand, M. 1998. "Regulation of Water Distribution in Argentina." Paper presented at the 12th Plenary Session of the Organisation for Economic Co-operation and Development (OECD) Advisory Group on Privatization, 17–18 September, Helsinki, Finland.

Cowan, S. 1997. "Competition in the Water Industry." *Oxford Review of Economic Policy* 13 (1): 83–92.

———. 2002. "Price-Cap Regulation." *Swedish Economic Policy Review* 9: 167–88.

Cowhey, P., and M. Klimenko. 1999. "The WTO Agreement and Communication Policy Reforms." University of California at San Diego, Graduate School of International Relations and Pacific Studies.

Crampes, C., and A. Estache. 1998. "Regulatory Trade-offs in Designing Concession Contracts for Infrastructure Networks." *Utilities Policy* 7 (1):1–13.

Criales, J., and W. Smith. 1997. "Bolivia's Regulatory Reforms." Paper presented at a World Bank Seminar on Bolivia's Capitalization Program, 23 June, Washington, D.C.

Delfino, J., and A. Casarin. 2001. "The Reform of the Utilities Sector in Argentina." Discussion Paper 2001/74. United Nations University, WIDER (World Institute for Development Economics Research), Stockholm, Sweden.

Demsetz, H. 1968. "Why Regulate Utilities?" *Journal of Law and Economics* 11 (1): 55–65.

Dewenter, K., and P. Malatesta. 2001. "State-Owned and Privately-Owned Firms: An Empirical Analysis of Profitability, Leverage, and Labor Intensity." *American Economic Review* 91 (1): 320–34.

Dinar, A. 2000. *The Political Economy of Water Pricing Reforms.* New York: Oxford University Press for the World Bank.

Di Tella, R., and A. Dyck. 2002. "Cost Reductions, Cost Padding and Stock Market Prices: The Chilean Experience with Price Cap Regulation." Harvard University, Harvard Business School, Cambridge, Mass.

Dnes, A. 1995. "Franchising and Privatization." Public Policy for the Private Sector Note 40. World Bank, Washington, D.C.

East European Constitutional Review. 1999. "Constitutional Watch." 8(3), New York University, School of Law.

ECMT (European Conference of Ministers of Transport). 2003. "Transport Policy: Successes, Failures, and New Challenges." CEMT/CM (2003)1, Paris.

Economides, N. 1998. "U.S. Telecommunications Today." *Business Economics* 33 (2): 7–13.

Edenor. 2001. *Annual Report.* Buenos Aires, Argentina.

Ehrhardt, D., and R. Burdon. 1999. "Free Entry in Infrastructure." Policy Research Working Paper 2093. World Bank, Washington, D.C.

EIA (Energy Information Administration). 1999. *International Energy Outlook 1999*. Washington, D.C.

———. 2002. *World Energy Projection System*. Washington, D.C.

Ergas, H., and J. Small. 2001. "Price Caps and Rate of Return Regulation." Network Economics Consulting Group, Kingston, Australia.

Esrey, S. 1996. "Water, Waste and Well-Being: A Multicountry Study." *American Journal of Epidemiology* 143 (6): 608–23.

Estache, A. 1997. "Designing Regulatory Institutions for Infrastructure—Lessons from Argentina." Public Policy for the Private Sector Note 114. World Bank, Washington, D.C.

———. 2001. "Privatization and Regulation of Transport Infrastructure in the 1990s." *The World Bank Research Observer* 16 (1): 85–107.

———. 2002. "Argentina's 1990s Utilities Privatization: A Cure or a Disease?" World Bank, Washington, D.C.

Estache, A., and J. Carbajo. 1996. "Competing Private Ports—Lessons from Argentina." Public Policy for the Private Sector Note 100. World Bank, Washington, D.C.

Estache, A., and G. de Rus. 2000. *Privatization and Regulation of Transport Infrastructure*. Washington, D.C.: World Bank.

Estache, A., and E. Kouassi. 2002. "Sector Organization, Governance and the Inefficiency of African Water Utilities." Policy Research Working Paper 2890. World Bank, Washington, D.C.

Estache, A., and D. Martimort. 1999. "Politics, Transaction Costs, and the Design of Regulatory Institutions." Policy Research Working Paper 2073. World Bank, Washington, D.C.

Estache, A., and L. Quesada. 2001. "Concession Contract Renegotiations: Some Efficiency versus Equity Dilemmas." Policy Research Working Paper 2705. World Bank, Washington, D.C.

Estache, A., and M. Rodriguez-Pardina. 1999. "Light and Lightning at the End of the Public Tunnel: Reform of Electricity Sector in the Southern Cone." Policy Research Working Paper 2074. World Bank, Washington, D.C.

Estache, A., and M. Rossi. 2001. "Comparing the Performance of Public and Private Water Companies in Asia and Pacific Region: What a Stochastic Costs Frontier Shows." Policy Research Working Paper 2152. World Bank, Washington, DC.

Estache, A., J. Carbajo, and G. de Rus. 1999. "Argentina's Transport Privatization and Re-Regulation. Ups and Downs of a Daring Decade-Long Experience." Policy Research Working Paper 2249. World Bank, Washington, D.C.

Estache, A., J. de Azevedo, and E. Sydenstricker. 2000. "Labor Redundancy, Retraining, and Outplacement during Privatization: The Experience of Brazil's Federal Railway." Policy Research Working Paper 2460. World Bank, Washington, D.C.

Estache, A., V. Foster, and Q. Wodon. 2002. *Accounting for Poverty in Infrastructure Reform—*

Learning from Latin America's Experience. Washington, D.C.: World Bank Institute.

Estache, A., M. Gonzalez, and L. Trujillo. 2001. "Technical Efficiency Gains from Port Reform: The Potential for Yardstick Competition in Mexico." Policy Research Working Paper 2637. World Bank, Washington, D.C.

Estache, A., M. Gonzalez, and L. Trujillo. 2002a. "Railways Reform in Brazil." *The Journal of Industry, Competition and Trade* 1 (2): 203–35.

Estache, A., M. Gonzalez, and L. Trujillo. 2002b. "What Does 'Privatization' Do for Efficiency? Evidence from Argentina's and Brazil's Railways." *World Development* 30 (11): 1885–97.

Estache, A., Guasch, J., and L. Trujillo. 2003. "Price Caps, Efficiency Payoffs and Infrastructure Contract Renegotiation in Latin America." Policy Research Working Paper 3129. World Bank, Washington, D.C.

Fare, R., S. Grosskopf, and J. Logan. 1985. "The Relative Performance of Private Mixed and State-Owned Enterprises." *Journal of Public Economics* 26 (1): 89–106.

Faulhaber, G. 2003. "Policy-Induced Competition: The Telecommunications Experiments." *Information Economics and Policy* 15 (1): 73–97.

Feler, L. 2001. "Electricity Privatization in Argentina." World Bank, Washington, D.C.

Fink, C., A. Mattoo, and R. Rathindran. 2002. "An Assessment of Telecommunications Reform in Developing Countries." Policy Research Working Paper 2909. World Bank, Washington, D.C.

Fischer, R., and A. Galetovic. 2000. "Regulatory Governance and Chile's 1998–1999 Electricity Shortage." Seria Economia 84. University of Chile, Department of Economics, Santiago.

Fischer, R., and P. Serra. 2000. "Regulating the Electricity Sector in Latin America." Serie Economia 86. University of Chile, Department of Economics, Santiago.

Fischer, R., R. Gutierrez, and P. Serra. 2003. "The Effects of Privatization on Firms and on Social Welfare: The Chilean Case." Research Network Paper R-456. Inter-American Development Bank, Washington, D.C.

Foster, V. 1996. *Policy Issues for the Water and Sanitation Sectors.* Washington, D.C.: Inter-American Development Bank

Foster, V., and O. Irusta. 2003. "Does Infrastructure Reform Work for the Poor? A Case Study on the Cities of La Paz and El Alto in Bolivia." Policy Research Working Paper 3177. World Bank, Washington, D.C.

Foster, V., A. Gomez-Lobo, and J. Halpern. 2000a. "Designing Direct Subsidies for the Poor— A Water and Sanitation Case Study." Public Policy for the Private Sector Note 211. World Bank, Washington, D.C.

———. 2000b. "Information and Modeling Issues in Designing Water and Sanitation Subsidy Schemes." Policy Research Working Paper 2345. World Bank, Washington, D.C.

Foster, V., S. Pattanayak, and L. Prokopy. 2003. "Water Tariffs and Subsidies: Can Subsidies Be Better Targeted?" Paper 5. Public-Private Infrastructure Advisory Facility and Water and Sanitation Program. World Bank, Washington, D.C.

Foxley, J., and J. Mardones. 2000. "Port Concessions in Chile." Public Policy for the Private Sector Note 223. World Bank, Washington, D.C.

Galal, A., L. Jones, P. Tandon, and O. Vogelsang. 1994. *Welfare Consequences of Selling Public Enterprises: An Empirical Analysis.* Oxford: Oxford University Press.

Gaviria, J. 1998. "Port Privatization and Competition in Colombia." Public Policy for the Private Sector Note 167. World Bank, Washington, D.C.

Gómez-Ibáñez, J. 1999. "Regulating Coordination: The Promise and Problems of Vertically Unbundling Private Infrastructure." Discussion Paper. Harvard University, Kennedy School of Government, Taubman Center for State and Local Government, Cambridge, Mass.

Gómez-Ibáñez, J., and J. Meyer. 1993. *Going Private: The International Experience with Transport Privatization.* Washington, D.C.: Brookings Institution.

Gonenc, R., Maher, M., and G. Nicoletti. 2001. "The Implementation and the Effects of Regulatory Reform: Past Experience and Current Issues." *OECD Economic Studies* 32 (11). Organisation for Economic Co-operation and Development, Paris.

Gray, P. 1998. "Utility Regulators—Supporting Nascent Institutions in the Developing World." Public Policy for the Private Sector Note 153. World Bank, Washington, D.C.

————. 2001. "Private Participation in Infrastructure: A Review of the Evidence." World Bank, Washington, D.C.

Gray, P., and M. Klein. 1997. "Competition in Network Industries—Where and How to Introduce It." Public Policy for the Private Sector Note 104. World Bank, Washington, D.C.

Grimm, C., and C. Winston. 2000. "Competition in the Deregulated Railroad Industry: Sources, Effects, and Policy Issues." In S. Peltzman and C. Winston, eds., *Deregulation of Network Industries: What's Next?* Washington, D.C.: American Enterprise Institute-Brookings Joint Center for Regulatory Studies.

Guasch, J. 2001. "Concessions and Regulatory Design: Determinants of Performance—Fifteen Years of Evidence." World Bank, Washington D.C.

Guasch, J., and C. Blitzer. 1993. "State-Owned Monopolies: Horizontal and Vertical Restructuring and Private Sector Access Issues." World Bank, Latin American and the Caribbean Technical Department, Washington, D.C.

Guasch, J., and R. Hahn. 1999. "The Costs and Benefits of Regulation: Implications for Developing Countries." *The World Bank Research Observer* 14 (1): 137–58.

Guasch, J., and J. Kogan. 2003. "Just-in-Case Inventories: A Cross-Country Analysis." Policy

Research Working Paper 3012. World Bank, Washington, D.C.

Guasch, J., A. Kartacheva, and L. Quesada. 2000. "Concessions Contracts Renegotiations in Latin America and Caribbean Region: An Economic Analysis and Empirical Evidence." World Bank, Washington, D.C.

Guasch, J., J-J. Laffont, and S. Straub. 2003. "Renegotiation of Concession Contracts in Latin America." Policy Research Working Paper 3011. World Bank, Washington, D.C.

Guislain, P. 1992. *Divestiture of State Enterprises: An Overview of the Legal Framework.* World Bank Technical Paper 186. Washington, D.C.

Gutierrez, L. 2002. "Regulatory Governance in the Latin American Telecommunications Sector." Serie Documentos 26. Universidad del Rosario, Santa Fe de Bogota, Colombia.

Gwilliam, K. 2001. "Regulation of Private Participation in the Transport Sector." World Bank, Washington, D.C.

Haarmeyer, D., and D. Coy. 2002. "An Overview of Private Sector Participation in the Global and US Water and Wastewater Sector." In P. Seidenstat, D. Haarmeyer, and S. Hakim, eds., *Reinventing Water and Wastewater Systems: Global Lessons for Improving Water Management.* Etobicoke, Ontario, Canada: John Wiley and Sons.

Haarmeyer, D., and P. Yorke. 1993. "Port Privatization: An International Perspective." Policy Study 156. Reason Foundation, Los Angeles, Calif.

Haggarty, L., P. Brook, and A. Zuluaga. 1999. "Thirst for Reform? Private Sector Participation in Mexico City's Water Sector." Policy Research Working Paper 2654. World Bank, Washington, D.C.

Haggarty, L., M. Shirley, and S. Wallsten. 2002. "Telecommunication Reform in Ghana." Policy Research Working Paper 2983. World Bank, Washington, D.C.

Hall, D. 1997. "Public Partnership and Private Control—Ownership, Control and Regulation in Water Concessions in Central Europe." PSIRU Report 9705-W-EUR-JV. University of Greenwich, Public Services International Research Unit, London.

———. 1998. "Public Enterprise in Europe." In G. Holtham, ed., *Freedom with Responsibility—Can We Unshackle Public Enterprise?* London: Institute for Public Policy Research.

Hall, D., and E. Lobina. 2002. "Water Privatisation in Latin America, 2002." Paper presented at PSI America's Water Conference, July, San Jose, Costa Rica. University of Greenwich, Public Services International Research Unit, London.

Hankins, M. 2000. "A Case Study on Private Provision of Photovoltaic Systems in Kenya." In *Energy and Development Report 2000: Energy Service for the World's Poor.* Washington, D.C.: World Bank.

Harris, C. 2003. *Private Participation in Infrastructure in Developing Countries: Trends, Impacts, and Policy Lessons.* Washington, D.C.: World Bank.

Harris, C., J. Hodges, M. Schur, and P. Shukla. 2003. "Infrastructure Projects." Public Policy for the Private Sector Note 252. World Bank, Washington, D.C.

Hart, O. 1995. *Firms, Contracts and Financial Structure.* Oxford: Oxford University Press.

Helm, D. 1994. "British Utility Regulation: Theory, Practice and Reform." *Oxford Review of Economic Policy* 10 (3): 17–19.

Henisz, W., and B. Zelner. 2001. "The Political Economy of Private Electricity Provision in Southeast Asia." *East Asian Economic Perspectives* 15 (1): 10–36.

Hewett, P., and M. Montgomery. 2002. "Poverty and Public Services in Developing Country Cities." Working Paper 154. Population Council, Policy Research Division, New York.

Hoffman, J. 1999. "Las privatizaciones portuarias en America Latina en los 90: Determinantes y Resultados." Paper presented at a World Bank seminar, Las Palmas, Spain.

————. 2001. "Latin American Ports: Results and Determinants of Private Sector Participation." *International Journal of Maritime Economics* 3: 221–41.

Hunt, S., and G. Shuttleworth. 1996. *Competition and Choice in Electricity.* Chichester, U.K.: John Wiley and Sons.

IADB (Inter-American Development Bank). 1999. "Profiles of Power Sector Reform in Selected Latin American and Caribbean Countries." Washington, D.C.

Idelovitch, E., and K. Ringskog. 1995. *Private Sector Participation in Water Supply and Sanitation in Latin America.* Washington, D.C.: World Bank.

ICC (Interstate Commerce Commission). 1985. Coal Rate Guidelines—Nationwide. 1 ICC 2d 520. Washington, D.C.

IEA (International Energy Agency). 1999. *Electricity Market Reform: An IEA Handbook.* Paris: Organisation for Economic Co-operation and Development.

IIED (International Institute for Environment and Development). 2003. *Local Action for Global Water Goals: Addressing Inadequate Water and Sanitation in Urban Areas.* Prepared for UN Habitat. London: Earthscan.

International Railway Journal. 2000. "Privatization Sees Rail's Market Share Increase." Editorial (September). Simmons-Boardman Publishing.

ITU (International Telecommunication Union). 1999. *Trends in Telecommunication Reform—Convergence and Regulation.* Geneva.

————. 2001a. "Effective Regulation—Case Study: Botswana." Geneva.

————. 2001b. "Effective Regulation—Case Study: Brazil." Geneva.

————. 2001c. "Effective Regulation—Case Study: Morocco." Geneva.

————. 2001d. "Effective Regulation—Case Study: Peru." Geneva.

———. 2001e. "ITU Lends Force to Pan-African Regulatory Cooperation." Press release, 3 October. Geneva.

———. 2002. *Trends in Telecommunication Reform—Effective Regulation.* Geneva.

———. 2003. *Trends in Telecommunication Reform—Promoting Universal Access to ICTs.* Geneva.

Ivaldi, M., and G. McCullough. 2001. "Density and Integration Effects on Class I U.S. Freight Railroads." *Journal of Regulatory Economics* 19 (2): 161–82.

Ivastorza, V. 2003. "Benchmarking for Distribution Utilities: A Problematic Approach to Defining Efficiency." *Electricity Journal* 16 (10).

Izaguirre, A. 2002. "Private Infrastructure: A Review of Projects with Private Participation, 1990–2001." Public Policy for the Private Sector Note 250. World Bank, Washington, D.C.

Jacobs, S. 1999. "The Second Generation of Regulatory Reforms." Paper presented at an International Monetary Fund conference on Second Generation Reforms, Washington, D.C.

Jamasb, T. 2002. "Reform and Regulation of the Electricity Sector in Developing Countries." University of Cambridge, Department of Applied Economics, Cambridge, U.K.

Jamasb, T., and M. Pollitt. 2000. "Benchmarking and Regulation of Electricity Transmission and Distribution Utilities: Lessons from International Experience." Working paper. University of Cambridge, Department of Applied Economics, Cambridge, U.K.

Joskow, P. 1974. "Inflation and Environmental Concern: Change in the Process of Public Utility Price Regulation." *Journal of Law and Economics* 17 (2): 291–327.

———. 1998a. "Electricity Sectors in Transition." *Energy Journal* 19 (2): 25–62.

———. 1998b. "Regulatory Priorities for Reforming Infrastructure Sectors in Developing Countries." Paper presented at the Annual World Bank Conference on Development Economics, 20–21 April, Washington, D.C.

———. 1999. "Comments of Professor Paul L. Joskow." Docket RM99-2-000. Federal Energy Regulatory Commission, Washington, D.C.

———. 2000a. "Deregulation and Regulatory Reform in the U.S. Electric Power Sector." In Sam Peltzman and Clifford Winston, eds., *Deregulation of Network Industries: What's Next?* Washington, D.C.: Brookings Institution Press.

———. 2000b. "Why Do We Need Electricity Retailers? Or Can You Get It Cheaper Wholesale?" Massachusetts Institute of Technology, Center for Energy and Environmental Policy Research, Cambridge, Mass.

———. 2001 "California's Electricity Crisis." NBER Working Paper 8442. National Bureau of Economic Research, Cambridge, Mass.

———. 2003. "Electricity Sector Restructuring and Competition: Lessons Learned." *Cuadernos de Economia* Ano 40 (121): 548–58.

Joskow, P., and R. Noll. 1994. "Deregulation and Regulatory Reform during the 1980s." In M. Feldstein, ed., *American Economic Policy during the 1980s.* Chicago, Ill.: University of Chicago Press.

Joskow, P., and R. Schmalensee. 1986. "Incentive Regulation for Electric Utilities." *Yale Journal on Regulation* 4 (1): 1–49.

Juhel, M. 1998. "Globalization, Privatization & Restructuring of Ports" Paper presented at the 10th Annual Australasian Summit on Ports, Shipping and Waterfront Reform. 9–10 February, Sydney, Australia.

Kahn, A.1984. "The Road to More Intelligent Telephone Pricing." *Yale Journal on Regulation* 1 (2): 139–57.

———. 1988. *The Economics of Regulation: Principles and Institutions.* Cambridge, Mass.: MIT Press.

———. 1996. "Argentina—The Reform of Regulation: An Overview." World Bank, Washington, D.C.

———. 2001. *Whom the Gods Would Destroy, or How Not to Deregulate.* Washington D.C.: American Enterprise Institute-Brookings Joint Center for Regulatory Studies.

Kahn, A., and W. Taylor. 1994. "The Pricing of Inputs Sold to Competitors: A Comment." *Yale Journal on Regulation* 11 (1): 225–40.

Karekezi, S., and J. Kimani. 2001. "Introduction." In *Power Sector Reform in Africa: Proceedings of a Regional Policy Seminar,* 24–25 April 2001, Nairobi, Kenya: AFREPREN.

Kay, J. 2001. "Privatization in the United Kingdom, 1979–1999." [www.johnkay.com].

Kebede, B. 2002. "Are Subsidies Decisive in the Provision of Energy to the Urban Poor? The Cases of Kerosene and Electricity in Ethiopia." Oxford University, Centre for the Study of African Economies and St. Anthony's College.

Kennedy, D., S. Fankhauser, and M. Raiser. 2003. "Low Pressure, High Tension: The Energy-Water Nexus and Regional Co-Operation in the CIS-7 Countries." Paper prepared for the Lucerne conference of the CIS-7 Initiative, 20–22 January.

Kerf, M. 2000. "Do State Holding Companies Facilitate Private Participation in the Water Sector? Evidence from Côte d'Ivoire, the Gambia, Guinea and Senegal." Policy Research Working Paper 2513. World Bank, Washington, D.C.

Kerf, M., and W. Smith. 1996. *Privatizing Africa's Infrastructure—Promise and Challenges.* World Bank Technical Paper 337. Washington, D.C.

Kessides, I. 1997. "Regulation of the Argentine Network Utilities: Issues and Options for the National Government." Country Department I, Latin America and the Caribbean Region, Economic Notes (No 16). World Bank, Washington, D.C.

Kessides, I., and J. Ordover. 2000. "The Czech Telecommunications Sector: An Economic Assessment." In I. Kessides, ed., *Czech Republic: Economic Principles to Guide Reform in the Czech Infrastructure Sectors.* Report 20545 CZ. Washington, D.C.: World Bank.

Kessides, I., and R. Willig. 1995. "Restructuring Regulation of the Rail Industry for the Public Interest." Policy Research Working Paper 1506. World Bank, Washington, D.C.

Kessides, I., J. Ordover, and R. Willig. 1999. "The Access Pricing Problem: Some Practical Rules in Telecommunications." World Bank, Washington, D.C.

Klass, M., and M. Salinger. 1995. "Do New Theories of Vertical Foreclosure Provide Sound Guidance for Consent Agreement in Vertical Merger Cases?" *The Antitrust Bulletin* (fall).

Klein, M. 1996a. "Competition in Network Industries." Policy Research Working Paper 1591. World Bank, Washington, D.C.

———. 1996b. "Economic Regulation of Water Companies." Policy Research Working Paper 1649. World Bank, Washington, D.C.

———. 1998a. "Infrastructure Concessions—To Auction or Not to Auction?" Public Policy for the Private Sector Note 159. World Bank, Washington, D.C.

———. 1998b. "Rebidding for Concessions." Public Policy for the Private Sector Note 161. World Bank, Washington, D.C.

———. 2003. "Where Do We Stand Today with Private Infrastructure?" *Development Outreach.* World Bank Institute, Washington, D.C.

Klein, M., and N. Roger. 1994. "Back to the Future: The Potential in Infrastructure Privati-

zation." In R. O'Brien, ed., *Finance and the International Economy.* Oxford: Oxford University Press.

Kleit, A., and D. Terrell. 2001. "Measuring Potential Efficiency Gains from Deregulation of Electricity Generation: A Bayesian Approach." *Review of Economics and Statistics* 83 (3): 523–30.

Komives, K. 1999. "Designing Pro-Poor Water and Sewer Concessions: Early Lessons from Bolivia." Policy Research Working Paper 2243. World Bank, Washington, D.C.

Komives, K., D. Whittington, and X. Wu. 2001. "Infrastructure Coverage and the Poor: A Global Perspective." Policy Research Working Paper 2551. World Bank, Washington, D.C.

Kopicki, R., and L. Thompson. 1995. *Best Methods of Railway Restructuring and Privatization.* World Bank Discussion Paper 111. Washington, D.C.

Kraay, A., and D. Dollar. 2000. "Growth Is Good for the Poor." Policy Research Working Paper 2587. World Bank, Washington, D.C.

Kwoka, J. 1996. *Power Structure, Ownership, Integration and Competition in the US Electricity Industry.* Boston, Mass.: Kluwer.

Laffont, J-J. 1996. "Regulation, Privatization, and Incentives in Developing Countries." In M. G. Quibira and J. M. Dowling, eds., *Current Issues in Economic Development—An Asian Perspective.* Oxford: Oxford University Press.

———. 2000. "Regulation of Infrastructure in Developing Countries." In G. Kochendorfer-

Lucius and B. Pleskovic, eds., *The Institutional Foundations of a Market Economy.* Berlin: German Foundation for Economic Development.

———. 2003. "Enforcement, Regulation and Development." *Journal of African Economies* 12 (supplement 2): 193–211.

———. 2004. *Regulation and Development.* Forthcoming. Cambridge: Cambridge University Press.

Laffont, J-J., and J. Tirole. 1991. "Privatization and Incentives." *Journal of Law, Economics, and Organization* 7:84–105.

———. 1993. *A Theory of Incentives in Procurement and Regulation.* Cambridge, Mass.: MIT Press.

———. 1994. "Access Pricing and Competition." *European Economic Review* 38 (9): 1673–1710.

———. 1996. "Creating Competition through Interconnection: Theory and Practice." *Journal of Regulatory Economics* 10 (3): 227–56.

———. 2000. *Competition in Telecommunications.* Cambridge, Mass.: MIT Press.

Laffont, J-J., and A. N'Gbo. 2000. "Cross-Subsidies and Network Expansion in Developing Countries." *European Economic Review* 44 (4–6): 797–805.

Laffont, J-J., and T. N'Guessan. 2002. "Telecommunications Reform in Côte d' Ivoire." Policy Research Working Paper 2895, World Bank, Washington, D.C.

Laffont, J-J., and W. Zantman. 1999. "Information Acquisition, Political Game and the Delegation of Authority." Working paper. University of Toulouse, Group de Recherche en Économie Mathématique et Quantitative, Toulouse, France.

Landau, G. 2002. "The Regulatory-Normative Framework in Brazil." Policy Papers on the Americas, vol. 13, study 2. Center for Strategic and International Studies, Washington, D.C.

Latinobarometro. 2002. "The Market and the State." Latinobarometro Time Series. Santiago, Chile.

Lee, H. 2003. "Assessing the Challenges Confronting Distributive Electricity Generation." Discussion Paper 2003-03, Belfer Center for Science and International Affairs, Kennedy School of Government, Harvard University.

Levy, B., and P. Spiller. 1996. *Regulations, Institutions, and Commitment: Comparative Studies of Telecommunications.* Cambridge: Cambridge University Press.

Li, W., and L. Xu. 2001. "Liberalization and Performance in the Telecommunications Sector around the World." World Bank, Washington, D.C.

Lieberman, I. 1997. "Privatization: What We Have Learned in the Last Seven Years." World Bank, Washington, D.C.

Littlechild, S. 2000. "Why We Need Electricity Retailers: A Reply to Joskow on Wholesale Spot Price Pass-Through." Cambridge Working

Papers in Economics (No 0008). University of Cambridge, Department of Applied Economics.

Lobina, E. 2001. "Water Privatization and Restructuring in Central and Eastern Europe, 2001." University of Greenwich, Public Services International Research Unit, London.

Lobina, E., and D. Hall. 1999. "Public Sector Alternatives to Water Supply and Sewerage Privatisation: Case Studies." PSIRU Report 9908-W-U-Pubalt.doc. University of Greenwich, Public Services International Research Unit, London.

Lovei, L. 2000. "The Single Buyer Model: A Dangerous Path toward Competitive Electricity Markets." Public Policy for the Private Sector Note 225. World Bank, Washington D.C.

Lovei, L., E. Gurenko, M. Haney, P. O'Keefe, and M. Shkaratan. 2000. "Scorecard for Subsidies." Public Policy for the Private Sector Note 218. World Bank, Washington, D.C.

Mangwengwende, S. 2002. "Tariffs and Subsidies in Zimbabwe's Reforming Electricity Industry: Steering a Utility through Turbulent Times." Energy Policy 30 (11–12): 947–58.

Martin, B. 2002. "Derailed—The UK's Disastrous Experience with Railway Privatization." Multinational Monitor 23 (1–2).

McCubbins, M., R. Noll, and B. Weingast. 1987. "Administrative Procedures as Instruments of Political Control." Journal of Law, Economics, and Organization 3: 243–77.

McKenzie, D., and D. Mookherjee. 2003. "Distributive Impact of Privatization in Latin America: An Overview of Evidence from Four Countries." Economia 3 (2): 161–218.

McLeod, N. 2002. "Water Supply in South Africa." Paper presented at the World Bank Urban Research Symposium, 10 December, Washington, D.C.

Meersman, H., E. Van de Voorde, and T. Vanelslander. 2002. "Port Pricing Issues—Considerations on Economic Principles, Competition and Wishful Thinking." Paper prepared for the second seminar of the IMPRINT-EUROPE Thematic Network: "Implementing Reform of Transport Pricing: Identifying Mode-Specific Issues," 14–15 May, Brussels.

Megginson, W., and J. Netter. 2001. "From State to Market: A Survey of Empirical Studies of Privatization." Journal of Economic Literature 39 (2): 321–89.

Menard, C., and G. Clarke. 2000. "A Transitory Regime: Water Supply in Conakry, Guinea." Policy Research Working Paper 2362. World Bank, Washington, D.C.

Menard, C., and M. Shirley. 2001. "Reforming Public Utilities: Lessons from Urban Water Supply in Developing Countries." World Bank, Washington, D.C.

Micco, A., and N. Perez. 2001. "Maritime Transport Costs and Port Efficiency." Paper prepared for the seminar "Towards Competitiveness: The Institutional Path," Annual Meeting of the Board of Governors of the Inter American Development Bank and

Inter American Investment Corporation, 16 March, Santiago, Chile.

Millan, J., E. Lora, and A. Micco. 2001 "Sustainability of the Electricity Sector Reforms in Latin America." Inter-American Development Bank, Research Department, Santiago, Chile. [http://www.iadb.org/res/seminars_events.htm].

Monson, C., and J. Rohlfs. 1993. "The $20 Billion Impact of Local Competition in Telecommunications." Strategic Policy Research, Bethesda, Md.

Mota, R. 2003. "The Restructuring and Privatization of Electricity Distribution and Supply Business in Brazil: A Social Cost-Benefit Analysis." DAE Working Paper 0309. University of Cambridge, Department of Applied Economics, Cambridge, U.K.

Nash, C., and J. Toner. 1998. "Railways: Structure, Regulation and Competition Policy." Organisation for Economic Co-operation and Development, Paris.

Navajas, F. 2000. "El impacto distributivo de los cambios en los precios relativos en la Argentina entre 1988–1998 y los efectos de la privatizaciones y la desregulacion economica." Fundación de Investigaciones Economicas Latinoamericanas, La Distribución del Ingraso en la Argentina, Buenos Aires, Argentina.

NERA (National Economic Research Associates). 1999. *Global Energy Regulation Newsletter* (1). London.

Newbery, D. 1997. "Privatization and Liberalization of Network Utilities." *European Economic Review* 41 (3-5): 357–83.

———. 2000a. *Privatization, Restructuring and Regulation of Network Utilities*. Cambridge, Mass.: MIT Press.

———. 2000b. "Romania: Oil and Gas Reform." In I. Kessides, ed., *Romania: Regulatory and Structural Assessment in the Network Utilities*. Report 20546-RO. Washington, D.C.: World Bank.

———. 2000c. "The Bulgarian Energy Sector." World Bank, Washington, D.C.

———. 2000d. "The Czech Energy Sector." In I. Kessides, ed., *Czech Republic: Economic Principles to Guide Reform in the Czech Infrastructure Sectors*. Report 20545-CZ. Washington, D.C.: World Bank.

———. 2000e. "The Oil and Gas Sector." In I. Kessides, ed., *Hungary: A Regulatory and Structural Review of Selected Infrastructure Sectors*. Washington, D.C.: World Bank.

———. 2001. "Issues and Options for Restructuring the ESI." University of Cambridge, Department of Applied Economics, Cambridge, U.K.

———. 2002. "Regulating Unbundled Network Utilities." *The Economic and Social Review* 33 (1): 23–41.

———. 2003. "The Relationship between Regulation and Competition Policy for Network Utilities." University of Cambridge, Department of Applied Economics, Cambridge, U.K.

Nickson, A. 2001. "The Cordoba Water Concession in Argentina." Working Paper 442 05. GHK International and University of Birmingham, Birmingham, U.K.

Noll, R. 1995. "The Role of Antitrust in Telecommunications." *Antitrust Bulletin* 40 (3): 501–28.

———. 1999. *The Economics and Politics of the Slowdown in Regulatory Reform.* Washington, D.C.: American Enterprise Institute-Brookings Joint Center for Regulatory Studies.

———. 2000a. "Note on Privatizing Infrastructure Industries." World Bank, Washington, D.C.

———. 2000b. "Regulatory Reform and International Trade Policy." In T. Ito and A. Krueger, eds., *Deregulation and Independence in the Asia-Pacific Region: NBER-East Asia Seminar on Economics*, vol. 8. Chicago, Ill.: University of Chicago Press.

———. 2000c. "Telecommunications Reform in Developing Countries." In A. Krueger, ed., *Economic Policy Reform: The Second Stage.* Chicago, Ill.: University of Chicago Press.

———. 2000d. "Telecommunications Reform in Romania." In I. Kessides, ed., *Romania: Regulatory and Structural Assessment in the Network Utilities.* Report 20546-RO. Washington, D.C.: World Bank.

———. 2001. "Progress in Telecommunications Reform in Mexico." World Bank, Washington, D.C.

Noll, R., M. Shirley, and S. Cowan. 2000. "Reforming Urban Water Systems in Developing Countries." SIEPR Discussion Paper 99-32. Stanford University, Stanford Institute for Economic Policy Research, Palo Alto, Calif.

Oates, W. 1999. "An Essay on Fiscal Federalism." *Journal of Economic Literature* 37 (3): 1120–49.

Ordover, J., and R. Pittman. 1994. "Restructuring the Railway for Competition." Paper presented at an Organisation for Economic Cooperation and Development–World Bank conference on Competition and Regulation in Network Infrastructure Industries, 28 June–1 July, Budapest, Hungary.

Ordover, J., A. Sykes, and R. Willig. 1985. "Non-Price Anticompetitive Behavior by Dominant Firms toward the Producer of Complementary Products." In F. Fisher, ed., *Antitrust and Regulation: Essays in Memory of John McGowan.* Cambridge, Mass.: MIT Press.

Oster, C., and J. Strong. 2000. "Transport Restructuring and Reform in an International Context." *Transportation Journal* 39 (3): 18–32.

Peters, H. 1995. "Private Sector Involvement in East and Southeast Asian Ports—An Overview of Contractual Agreements." Infrastructure Notes, Transport PS-10. World Bank, Washington, D.C.

Petrazzini, B. 1997. "Regulating Communications Services in Developing Countries." In W. Melody, ed., *Telecom Reform: Principles, Policies and Regulatory Practices.* Lyngby: Technical University of Denmark, Den Private Ingenirrfond.

Pettersen-Strandenes, S., and P. Marlow. 2000. "Port Pricing and Competitiveness in Short Sea Shipping." *International Journal of Transport Economics* 27 (3): 315–34.

Pittman, R. 2001. "Railway Competition: Options for the Russian Federation." Working Paper 111003. University of Washington, St. Louis, Mo.

————. 2003. "Vertical Restructuring (or Not) of the Infrastructure Sectors of Transition Economies." *Journal of Industry, Competition and Trade* 3 (1–2): 5–26.

Platts. 2002. "More Energy Companies Hit Bottom in Argentina." *Platts—Power in Latin America* 86, 3 May.

Pollitt, M. 2003. "Electricity Reform in Argentina—Lessons for Developing Countries." World Bank, Washington, D.C.

PPIAF (Public–Private Infrastructure Advisory Facility). 2001. *Private Solutions for Infrastructure—Opportunities for Uganda. A Country Framework Report.* Washington, D.C.: World Bank.

PPIAF (Public–Private Infrastructure Advisory Facility) and WSP (Water and Sanitation Program). 2001. *New Designs for Water and Sanitation Transactions: Making Private Sector Participation Work for the Poor.* Washington, D.C.: World Bank.

Prayas Energy Group. 2003. "Performance of Private Electricity Distribution Utilities in India: Need for In-Depth Review & Benchmarking." Occasional Report. Pune, India.

Public Services International. 2000. "World Water Briefing: Privatization and Transparency." University of Greenwich.

Pyramid Research. 1999. *Privatizing Telecoms Markets.* Boston, Mass.: The Economist Intelligence Unit.

————. 2001. *Communications Markets in Mexico—Blurring Barriers and Escalating Competition.* Boston, Mass.: The Economist Intelligence Unit.

Ramamurti, R. 1996. "The New Frontier of Privatization." In R. Ramamurti, ed., *Privatizing Monopolies: Lessons from the Telecommunications and Transport Sectors in Latin America.* Baltimore, Md.: The Johns Hopkins University Press.

Ringskog, K. 1998. "Private Sector Participation in Water Supply and Wastewater: Case Studies." World Bank, Washington, D.C.

Roger, N. 1999. "Recent Trends in Private Participation in Infrastructure." Public Policy for the Private Sector Note 196. World Bank, Washington, D.C.

Rohlfs, J., K. Pehrsson, C-M. Rossoto, and M. Kerf. 2000. "Effects of the Entrance of a Second GSM Operator on the Cellular Telecommunications Market and on the Incumbent Operator." Paper presented at the 28th Annual Telecommunications Policy Research Conference, 24 September, Alexandria, Va.

Ros, A. 1999. "Does Ownership or Competition Matter? The Effects of Telecommunications Reform on Network Expansion and Efficiency." *Journal of Regulatory Economics* 15 (1): 65–92.

———. 2001. "Principles and Practice of Price Cap Regulation—An Application to the Peruvian Context." National Economic Research Associates, Cambridge, Mass.

Rosston, G. 2000. "The Telecommunications Sector." In I. Kessides, ed., *Hungary: A Regulatory and Structural Review of Selected Infrastructure Sectors*. Washington, D.C.: World Bank.

Rudnick, H. 1998. "Competitive Markets in Electricity Supply: Assessment of the South American Experience." *Revista ABANTE* 1 (2): 189–211.

Rudnick, H., and J. Zolezzi. 2001. "Electric Sector Deregulation and Restructuring in Latin America: Lessons to be Learnt and Possible Ways Forward." In *IEEE Proceedings: Generation, Transmission and Distribution* 148: 180–84.

Saavedra, E. 2001. "Opportunistic Behavior and Legal Disputes in the Chilean Electricity Sector." ILADES (Instituto Latinoamericano de Doctrim y Estudios Sociales)-Georgetown University Working Papers (No. 130). Georgetown University, Department of Economics, Washington, D.C.

Saleth, R., and A. Dinar. 1999. "Water Challenge and Institutional Response: A Cross-Country Perspective." Policy Research Working Paper 2045. World Bank, Washington, D.C.

Samarajiva, R. 2001. "Regulating in an Imperfect World: Building Independence through Legitimacy." *Policy Forum* 1 (2): 363–68.

Samarajiva, R., A. Mahan, and A. Barendse. 2002. "Multisector Utility Regulation." Discussion Paper 23. Technical University of Denmark, World Dialogue on Regulation for Network Economies, Copenhagen.

Sappington, D. 2002. "Pricing of Regulated Retail Services in the Telecommunications Industry." Paper prepared for the President's Commission on the United States Postal Service. University of Florida, Gainesville.

Sappington, D., and D. Weisman. 1996. *Designing Incentive Regulation for the Telecommunications Industry*. Cambridge, Mass.: MIT Press.

Scherer, F. 1980. *Industrial Market Structure and Economic Performance*. Boston, Mass.: Houghton Mifflin.

Schmalensee, R. 1989. "Good Regulatory Regimes." *Rand Journal of Economics* 20 (3): 417–36.

Shapiro, C., and R. Willig. 1990. "Economic Rationales for the Scope of Privatization." In E. Suleiman and J. Waterbury, eds., *The Political Economy of Public Sector Reform and Privatization*. London: Westview.

Sheshinski, E., and L. Lopez-Calva. 2000. "Privatization and Its Benefits: Theory, Evidence, and Challenges." Center for Applied Energy Research Discussion Paper 35. Harvard University, Harvard Institute for International Development, Cambridge, Mass.

Shirley, M., and C. Menard. 2002. "Cities Awash: Reforming Urban Water Systems in Developing Countries." In M. Shirley, ed., *Thirsting for Efficiency: The Economics and Politics of Urban Water System Reform*. Oxford: Elsevier Press.

Shirley M., and P. Walsh. 2001. "Public versus Private Ownership: The Current State of the Debate." Policy Research Working Paper 2420. World Bank, Washington, D.C.

Shirley, M., F. Tusubira, F. Gebreab, and L. Haggarty. 2002. "Telecommunications Reform in Uganda." Policy Research Working Paper 2864. World Bank, Washington, D.C.

Shleifer, A. 1985. "A Theory of Yardstick Competition." *Rand Journal of Economics* 16 (3): 319–27.

Shuttleworth, G. 1999. "Regulatory Benchmarking: A Way Forward or a Dead-End?" *Energy Regulation Brief* 3. National Economic Research Associates, London.

Siemens. 2001. *International Telecom Statistics*. Munich, Germany.

Smith, P., and B. Wellenius. 1999. "Mitigating Regulatory Risk in Telecommunications." Public Policy for the Private Sector Note 189. World Bank, Washington, D.C.

Smith, W. 1997a. "Utility Regulators—Decisionmaking, Structures, Resources, and Start-up Strategy." Public Policy for the Private Sector Note 129. World Bank, Washington, D.C.

———. 1997b. "Utility Regulators—Roles and Responsibilities." Public Policy for the Private Sector Note 128. World Bank, Washington, D.C.

———. 1997c. "Utility Regulators—The Independence Debate." Public Policy for the Private

Sector Note 127. World Bank, Washington, D.C.

———. 2000a. "Regulating Infrastructure for the Poor: Perspectives on Regulatory System Design." Paper presented at the Public-Private Infrastructure Advisory Facility, U.K. Government, and World Bank Conference on Infrastructure and Development: Private Solutions and the Poor, 31 May–2 June, London.

———. 2000b. "Regulating Utilities: Thinking about Location Questions." Paper presented at the World Bank's *World Development Report 2002* Summer Research Workshop, 17–19 July, Washington, D.C.

Solo, T. 1998. "Competition in Water and Sanitation: The Role of Small-Scale Entrepreneurs." Public Policy for the Private Sector Note 165. World Bank, Washington, D.C.

Spiller, P. 1992. "Institutions and Regulatory Commitment in Utilities Privatization." Working Paper IPR51. Institute for Policy Reform, Washington, D.C.

———. 1996. "Electricity Regulation in Argentina, Brazil, Uruguay and Chile." In R. J. Gilbert and E. P. Kahn, eds., *International Comparisons of Electricity Regulation*. New York: Cambridge University Press.

Spiller, P., and L. Martorell. 1996. "How Should It Be Done? Electricity Regulation in Argentina, Brazil, Uruguay and Chile." In R. Gilbert and A. E. Kahn, eds., *International Comparisons of Electricity Regulation*. Cambridge: Cambridge University Press.

Spiller, P., and W. Savedoff. 1999. "Commitment and Governance in Infrastructure Sectors." In F. Besanes, E. M. Uribe, and R. Willig, eds., *Can Privatization Deliver? Infrastructure for Latin America.* Washington, D.C.: Inter-American Development Bank and Baltimore, Md.: The Johns Hopkins University Press.

Stern, J. 1997. "What Makes an Independent Regulator Independent?" *Business Strategy Review* 8 (2): 67–74.

———. 1999. "Styles of Regulation: The Choice of Approach to Utility Regulation in Central and Eastern Europe." Regulation Initiative Working Paper 34. London Business School, London.

———. 2000. "Electricity and Telecommunications Regulatory Institutions in Small and Developing Countries." *Utilities Policy* 9 (3): 131–57.

———. 2002. "Retrospect and Prospects for 2002." In *Central and Eastern Europe & FSU Electricity Prospects for 2002.* London: Platts.

———. 2003. "Regulation and Contracts for Utility Services: Substitutes or Complements? Lessons from UK Historical Experience." Regulation Initiative Working Paper 54. London Business School, London.

Stern, J., and S. Holder. 1999. "Regulatory Governance: Criteria for Assessing the Performance of Regulatory Systems: An Application to Infrastructure Industries in the Developing Countries of Asia." *Utilities Policy* 8 (1): 33–50.

Stiglitz, J. E. 1999. "Wither Reform? Ten Years of the Transition." Keynote address. Annual World Bank Conference on Development Economics, 28–30 April, Washington, D.C.

Stirton, L., and M. Lodge. 2001. "Telecommunications Reform in Jamaica: Toward Embedded Regulatory Autonomy?" Paper presented at the Development Studies Association annual conference, University of Manchester, 10–12 September, Manchester, U.K.

Suding, P. 1996. "Opening Up and Transition, Success and Problems: Financing and Reforms in the Electric Power Sector in Latin America and the Caribbean." *Energy Policy* 24 (5): 437–45.

Taud, R., J. Karg, and D. O'Leary. 1999. "Gas Turbine Power Plants: A Technology of Growing Importance for Developing Countries." Energy Issues 20. World Bank, Washington, D.C.

Thomas, R., and T. Schneider. 1997. "Underlying Technical Issues in Electricity Deregulation." Paper presented at the 30th Hawaii International Conference on System Sciences, 7–10 January, Maui, Hawaii.

Thompson, L. 1997. "The Benefits of Separating Rail Infrastructure from Operations." Public Policy for the Private Sector Note 135. World Bank, Washington, D.C.

———. 2001a. "Railways in Eastern Europe." World Bank, Washington, D.C.

———. 2001b. "Railways Regional and Suburban Services: Why Are They Important?" Paper presented at the workshop "Better Ways to

Deliver and Fund Regional and Suburban Passenger Rail Services," 13–15 June, Colmar, France.

———. 2003. "Changing Railway Structure and Ownership: Is Anything Working?" *Transport Reviews* 23 (3): 311–56.

Thompson, L., and K-J. Budin. 2001. "Directions of Railway Reform." Paper presented at the International Railway Congress Association meeting, 25–28 September, Vienna, Austria.

Thompson, L., K-J. Budin, and A. Estache. 2001. "Private Investment in Railways: Experience from South and North America, Africa and New Zealand." Paper presented at the Association for European Transport European Transport Conference, 12–13 September, Cambridge, U.K.

Tiebout, C. 1956. "A Pure Theory of Local Expenditures." *Journal of Political Economy* 64 (5): 416–24.

Torero, M., and A. Pasco-Font. 2001. "The Social Impact of Privatization and Regulation of Utilities in Peru." Discussion Paper 2001/17. United Nations University, WIDER (World Institute for Development Economics Research), Stockholm, Sweden.

Torp, J., and P. Revke. 1998. "Privatization in Developing Countries: Lessons to Be Learnt from the Mozambican Case." *Transformation* 36: 73–92.

Tremolet, S. 2002. "Rural Water Service." Public Policy for the Private Sector Note 249. World Bank, Washington, D.C.

Tremolet, S., S. Browning, and C. Howard. 2002. *Emerging Lessons in Private Provision of Infrastructure Services in Rural Areas: Water Services in Côte d'Ivoire and Senegal.* Reference 8524. Washington, D.C.: Public–Private Infrastructure Advisory Facility and London: Environmental Resources Management.

Trujillo, L., and G. Nombela. 2000a. "Multiservice Infrastructure." Public Policy for the Private Sector Note 222. World Bank, Washington, D.C.

———. 2000b. "Seaports." In A. Estache and G. de Rus, eds., *Privatization and Regulation of Transport Infrastructure.* Washington, D.C.: World Bank.

Tsaplin, V. 2001. "An Evaluation of the Efficiency of Energy Regulation in Ukraine." M.A. diss. National University of Kyiv, Mohyla Academy, Kyiv, Ukraine.

Tull, M., and J. Reveley. 2001. "Privatization of Ports: A Malaysian Case Study." Working Paper 182. Murdoch University, School of Economics, Perth, Australia.

Turvey, R. 1968. *Optimal Pricing and Investment in Electricity Supply.* London: Allen & Unwin.

Tynan, N. 1999. "Private Participation in the Rail Sector—Recent Trends." Public Policy for the Private Sector Note 186. World Bank, Washington, D.C.

———. 2000. "Private Participation in Infrastructure and the Poor: Water and Sanitation." Paper presented at the International Conference on Infrastructure for Development: Private Solutions and the Poor, 31 May–2 June, London.

————. 2002. "Role and Design of Free Entry Policies: Expanding Service Options for Low-Income Households." Paper prepared for the PPIAF/ADB Conference on Infrastructure Development—Private Solutions for the Poor: The Asian Perspective, 28–30 October, Manila.

Urbiztondo, S. 2003. "Renegotiation with Public Utilities in Argentina: Analysis and Proposal." Latin American University, Buenos Aires.

Uribe, E. 2000. "Building Regulatory Institutions in Latin America: From Penalties to Incentives." Inter-American Development Bank, Sustainable Development Department, Washington, D.C.

Valetti, T., and A. Estache. 1998. "The Theory of Access Pricing: An Overview for Infrastructure Regulators." Policy Research Working Paper 2097. World Bank, Washington, D.C.

Vanags, A. 2001. "Latvia's New Super-Regulators Have a Mission." *Transition Newsletter* 12 (4): 35–36.

van den Berg, C. 2000. "Water Concessions: Who Wins, Who Loses, and What To Do About It." Public Policy for the Private Sector Note 217. World Bank, Washington, D.C.

van der Veer, J. 2001. "Private Sector Involvement in Ports: Economics and Policy." *Topics 24.* National Economic Research Associates, London.

Vickers, J., and G. Yarrow. 1991. "Economic Perspectives on Privatization." *Journal of Economic Perspectives* 5 (2): 111–32.

Villalonga, B. 2000. "Privatization and Efficiency: Differentiating Ownership Effects from Political, Organizational, and Dynamic Effects." *Journal of Economic Behaviour & Organization* 42 (1): 43–74.

Vogelsang, I. 2002. "Optimal Price Regulation for Natural and Legal Monopolies." Boston University, Boston, Mass.

Vogelsang, I., and B. Mitchell. 1997. *Telecommunications Competition: The Last Ten Miles.* Cambridge, Mass.: MIT Press.

von Hirschhausen, C., and B. Meinhart. 2001. "Infrastructure Policies and Liberalization in the East European Transition Countries—Would Less Have Been More?" *Internet Journal of the Centre for Energy, Petroleum and Mineral Law Policy* 9.

von Hirschhausen, C., and P. Opitz. 2001. "Power Utility Re-Regulation in East European and CIS Transformation Countries: An Institutional Interpretation." Paper presented at the International Society for New Institutional Economics Conference, 13–15 September, Berkeley, Calif.

Wallsten, S. 2000. "Telecommunications Privatization in Developing Countries: The Real Effects of Exclusivity Periods." Stanford University, Palo Alto, Calif.

————. 2001. "An Econometric Analysis of Telecom Competition, Privatization, and Regulation in Africa and Latin America." *The Journal of Industrial Economics* 49 (1): 1–19.

Walters, B. 1979. *Port Pricing and Investment Policy for Developing Countries.* Oxford: Oxford University Press.

303

Weisman, D. 2001. "Is There 'Hope' for Price Cap Regulation?" Kansas State University, Department of Economics, Kansas City.

Wellenius, B. 1997. "Telecommunications Reform—How to Succeed." Public Policy for the Private Sector Note 130. World Bank, Washington, D.C.

———. 1999. "Introducing Telecommunications Competition through a Wireless License—Lessons from Morocco." Public Policy for the Private Sector Note 199. World Bank, Washington, D.C.

Whittington, D. 1992. "Possible Adverse Effects of Increasing Block Water Tariffs in Developing Countries." *Economic Development and Cultural Change* 41 (1): 75–87.

Whittington, D., J. Boland, and V. Foster. 2002. "Water Tariffs and Subsidies: Understanding the Basics?" Paper 1. World Bank, Public–Private Infrastructure Advisory Facility and Water and Sanitation Program, Washington, D.C.

WHO (World Health Organization), UNICEF (United Nations Children's Fund), and WSSCC (Water Supply and Sanitation Collaborative Council). 2000. *Global Water Supply and Sanitation Assessment, 2000 Report.* New York: WHO and UNICEF.

Williamson, B., and S. Toft. 2001. "The Appropriate Role of Yardstick Methods in Regulation." National Economic Research Associates, London.

Williamson, O. 1976. "Franchise Bidding for Natural Monopolies—In General and with Re-

spect to CATV." *The Bell Journal of Economics* 7 (1): 73–104.

Willig, R. 1992. "Anti-Monopoly Policies and Institutions." In C. Clague and G. Rausser, eds., *The Emergence of Market Economies in Eastern Europe.* Cambridge, Mass., and Oxford: Blackwell.

———. 1994a. "Before the (New York) Public Service Commission." PSC Case 94-E-0136. New York.

———. 1994b. "Public versus Regulated Private Enterprise." Paper presented at the Annual World Bank Conference on Development Economics, 3–4 May 1993, Washington, D.C., Washington, D.C.

———. 1995. "Current and Forthcoming Issues in the Argentine Network Utilities." World Bank, Washington, D.C.

———. 1999. "Economic Principles to Guide Post-Privatization Governance." In F. Besanes, E. M. Uribe, and R. Willig, eds., *Can Privatization Deliver? Infrastructure for Latin America.* Washington, D.C.: Inter-American Development Bank and Baltimore, Md.: The Johns Hopkins University Press.

Wilson, W. W. 1997. "Cost Savings and Productivity in the Railroad Industry." *Journal of Regulatory Economics* 11 (1): 21–40.

WMO (World Meteorological Organization). 1992. "The Dublin Statement and Report of the Conference." Presented at the United Nations International Conference on Water and the Environment: Development Issues for the 21st Century, 26–31 January, Dubin, Ireland.

Wolak, F. 2000. "Report on Electricity Industry Restructuring in Romania." In I. Kessides, ed., *Romania: Regulatory and Structural Assessment in the Network Utilities*. Report 20546-RO. Washington, D.C.: World Bank.

———. 2001. "Designing a Competitive Wholesale Electricity Market That Benefits Consumers." Stanford University, Palo Alto, Calif.

———. 2003. "Designing Competitive Wholesale Electricity Markets for Latin American Countries." Paper prepared for the First Meeting of the Latin American Competition Forum, sponsored by the Organisation for Economic Co-operation and Development and the Inter-American Development Bank, 7–8 April, Paris.

Wolak, F., and R. Nordhaus. 2001. "Comments on 'Staff Recommendation on Prospective Market Monitoring and Mitigation for the California Wholesale Electricity Market.' " California Independent System Operator, Market Surveillance Committee, Sacramento.

Wolak, F., R. Nordhaus, and C. Shapiro. 2000. "An Analysis of the June 2000 Price Spikes in the California ISO's Energy and Ancillary Services Markets." [http://www.caiso.com/docs/2000/09/14/200009141610025714.html].

World Bank. 1992. "Brazil—Reforming the Telecommunications Sector: Policy Issues and Options for the 1990s." Latin America and the Caribbean Region, Washington, D.C.

———. 1994a. *The Brazilian Railroad Industry: Options for Organizational Restructuring*. Report 11752-BR. Washington, D.C.

———. 1994b. *World Development Report 1994: Infrastructure for Development*. New York: Oxford University Press.

———. 1995. *Bureaucrats in Business: The Economics and Politics of Government Ownership*. A Policy Research Report. Washington, D.C.

———. 1997. "Project Appraisal Document—On a Proposed Loan in the Amount of US$60 Million Equivalent to India for a Haryana Power Sector Restructuring Project." Report 17234-IN. World Bank, Washington, D.C.

———. 1999a. *Energy and Development Report 1999: Energy after the Financial Crises*. Washington, D.C.

———. 1999b. *India: Country Framework Report for Private Participation in Infrastructure*. Washington, D.C.

———. 2000. "Regulatory Issues in the Latvian Infrastructure Sectors." *Programmatic Structural Adjustment Loan to the Republic of Latvia*. Report P7352-LV. Washington, D.C.

———. 2001a. *Bulgaria—The Dual Challenge of Transition and Accession*. Europe and Central Asia Region, Poverty Reduction and Economic Management Unit, Washington, D.C.

———. 2001b. *Greening Industry*. A Policy Research Report. Washington, D.C.

———. 2001c. *Mexico—Private Participation in Infrastructure: Investment and Performance Challenges.* Washington, D.C.

———. 2001d. *Port Reform.* A Privatization Toolkit. Washington, D.C.

———. 2001e. "Survey of Telecommunications Regulators in Developing and Transition Economies." Development Economics Group, Competition and Regulation Unit, Washington, D.C.

———. 2002a. "Survey of Energy Telecommunications Regulators in Developing and Transition Economies." Development Economics Group, Competition and Regulation Unit, Washington, D.C.

———. 2002b. *World Development Report 2002: Building Institutions for Markets.* New York: Oxford University Press.

———. 2003. *World Bank Development Indicators 2003.* Washington, D.C.

Woroch, G. A. 2002. "Local Network Competition." In M. Cave, S. Majumdar, and I. Vogelsang, eds., *Handbook of Telecommunications Economics.* Amsterdam: Elsevier.

Yvrande, A. 2000. "The New British Railways Structure: A Transaction Cost Economic Analysis." DRUID Working Paper 2000-5. Copenhagen Business School, Department of Industrial Economics and Strategy, Danish Research Unit for Industrial Dynamics, Copenhagen, Denmark.

Zelner, B., and W. Henisz. 2000. "Politics and Infrastructure Investment." Georgetown University, Washington D.C.

Zhang, Y-F., Parker, D., and C. Kirkpatrick. 2002. "Electricity Sector Reform in Developing Countries: An Econometric Assessment of the Effects of Privatization, Competition and Regulation." CRC Working Paper 31. Center on Regulation and Competition, Manchester, U.K.

Zupan, M. 1989. "The Efficiency of Franchise Bidding Schemes in the Case of Cable Television: Some Systematic Evidence." *Journal of Law and Economics* 32: 401–56.